THERE'S BEEN A LIFE!

ALEX NORTON

There's Been A Life!

MY AUTOBIOGRAPHY

BLACK & WHITE PUBLISHING

First published 2014
by Black & White Publishing Ltd
29 Ocean Drive, Edinburgh EH6 6JL

1 3 5 7 9 10 8 6 4 2   14 15 16 17

ISBN: 978 1 84502 949 4

This book is a work of non-fiction based on the life, experiences and recollections of
Alex Norton. In some limited cases names have been changed solely to protect the privacy
of others. The author has stated to the publishers that, except in minor respects not
affecting the substantial accuracy of the work, the contents of this book are true.

The publisher has made every reasonable effort to contact copyright holders
of images in the picture section. Any errors are inadvertent and anyone who for
any reason has not been contacted is invited to write to the publisher so that a
full acknowledgement can be made in subsequent editions of this work.

A CIP catalogue record for this book is available from the British Library.

Typeset by RefineCatch Limited, Bungay, Suffolk
Printed and bound by ScandBook AB, Sweden

For my parents, John and Sarah, my wife, Sally, and my three sons, Jock, Rory and Jamie

'This above all: to thine own self be true,
and it must follow, as the night the day,
thou canst not then be false to any man.'

William Shakespeare, *Hamlet*

'Much of what follows is true.'

William Goldman, *Butch Cassidy and the Sundance Kid*

INTRODUCTION

I never gave a thought to the notion of putting my life down on paper until the day I walked into the reception area of a recording studio in Soho to do (as I thought) a voice test for a series of Baxters soup commercials. Other than me, the only person in the foyer was a man sitting on the sofa reading a newspaper, holding it up in front of his face like a spy in an old war film. I barely gave him a second glance as I told the receptionist who I was and why I was there. She said the copywriters were running a bit late with the script and asked if I would mind taking a seat until the rewrite was ready. I settled myself on the sofa next to the solitary reader, who lowered his paper and gave me a friendly smile. I was slightly surprised to see it was Michael Aspel – but then there was nothing particularly unusual about that; I often bumped into famous faces in voice-over studios. What *was* unusual was that although we'd never met before, he seemed to know who I was. 'Hello, Alex,' he said with a friendly smile. Before I got a chance to say 'Hello, Michael', the boundaries of reality disintegrated as a film crew appeared from nowhere, pointing their cameras at my astonished face. Mike Aspel seemed to be saying something about *Taggart*, and as he handed me a big red book, the penny dropped: I was about to be the subject of *This Is Your Life*.

I remember thinking that there must have been some kind of mistake. *This Is Your Life* was for Famous Celebrities, not journeymen actors like me. If Mike Aspel had peeled off his face to reveal he was really an alien in disguise, and beamed me up to a waiting UFO, I couldn't have been more incredulous. I managed to stammer, 'This is the most surreal thing that's ever happened in my life – and it's all been pretty bloody surreal up to now!'

Still reeling from the weirdness of what had just happened, I was whisked off to BBC Television Centre, bundled in through a side door and shut away in a dressing room to make sure I didn't accidentally catch sight of any of the show's guests. After about an hour of solitary confinement, the door was thrown open and a couple of security guards led me along a long corridor towards the studio. As my mind raced with thoughts of who the guests might be and what they would say, the creepy parallels with the walk from the condemned cell to execution shed didn't escape me. Standing in the darkness at the back of the set listening to Mike Aspel's introduction, the magnitude of what I was about to undergo hit home and a swarm of butterflies started performing aerobatics in my stomach. Seconds later the sliding doors parted and I walked forward to a huge round of applause and a sea of beaming faces that seemed to include just about everyone I had ever known in this life, and several previous ones. The array of guests who took part that evening included Billy Connolly, Peter Capaldi, Robbie Coltrane, Jeremy Beadle and Bill Paterson. The surprise of the evening was that Ronnie Christie, my old classmate who had given me my first guitar lessons and introduced me to the heady world of show business, had been flown in all the way from Australia. To hell with glittering trophies and meaningless plaques: for me *This Is Your Life*, a show that I had watched since I was a boy, was the highest accolade I could wish for – infinitely better than some statuette gathering dust on a shelf in the spare room.

The experience of having my life flash before my eyes without having to die at the end got me thinking back over the seemingly random chain of events that made me the person I am. Calling me up the following day to say what a fantastic evening it had been, my old and much-missed chum Jeremy Beadle suggested that I should think seriously about writing my life story. At first I laughed it off as just another of his daft notions, but as I thought about the wonderful tribute I had just been paid, and the famous friends and acquaintances who had turned up to share my half-hour in the limelight, it dawned on me that my life has been pretty extraordinary by any standards. From improvised school shows and fit-up tours around Highland halls to working for some of the major Hollywood studios, I've followed a dream that began more than fifty years ago. Over that time I've performed with some of the biggest names in the business, as well as names that may have been forgotten by the public, but not by me. Along the way I've gathered a fair share of tales and anecdotes, not all of them humorous and some of which may raise an eyebrow from those who know me only as the dour DCI from STV's long-running detective series, *Taggart*.

Before deciding to pen the tale of a plumber's son from the Gorbals who desperately wanted more from life than was pencilled in for him (and who still lives in daily expectation of a wee guy in a greasy biler suit and frayed bunnet, tapping him on the shoulder and saying 'Right son, ye've had yer fun an' games. Now back tae yer work'), I asked myself a variation of the question I always ask when deciding whether or not to accept a job offer: 'Would people pay good money to watch me in this?' This time my question was: 'Would people pay good money to read about me in this?'

If you've done just that, you have my sincere thanks, and I hope the little voice in my head that said 'Yes, they would' wasn't Jeremy Beadle having a last laugh at my expense.

PREFACE

Every profession has its own 'in' jokes. Most are, at best, not very funny or, at worst, virtually impenetrable to outsiders. In my view, however, the best ones illuminate a shared awareness of the unspoken absurdity of any particular profession. Here are a couple of my favourite 'in' jokes that beneath their comical facade reveal a deep truth about the supposedly glamorous world of show business.

Three recently deceased souls are standing outside the pearly gates. St Peter welcomes them and explains that they've recently introduced a new system in Heaven, and where you spend eternity is now linked to your previous year's income on Earth. 'So,' he says to the first man, 'may I ask what you earned last year?'

'Oh, around one and a half million plus bonuses and stock options,' he replies.

'Splendid,' says St Peter, 'you'll be in Zone A, along with senior executives, hedge fund managers and dot com entrepreneurs.'

Turning to the next man he asks him the same question.

'Around two hundred and fifty thousand,' he answers.

'Excellent,' says St Peter, 'you'll be in Zone B along with middle management, double-glazing salesmen and used-car dealers.

Turning to the third guy, he says, 'And how much did you earn last year?'

'About five and a half grand,' the man replies.

'Really?' says St Peter. 'And might I have seen you in something . . . ?'

A guy bursts into the office of a top variety agent one morning. Before the startled agent can utter a word, the guy announces, 'I am the most amazing act you have ever seen in your life! You have to take me on.'

'I'm sorry,' says the agent tactfully. 'I never see anyone without an appointment. Now would you please leave.'

'No,' says the guy. 'You don't understand. I am the most original and exciting act in the world. All I'm asking is just five minutes of your time.'

'I won't tell you again. If you don't leave my office right now, I'll—'

'Look. Four minutes, OK? What's four minutes? I promise you, you've never seen anything like my act before. It's absolutely unique.'

'OK, OK,' says the agent reluctantly. 'What do you do?'

'I am The Man Who Feels No Pain,' the guy replies.

'Aw for f—' the agent groans. 'Out! Now!'

'All right, *three* minutes then. If you're not convinced in three minutes that I am the most incredible act you've ever seen, I'll turn around and leave and never bother you again. Please. Just three minutes.'

'Two minutes,' growls the agent, checking his watch. 'And if you're still here after that, I'll have you thrown out.'

'Thank you so much, sir. You'll never regret this decision, I promise you.'

As the agent sits back down behind his desk, the guy opens his bag and takes out a large builder's hammer. 'Now,' he says to the agent, 'hit me on the forehead with this as hard as you possibly can.'

'No bloody way!' says the agent.

'No, no. It's OK,' says the guy, as he takes up a stance ready to receive the blow. 'I am The Man Who Feels No Pain. Just hit me right here – right between the eyes, as hard as you like, and prepare to be astounded!'

Against his better judgement, but at the same time not wanting to lose out on the possibility of a potentially amazing act, the agent reluctantly draws back the hefty club hammer and lets fly. WHACK!

With all his strength he smacks the guy squarely in the centre of his forehead. The Man Who Feels No Pain flies backwards and slams against the wall. His eyes roll back in their sockets as he slides unconscious to the floor, great gouts of blood welling up from the deep, perfectly square indentation in the centre of his skull. The agent is totally panic-stricken. He dials 999 and somehow manages to stutter out his story. An ambulance arrives and whisks the guy away for emergency surgery. Barely alive, he is in a deep coma and the prognosis is not hopeful. The poor agent is so mortified by what he's done that he pays out of his own pocket for a private room in the intensive-care wing of a top hospital and holds a round-the-clock bedside vigil. Day and night he sits holding the guy's hand, listening to the faint and irregular beeping of the life-monitoring machines on the wall. Weeks pass with no signs of recovery, then, one evening, he feels a faint tug on his sleeve. Hardly daring to hope his prayers have been answered, he glances down at the bed. The Man Who Feels No Pain looks up at him with a triumphant grin, spreads his arms wide and goes: 'Tah Daahhh!'

I thought of calling my autobiography *Tah Daahhh!* because, for me, that joke tells you all you need to know about showbusiness. If you don't believe me, watch a few episodes of *Britain's Got Talent* or some such show to see just how delusional people can be in their desire to achieve public acclaim. The reason The Man Who Feels No Pain never fails to get a huge reaction when I tell it to a fellow performer is that for a lot of our working lives, we're seldom a kick in the backside away from that level of desperation ourselves.

I've read a lot of autobiographies from other actors in 'The Business' and I'm endlessly curious about what motivated them to become actors or directors or screenwriters, how they struggled for recognition and how they found themselves in the position of being famous enough to justify writing their life stories. Of the autobiographies I've read all the way through (and there have been quite a few I've thrown in the bin after a couple of wasted hours), I've always found the opening chapters the most boring. Who gives a toss about how their parents met, or how their great-grandparents fled the Steppes to escape the pogroms? The thing is, I just don't think I can tell my story properly without sharing at least some of my background, since it has played such an integral role in shaping my life. If all that 'formative years' sort of stuff bores you as often as it bores me, then by all means skip the first few chapters with my blessing. If, on the other hand, you want to know what prompted me to join the ranks of rogues and vagabonds (as actors were once legally defined), stick with it – there are some entertaining reminiscences along the way.

Contents

CONTENTS

1

Hooray for Househillwood

I'm a real mongrel. On my mother's side my grandfather was English and my granny Irish. They were, respectively, Hugh Douglas, a Londoner born within the sound of Bow bells, whose Scottish parents got homesick and returned to live in Glasgow, bringing their young son with them, and Elizabeth Devancy, who, along with her nine brothers and sisters, had emigrated from County Sligo in Ireland to seek a better future in the wealthy and flourishing city of Glasgow. Elizabeth's brothers found work as dockers on busy Clydeside, while she and her sisters went into domestic service. Hugh, after serving in the merchant Marines during the First World War, found a job as a marker in a billiard hall. Somewhere, somehow, Hugh Douglas met Lizzie Devaney, and despite Hugh being a Protestant and Lizzie a Catholic (no small obstacle to wedded bliss in Glasgow at that time), they married and produced five children: Hughie, Betty, Sarah (my mother), Jim and Willie.

My dad's parents, Alex and Jenny Norton, raised their family of five sons – Alec, Bobby, Willie, Tommy and my father John – in a room and kitchen in Fauldhouse Street, Oatlands, until the Corporation re-housed them in Carnwadric, a good-quality housing scheme near Rouken Glen Park on Glasgow's south side – or sou'side, as my dad always called it. The brothers all became qualified tradesmen – electricians, engineers and, in my dad's case, a plumber. Their parents' spacious and airy new house was even

1

big enough to cope with an extra family member. My dad used to tell me how wee Johnny Cameron, a workmate and pal of Uncle Alec, found himself temporarily homeless. Alec invited him back for his tea and, thanks to the legendary generosity of 'Big Jenny', wee Johnny the lodger stayed with the family for the next twenty years or so.

My father, John Cameron Norton, met my mother, Sarah McConnell Douglas, at a dance in the Pollokshaws Burgh Halls one evening in 1947. Apart from being stone deaf in one ear, he had survived the war, serving as an artilleryman during the Italian campaign. I still have the Bible that was presented to him in grateful thanks for his contribution to saving civilisation from the forces of darkness. It must have been a great comfort to know that the Lord was watching out for him while he was in the Libyan desert firing howitzers at Mussolini's troops – which was more than you could say for the War Office, who rejected his claim for a disability pension, refusing to concede that his deafness just might have been caused by concussive shock waves from the high-explosive shells being discharged a few feet from his right ear. I can't help thinking a hearing aid and a few extra quid a week might have given him a damn sight more comfort than a Bible.

John and Sarah decided to get married and, like many other young Glasgow couples, they put their name down on the Corporation's housing list and waited. While they were waiting, they spent the first years of their married lives lodging with my mother's family in their red sandstone council flat in Brock Road, Househillwood, a pleasant wee spot on the south side, now almost completely obliterated by a giant shopping mall.[1] I was born in my granny's wee back bedroom on 27 January 1950 at half past four in the afternoon. Jim and Willie, my mum's younger brothers, were despatched to deliver the news to the pub where my dad and his

---

[1] In the unlikely event that anyone ever decided to put up a plaque saying 'Alex Norton was born here', they'd have to nail it to the wall nearest the wheeled-luggage section of TK Maxx . . .

mates were drinking to his imminent fatherhood. After a brief visit home to ascertain that mother and son were both fine, I'm told he went straight back to the pub to carry on the celebrations.

My earliest memories of life at my granny and granda's house are blissful. I was adored by everyone and wanted for nothing. I'm sure, looking back, things couldn't have been that easy for their extended family – there were four adults, three teenage boys (Betty had married Robbie, the handsome young ploughman she met during the war when she was a land girl, and had moved away to live on a farm near Kilbarchan) and a greetin' wean in a two-bedroomed house. I imagine they must all have lived with the belief that privacy was something reserved solely for the middle classes.

I remember our first flit. I was four years old when my parents finally got their own home – a single end in Moffat Street in the heart of the Gorbals. There have been plenty of other books chronicling life in Glasgow's most notorious slum, so I won't linger too long over the more lurid descriptions of life up a tenement close – although, until recently, I didn't appreciate how difficult it could be for someone with a middle-class upbringing to comprehend what living in a single end was actually like. My wife Sally and I were watching an episode of *Antiques Roadshow* where someone had brought along a Georgian screen that had a low dip at one end. The expert dealing with the piece explained that as Georgian houses had no indoor toilets, a screen such as this one would be set in a corner of the dining room with a chamber pot behind it, so that if one of the ladies present needed to relieve herself during the course of dinner, she would simply excuse herself from the table, go behind the screen and squat over the chamber pot, the dip at the end allowing her to continue conversing with her fellow diners. Sally, who hails from a fairly well-to-do background, was horrified. 'Oh my God!' she exclaimed. 'How could anyone live like that?' She seemed bewildered when I said that quite a lot of people continued to 'live like that' long after the Georgian era had ended. By way of an example, I told her that when we lived in our single end in the middle of the twentieth century, we kept an old, enamel chantie that my dad would regularly pee into. Sally's jaw dropped in amazement. 'But,' she gasped, 'surely not in the dining room?'

'Of course not!' I snapped back with mock indignation. 'He would retire to his study or, if the fancy took him, the library. But *never* in the dining room . . .'

The dining room! Not a clue that a single end was literally one room with a bed recess, a coal bunker, a stone sink with a gooseneck tap,[2] a gate-leg table and two fireside chairs, which served as kitchen, dining room, living room and bedroom combined. But then how could Sally, or anyone else who wasn't brought up with raw sewage oozing from under the doors of burst stairhead lavvies, or swarms of hungry rats running around the back courts, possibly have any idea what life in a single end was like? Yes, the Gorbals might once have been described as the 'second-worst slum in Europe, after Naples', but for weans like me it was where you felt safe and secure – where being poor didn't necessarily equate with being dirty and where, despite the decrepit state of the tenements themselves, the women took their weekly turn at scrubbing the close and used blocks of white pipe clay to decorate its edges with patterns of scallops, triangles or half-moons, where neighbours looked out for each other and where nothing you ever tasted during the rest of your life, no matter how posh, ever came close to your maw's mince and totties. For me and my pals the Gorbals was an enchanted realm where the back court that defined the boundaries of your little fiefdom provided a ready-made adventure playground with high, tile-capped walls on which to practise your climbing and tightrope-walking skills, and crumbling brick wash houses, the roofs of which were skilfully designed for serious thrill-seekers to hang from by their fingertips before letting go and plummeting earthwards – or 'dreepin' aff', as we called it.

Then, of course, there were the middens. Like every other kid in the Gorbals I was a devout midgie raker. Until you began to delve,

---

[2] Cold water only, of course, but the sweetest, purest, unchlorinated, un-buggered-up Loch Katrine water you could ever hope to taste.

you never knew what hidden treasures might be revealed beneath the layers of still-warm ash and the occasional jobby wrapped in a Late Night Final. If somebody had died and their worldly goods were discarded, or a family had done a moonlight flit and jettisoned their excess junk, the word that a lucky midden had been discovered raced round the back courts like a fiery cross, and hordes of scavenging weans would set off at the gallop, returning home clutching their booty and looking like small grey ghosts. 'Have you been at the midgie rakin' again?' my ma would demand. 'No, Mammy,' I would lie. The inevitable clout I received would detonate a mushroom cloud of fine ash particles that would fill the room before settling slowly over everything she had had just spent the best part of the day cleaning, which usually led to another clout. It never put me off, though – I'm still addicted to midgie raking. Even though I tend to get my fix these days at auction rooms and French flea markets, I still can't pass a roadside skip without taking a fly keek to see if there are any luckies peeking out from under the rubble. Aye, you can take the boy out of the Gorbals . . .

Once, many years ago, I travelled to a tiny village in Morocco's Atlas Mountains. As I often do on far-flung trips, I got up at dawn and went on a trek round the village with my camera, hoping to capture a few memorable snaps before the tourists woke up and spoiled the atmosphere. Turning a corner off a little alleyway, an old, familiar perfume caught me unawares. The hairs on the back of my neck stood on end. It was the unmistakable scent of our back court in Moffat Street. I was instantly transported back to my childhood as a flood of long-forgotten images overwhelmed my senses. It was an aroma I would come across a few more times in my life – in a remote African village, among the slums of Bombay and in a once-grand courtyard in the centre of Moscow at the tail end of the Soviet regime. So what exactly was it that triggered such a powerful reaction in me? Open middens, damp ground, dirty puddles, spent ashes, outside toilets, washing on a line – the scent of humanity. A scent that unites working people the world over.

My first school was in the Gorbals – Oatlands Primary, the same school my dad had gone to as a boy. My earliest memory of the place is of being taken by my mother at the age of five to register in the primary class. From that day on, I walked to school and back on my own, something my own children didn't do until they were around ten. Sadly, my most enduring memory of Oatlands primary school is of our teacher, a sour-faced, heartless woman who thought nothing of beating and humiliating five-year-old children if they made so much as a spelling mistake. Since I was reasonably clever, I usually escaped her attentions. Other classmates weren't so lucky. I remember David, a quiet and sensitive lad who sat next to me. He was 'awfy well turned oot', as they used to say (in my school photo he's wearing a shirt with a frilly front – I think his mammy really wanted a girl). In short, David was what was referred to at the time as 'a bit of a jessie'. As if the poor wee sowel's life wasn't difficult enough, it was made a living hell by our teacher belting him on a regular basis with a thick leather strap, or 'tawse'. What in God's name was she thinking? More to the point, why didn't anyone stop her? Did every other teacher at that school think that was how you treated children? Or were they, too, fully paid-up members of the national association of child abusers? A lot of people from my generation have similar stories of living in daily terror of a brutal teacher. Maybe back then parents were prepared to turn a blind eye if they wanted their sons and daughters to reap the benefits of the world-renowned Scottish education system. As my old friend Robin Harper, a former teacher turned MSP, once pointed out, 'If you made a roomful of dogs sit completely still for most of the day and hit them with a belt every time they barked, you'd be jailed!'

To this day I can't for the life of me imagine how our teacher justified her cruelty. All I know is that every time I hear the phrase 'the happiest days of your life', I have to grit my teeth. Still, I suppose it could have been worse. I could have been at public school . . .

One of the few happy memories I have of Oatlands Primary was the afternoon a woman from the Education Department came to inspect the class. I remember her dressed in a green uniform with brass buttons and that sort of Maw Broon shape that seemed to have no discernible female outline. She tested us on adding up and taking away, examined our handwriting and finished by asking to see some examples of our handwork. Now, handwork (or handiwork as we used to call it) usually consisted of our teacher having a fag break while her charges manipulated dauds of keech-coloured plasticine in cowed silence. So, the plasticine was duly doled out, and like a stately galleon under sail, the inspector slowly circumnavigated the classroom, nodding and making the odd affirmative grunt. She pulled up sharply when she reached my pal Rab Mathieson's desk. Rab lived up my close and was the class daftie (although someone with the ability to rift the Lord's Prayer all the way through on only three gulps of air couldn't have been all *that* daft). Rab had shaped his plasticine into the vaguely recognisable shape of a human figure, with one significant addition – it seemed to have an extra leg. The inspector leaned over to examine it more closely, a quizzical crease forming between her bushy eyebrows. 'What's this?' she enquired.

'Please, Miss,' said Rab, 'it's a man.'

An ominous cloud began to form above her head as she scrutinised Rab's squidgy lump. 'And why,' she asked, 'has he got three legs?'

'Please, Miss,' replied Rab, 'that's his cock.'

'I see,' she said in an eerily flat tone. 'Well, take it off at once and make it into a hat.' And shooting our mortified teacher a glare that was the naval equivalent of a full broadside, she weighed anchor and sailed swiftly and imperiously out the door.

Thank God I didn't laugh. Anyone daring so much as a snigger would have been flayed alive by our teacher, although over the years, I've more than made up for it each time I've recalled the look of shock and horror on her hatchet face.

2

The Big Picture

Theatre, Cinema, Television and the Lassies, four of the biggest influences on my life – though not necessarily in that order – were firmly established when I lived in the Gorbals. The Television part of it was because I think we must have been one of the first families in Moffat Street to have a telly installed. I remember coming home from school one Tuesday and there, in the corner of the room, was a squat brown Bakelite box with a screen on which ghostly images shimmered through a flurry of sparkly static. A man in a brown dustcoat was twiddling its controls while another man in dungarees was manipulating a long metal rod that was attached to the rear of the set with a length of cable. This, I understood from man one's instructions to man two, was called The Aerial. 'Try movin' it up a bit, Boab. Aye, that's you noo – ach naw, ye've loast the vertical hold. Try it a bit mair sideyweys. Aye that's – aw, bugger it – ye've went an' loast the horizontal hold an' a' noo.' Eventually both holds were attained and the aerial hammered home halfway up the wall. When the pair of them had gone, I sat down and watched my first telly programme – *Andy Pandy*. I was still glued to the set when my dad got home from his work. With a clatter, he emptied a hefty bag of lead, copper and brass scrap metal into the coalbunker. 'What's that for, Da?' I asked.

'That's what's peyin' fur the telly, son,' he answered with a wink at my mother.

Later that evening as we sat watching *In Town Tonight*, my ma glanced behind her and whispered, 'John – ye'd better draw the curtains.' As my da jumped up from his chair, I looked round to the window to see the crowd of faces who had been happily sharing our evening's viewing beat a hasty retreat.

For me, the telly was a window that looked out on to a far greater horizon than the wee window of our single end in Moffat Street. Despite there being just one channel, I think the quality of the programmes were of a higher standard than most of today's vapid offerings. Sir John Reith, who ran the BBC back then, had a streak of old-fashioned Scots Presbyterianism about him that manifested itself in the desire to educate as well as entertain. He certainly got that right – a tubby chef named Philip Harbin taught me that cooking wasn't only for women. Armand and Michaela Denis took me on exciting African safaris, while Hans and Lotte Hass, an Austrian husband and wife team, were my personal guides to the coral reefs and exotic creatures that live deep beneath our oceans. I promised myself that one day I would learn to cook, go on an African safari, and drop in on Hans and Lotte's undersea kingdom – and, thanks to the inspiration from the wee magic box in the corner, when I grew up I did just that.

I have a vivid memory of my first visit to the theatre – the old Metropole in Stockwell Street. What I remember so clearly is sitting between my parents in the dark and smoky auditorium and being mesmerised by the bright, colourful stage lights and the antics of the performers – I can still hear the gales of laughter and applause that accompanied their sketches and songs. I'll probably never know who I saw that night, but it's reasonable to assume that the principal 'turn' must have been one of the popular Glasgow comics of the era: Tommy Morgan perhaps, with his 'Big Beanie' character, or maybe one of the other greats – Jack Radcliffe, Jack Anthony, Tommy Lorne or wee Dave Willis, singing about his 'Wee Gas Mask'. Although my memory of that night may be a little vague, the impression of shared joy and laughter struck a deep chord that stayed with me long after the finale, where, as the cast took their curtain call, a bevy of lovely lassies in glittering tartan mini kilts posed on a rustic bridge over a Highland waterfall in full spate. I used to wonder whether it was something I had imagined, until I discovered years later that 'Currie's Waterfalls of Scotland' was a brilliant piece of aquatic engineering designed and built by a plumber from Barrhead named Jimmy Currie. When, in the late nineties, I was given the opportunity to direct the pantomimes at the King's Theatre, I tried to find out if Currie's Waterfalls were mouldering in a dusty storeroom somewhere, thinking they might still enthral a present-day audience. Sadly they seemed to have vanished, along with the May Moxon Merry Maids who graced their canvas rocks.

Speaking of the legendary May Moxon dancers, there's a wonderful if too-good-to-be-true story I heard years ago about one of her troupes travelling by train to Ayr for the panto season. The only other passenger in their compartment was a wee Church of Scotland minister, which slightly put a damper on their normally spicy gossip. After about half an hour of silence, the minister produced a packet of Pan Drops and attempted to break the ice by offering them to his travelling companions. As they sat sookin' away, he asked them where they were off to. 'We're gaun tae Ayr,' one of them replied.

'Really?' said the minister. 'And are you visiting friends, or is it just a wee day out for you?'

'Naw,' said their leader, 'we're workin' at the Ayr Gaiety. We're the dancers in the pantomime.'

'The pantomime?' said the minister. 'How fascinating. And what's this year's production, might I ask?'

'*Dick Whittington*,' she answered.

'*Dick Whittington*?' he said. 'That's my favourite pantomime. And tell me, which of you takes Dick?'

'Oh we a' dae,' came the rejoinder. 'But no' fur a Pan Drop . . .'

I saw my first film at the Paragon Picture House, a former Methodist hall in nearby Cumberland Street. I remember the thrill of sitting on my dad's shoulders and being transported through the dark and foggy streets to see Charlie Chaplin's comic masterpiece, *The Gold Rush*. I was spellbound from the moment the lights dimmed and the curtains opened. When the Little Fellow (as Chaplin called his tramp character) did his famous bread roll dance routine, I was in hysterics. Despite being a rather pompous and opinionated pain in the bum when he was older, there's no denying that Charles Spencer Chaplin pretty much invented the grammar of silent screen comedy.

On the way back from the pictures that night, as we turned off Crown Street, my dad stopped to show me the smoke and flames belching from the huge blast furnace of Dixon's Blazes, an iron foundry whose chimney dominated the Gorbals skyline. As I watched the night sky burn scarlet, my sense of awe was mixed with a degree of terror, since my mother had warned me that if I was a bad boy Auld Nick would reach up through the floor and drag me down to his Big Bad Burny Fire. (See – they really knew how to raise happy, well-adjusted kids in those days.) All the way back to our close, I clung a little tighter to my father's reassuring hand and sang cheery songs to keep scary thoughts of Auld Nick at bay, now I realised the lum for his Big Bad Burny Fire was just down the far end of Moffat Street.

As regards The Lassies, my old friend Carey Wilson once remarked, 'I first became interested in lassies when I realised I wasn't one.' And if I'm honest with myself, I would have to admit that a fondness for the lassies has probably been one of the prime motivating factors in my choice of career.[1] It all began the day I was in the back court, playing happily on my new three-wheeler bike, when a lassie about my own age appeared in front of me. 'Gie's a go on yer bike,' she said. 'Naw!' I answered brusquely. Undaunted,

---

[1] In fact, I don't think I've ever met a fellow actor who wouldn't deny that the thought of being adored by swarms of female fans had *some* influence over their decision to tread the boards.

she gave me a look that sent a curious tingle up my spine and whispered, 'If ye gie me a go on yer bike ah'll show ye ma fanny.' Now I honestly can't recall if I knew who, or even what, a fanny might be, or, if I did know, quite how I came by the knowledge. I'm fairly certain it couldn't have been from the telly – to the best of my knowledge, Sir Mortimer Wheeler had never displayed one on *Animal, Vegetable or Mineral*. Gilbert Harding had never asked on *What's My Line* if you could eat one, and David Nixon had almost definitely never sawn one in half on *Variety Bandbox*. Nevertheless, something deep and mysterious stirred within me and I agreed to the exchange, certain that this was an opportunity not to be missed. Slipping into a nearby wash house, she clambered on top of the old sink and, with a curiously detached air, fulfilled her part of the bargain. I might be mistaken, but I seem to remember a shaft of heavenly light beaming through the cracked windowpane, while the Glasgow Orpheus Choir sang the 'Hallelujah' chorus. Then, as swiftly as it appeared, the vision vanished – knickers up, frock down, show over. 'Right, that's yer lot,' she said. 'Noo gie's a go on yer bike.'

Sic transit gloria mundi right enough, eh?

3

Running Over

In 1957 Pollokshaws was still a fairly well-preserved burgh, whose roots stretched back to the seventeenth century. Its initial prosperity was built on the cloth trade – from the spinners and weavers (many of them Flemish immigrants, imported for their skills) to the bleaching and dyeing works that stretched along the banks of the River Cart. I celebrated my seventh birthday there a few weeks after we left the Gorbals and flitted to a room and kitchen at 5 Kirk Lane. For me, it was a major step up in life. I had my own bedroom with a zed-bed and an upturned orange box for a bedside table. In our kitchen, Spanish ladies with gold highlights fandangoed across the wallpaper, and the window above the sink looked directly into the yard of a noisy sawmill. If you leaned out and looked to the right, you could see into 'The Gravie', a high-walled graveyard filled with thrillingly creepy tombstones. I loved our new house. But who could have guessed that in the very year we moved there, Glasgow Corporation's planning department had just signed Pollokshaws' death warrant by designating it as Glasgow's 'Second Comprehensive Development Area'.

My life in the Shaws couldn't have been much happier and I look back to my time there with deep affection. Although we didn't have the luxury of a garden, the seemingly endless meadows and woodlands of Pollok Estate were a ten-minute walk away, while directly opposite my bedroom window was a derelict and overgrown patch of land, known to us as The Green – 'us' being me, John McGinlay from up the close, Billy McDermott who lived next door, Billy's wee brother Campbell and occasionally his cousin Agnes – a part-time Shirley MacLaine to our ragged-arsed Rat Pack. On the far side of The Green stood the Pollok Picture House – the kind of place that gave the term 'fleapit' a bad name. Nevertheless, my pals and I would go there as often as we could and settle down in the middle of the front row with a carton of Kia-Ora squash and a packet of Butterkist, eager to be whisked away from our little lives in grey and rainy Glasgow, to set sail with a pirate crew or gallop along with the rootin' tootin' cowboys of the Wild West, or take a trip to my favourite destination – Outer Space. I have a much-played DVD (and a poster, and a model of Robbie the Robot) of the greatest sci-fi film from that era, *Forbidden Planet*. In a plot borrowed from Shakespeare's *The Tempest*, Ariel was re-imagined as Robbie – a robot that resembled an ambulatory 1950s jukebox. It never entered my head for a moment that Robbie was anything other than a genuine robot – he clearly wasn't just another guy in a rubber suit. I could spot guys in rubber suits a mile off – the mostly human-shaped monsters who lurched and squelched their way through films whose titles all seemed to start with the word 'It'. Films such as *It Came from Beyond!* and *It Conquered the World!*[1] held no terrors for me. Well, that's not strictly true – the one X-rated film that scared the living daylights out of me at the time was that classic depiction of Cold War paranoia in small-town America: *Invasion of the Body Snatchers*. I was quite the thing, right up until the moment the first alien seedpod began to split apart, oozing out dodgy-looking foam. That was it – the Kia-Ora and the Butterkist went flying as I bolted for the exit before whatever was lurking inside those bubbles jumped out and grabbed me. Whatever it was, I was pretty bloody sure it wouldn't be a guy in a rubber suit . . .

---

[1] If the producer had managed to raise an extra few grand into the budget, the film's title would start with 'They' . . .

14

After the misery of Oatlands Primary, I was a bit hesitant when my mother took me along to Sir John Maxwell's school in nearby Bengal Street. Known locally as 'Sir Jake's', it was built in 1907 as a gift from the local landowner Sir John Stirling Maxwell. Up to the outbreak of the First World War, the great Socialist orator and Shaws resident John Maclean had held evening classes there, teaching Marxist economic theory to the workers – a development that must have had old Sir John spinning like a peerie in the family vault. After a brief interview with the headmistress, I was placed in Miss Gillespie's class. Miss Gillespie was gentle and kindly – the complete opposite of my teacher at Oatlands. I never remember her losing her temper or using the belt to keep her class in order. There was no need – we all adored her and were happy to do whatever she asked of us.

It was at Sir Jake's that I got my first experience of performing in front of an audience. The school was putting on a celebration to mark the anniversary of its founding, and our class were down to perform an entertaining little piece that involved us all popping up from behind a long white sheet running horizontally across the stage. The piece was a 'This is the house that Jack built' type of thing, where everyone had to repeat his or her little speech over and over as the list grew longer. I was a Member of Parliament, with a bowler hat, briefcase and rolled umbrella. Although quite shy by nature, I felt oddly at home as I crouched behind the sheet waiting for my cue. Was that the moment I realised my destiny lay in the exciting and glamorous world of the theatre? I doubt it. I certainly don't recall having an epiphany as I queued up to have my make-up wiped off with a damp dishcloth that stank of sour milk.

Most of the entertainment for Pollokshaws kids in the fifties usually came dished up with a spoonful – actually, make that a ladleful – of religion, like the weekly Bandy Hope meetings[2] in the Gospel Hall,

---

[2] I'd been going there for ages before I discovered it was actually called 'the Band of Hope'.

where we would all join in singing – with actions – jolly songs like
'Running Over':

Running over
Running over
My cup's full and running over.
Since the Lord saved me
I'm as happy as can be.
My cup's full and running over.

Then the lights would be switched off and we'd watch an ancient
slide show, usually about a poor but virtuous household that
rapidly degenerated into a disgusting hovel when the husband
was talked into downing 'the Fatal Glass of Beer'. When the lights
went on again, we'd be treated to the obligatory lecture about the
evils of drink and the joy of redemption through commitment to
the Band of Hope, after which we'd be asked to 'Sign the Pledge'
and swear our everlasting commitment to abstinence. As a finale,
the dodgy pair of zealots who ran the place would throw out
handfuls of sweeties, which, frankly, was the only thing that
guaranteed our regular attendance.

As a kid, I was a big fan of puppets, forever turning empty orange
boxes into theatres, cutting up old tea towels for curtains, painting
backdrops, making sets and putting on improvised puppet shows
for my pals. (I'd even won a Pelham Puppet as a first prize for my
puppetry skills in a competition at the Boys' and Girls' Exhibition
in the Kelvin Hall.) So picture my joy when a poster on the door of
the wee Salvation Army hall in Bengal Street announced a puppet
show the following evening. Buzzing with anticipation, my pals
and I turned up at the packed hall to find that the 'show' consisted
of a couple of badly made glove puppets dressed in Salvation Army
uniforms and banging on about – yes, you've guessed it – the evils
of drink and the joy of redemption through commitment to the
Salvation Army. The only way you could tell which puppet was
doing the talking was because its operator jiggled it a bit. After

about ten minutes of this, the swelling chorus of jeers and raspberries from the disgruntled audience finally forced the hapless puppeteers to depart from the script and try some snappy improvisation. 'Oh dear, Corporal Phillip,' jiggled the first puppet. 'These boys and girls aren't as well behaved as the boys and girls in Swindon, are they?'

'No, Captain Nigel,' the second puppet jiggled back in a voice that seemed tinged with an edge of panic, 'they're not nearly as quiet and polite as the boys and girls in Wolverhampton.' That's when I realised the pair of no-hopers were on the Scottish leg of a nationwide tour. They must have thought they were on a roll until the night they played Pollokshaws.

'Perhaps we should just stop the show right now and go back home,' squeaked the Captain Nigel puppet rather testily. Whether the Corporal Phillip puppet agreed or not I never found out, as its reply was lost beneath the thunderous roar of approval that greeted Captain Nigel's suggestion. From that point on things went rapidly downhill until, in a desperate attempt to prevent a full-scale riot, a Sally Army officer, his face purple with fury, screamed at us all to sit down and shut up. To cover the puppeteers' humiliation and distract us while they dismantled their booth and slunk out the exit, he led us in a spirited chorus of 'Join the Army', which, luckily enough, we all knew, since it was exactly the same tune as 'Running Over', back at the Bandy Hope:

> Join the Army
> Join the Army
> Boys and girls come join the Army
> For there's room for them all
> In the Pollokshaws Hall
> Boys and girls come join the Army.

After the singsong, I guessed the chance of free sweeties that night would be extremely slim indeed.

4

Going Through the Motions

Without doubt, the happiest times of my childhood began on the magical day when school closed for the summer holidays. Freed after years of incarceration on Devil's Island, Captain Dreyfus couldn't have felt more relieved than I did when the school gates clanged shut behind me. For six glorious weeks I was at liberty to roam the Pollok Estate or the Rouken Glen, taking turns at being Tom Sawyer, Huckleberry Finn, Robin Hood, William Tell, Rob Roy or the hero of whatever Disney film was currently showing at the Pollok Picture House. The absolute highlight of my summer holiday was the Glesca Fair, when for a fortnight my folks and I would decamp to a rented room in Saltcoats. It began with a ritual that must have been repeated all over the city – at teatime on Fair Friday, my mother would answer the door to a pair of drunk guys with an even drunker guy propped up between them. 'We've brought yer man back,' one of them would say, and without a word of reproach from my mother, Athos would be set down in his chair to sleep it off, while Porthos and Aramis staggered back to the nearest pub. The next morning, after my dad had, in time-honoured tradition, boaked in the sink and downed a couple of Askit powders, we would set off for Central Station.

Saltcoats got away with it for a long time. Since the nineteenth century, this Clyde coast resort had provided basic, if over-priced, accommodation for its annual influx of visitors from the manufacturing towns of Glasgow, Paisley and Kilmarnock. Then, in the late sixties, cheap package holidays to sun-soaked resorts like Benidorm became available, leaving the surprised locals blinking in bewilderment and wondering why on earth working folk would rather spend their two weeks of freedom in a place with good food, cheap booze, decent hotels, warm seas and guaranteed sunshine. Didn't they like the dingy pubs that shut at half past nine? The scattering of cafes whose bill of fare consisted solely of high fish tea with bread and butter? The rainy days huddled in a room even more dismal than the one they spent the rest of the year in? And what about the children? Wouldn't they miss their customary bouts of diarrhoea after eating whelks and mussels picked from the big, rusty sewage pipe with its outlet less than five yards from the shore? Or having their feet lacerated by the broken bottles cunningly concealed in the sand by smirking psychopaths?

Looking back, it's easy to knock Saltcoats, but at the time I thought a fortnight there was as close to heaven as you could get. The thrills began as we joined the throngs at Central Station. As the big clock ticked perilously close to our departure time, my mother and I would wait anxiously at the platform entrance, until with less than a couple of minutes to the guard's whistle, my Da would emerge from the buffet, having had a wee livener for the journey. Once, as we scurried along the platform looking for a relatively uncrowded compartment, we passed an empty first-class carriage. 'How do we always have to travel second class?' I whinged.

'Because there's nae thurd class,' said my da.

The Saltcoats train had carriages that were divided into single sections, each with two opposing rows of six seats. There was no corridor, hence no lavatories. Like my Da, most of the men on the journey would have sunk a couple of pints in the station buffet, and about half an hour into the journey would be feeling the need to empty their bladders. Thankfully, there was a long observed ritual whereby a gentleman would rise and lower the carriage window, which would be the signal for all the ladies to look the other way while he relieved himself. God help any weans in the following compartment who happened to be leaning out the window at the time. It was more than the warm summer breeze they got in their faces.

One time, inspired by the underwater expeditions of my TV hero Hans Hass, I spent a sizeable share of my 'fairing' – shillings and sixpences handed out to kids at the start of the Fair Fortnight by kindly neighbours – on a pair of flippers and a mask and snorkel combo from my favourite wee shop in Saltcoats, whose window display sported an enviable range of lethal-looking sheath knives along with kitsch shell figures, plastic donkeys that dispensed cigarettes out of their backsides and chrome-plated cruet sets with 'A present from Bonny Scotland' on the front, and 'Made in England' on the base. Quivering with anticipation, I strapped on my fins, pulled my mask over my face and waded in for my first encounter with – as Hans often put it – 'ze denizens of ze deep'. As the chilly waters of the Clyde estuary closed over my head I gasped with amazement. I had achieved one of my most cherished ambitions – I was actually breathing underwater. As I finned away from the shore, I could hear Hans' heavily accented narration running through my head. 'Lotte und I vere on ze adventure of a lifetime – who knows vot extraordinary creatures ve might come across on our visit to zeir mysterious undervater realm.' As I peered through the grey murk, thrilled by the thought of swimming alongside curious seals, shy turtles and playful dolphins, a big, perfectly formed jobby drifted lazily by, inches from my mask. With a muffled shriek, I was out of zat mysterious undervater realm and tearing up the beach, quicker than Hans tearing up his war diaries after VE day.

5

The Escapologist

I can't recall when I first became aware that my mother wasn't well. Each time she would send me out to buy her five Woodbines, she would always tell me to get a couple of Askit powders as well. As time went on, the number of Askits increased until she must have been downing anything up to eight a day. Askit powders were manufactured in a Glasgow factory under licence from a Swedish pharmaceutical company who had been marketing them since the end of the First World War. 'Dr. Hjorton's Powders' proved to be a big seller among the dockworkers in Malmo who drank heavily and consequently suffered from ferocious hangovers, and these little packets of bitter-tasting powder seemed to be the answer to their prayers. Swallow a couple of them on the way to work in the morning and in no time they'd be right as rain – except they weren't really. The secret of Dr. Hjorton's magic formula that cured your hangover, and gave you a wee bit of a buzz into the bargain, was a chemical compound called phenacetin. Unfortunately, as a great many dockers would discover, phenacetin had something of a down side – it destroyed their kidneys, leading to an early and agonising death – an annoying little side effect the Askit Powder Company chose not to disclose to its many devotees.

One of the shops I would often go to for my mother's Askits was Wendy's café in Shawbridge Street. It had a jukebox and sold frothy coffee and I thought it was the last word in sophistication. Cool and aloof, the eponymous Wendy seemed to have jetted in from some chic East Village hangout. She wore her hair in a modish Audrey Hepburn bouffant, her dark eyes enhanced by a swish of black liner. A pair of skin-tight matador pants, kitten heels and a black polo-neck sweater completed her New York beat look. Needless to say, even at the tender age of ten, I was completely smitten.

I took to hanging out at Wendy's café whenever I had collected enough empty ginger bottles to pay for a glass of Creamola Foam and a Blue Riband. If I was particularly flush, I would slip a tanner into the jukebox and play Shirley Bassey singing *Kiss Me Honey Honey Kiss Me*. Young as I was, I confess I nurtured a secret fantasy which involved Wendy and me in some exotic location like *Hernando's Hideaway* where, after a couple of *Cocktails for Two* and a wee turn at the *Mambo Italiano*, we would stroll hand in hand to *My Little Wooden Hut*, where we would snib the door and . . . Well, to be honest, I wasn't sure quite what we'd do after we'd snibbed the door. But I imagined Wendy, *The Naughty Lady of Shady Lane*, would hopefully steer me in the right direction.

Sadly, my dream never came to pass. The vision of Wendy and me spending the Fair Fortnight on a tropical isle ended tragically when, in the café one day, I pointed to the trays of sweeties that were arranged behind the glass-fronted counter in order of price. 'What can I get for tuppence?' I asked, hoping the answer would be far, far, beyond my wildest imaginings. 'Well,' replied Wendy, indicating the trays. 'You can have one of these, or two of those, or you could have four of these, or several of these.' I blinked in surprise at this unfamiliar word. Obviously I must have misheard her.

'Seven?' I asked.

'Several,' she repeated.

There was a slight pause as I tried to grasp how I could have misheard her twice in a row. I knew there was no such word as 'several'. What else could she conceivably be saying *but* seven? I had no option other but to ask her again.

'Seven?' I ventured nervously.

'Several!' she hissed through tightly pursed lips.

A terrible feeling of panic began to overwhelm me. I felt trapped with no way out other than to stumble deeper into the fathomless pit I was digging for myself.

'Seven?' I squeaked, in a tiny voice that seemed somehow not to be my own.

'*Six!*' snapped Wendy, grabbing my tuppence and stuffing a handful of random sweets into a paper poke. Swivelling on her kitten heels she marched into the back shop, casting not a backward glance as I slithered out beneath the door. My feelings for Wendy were never quite the same after that, especially when I opened my poke of sweeties to find there were only five.

I was eight when I transferred from Sir Jake's to Pollok Academy. Wee Pollok Primary, as it was known, was a small parish school, designed in the Italianate style by the great Glasgow architect Alexander 'Greek' Thomson.[1] Although the classes were mixed, the playgrounds were strictly segregated. In the girls' playground the games involved skipping or bouncing tennis balls off a wall and catching them with amazing dexterity. In the boys' playground our games usually involved fighting each other with imaginary weapons. Who fought who depended on what film was currently showing at the Pollok Picture House – British and Germans, Highlanders and Redcoats, pirates and, er, other pirates. The great thing was, it didn't matter how often you were slain: as soon as one of your team touched you and said tig, you leaped back into the fray, good as new.

I remember once watching four lads galloping round the playground; there were two at the front with their arms round each other's shoulders. Behind them, bent forward and clinging onto

---

[1] Along with so much of what Sir John Betjeman called 'the most perfect Victorian city in Britain', Wee Pollok school was demolished in the sixties. The collection of third-rate architects, second-rate planners and first-rate duds that made up the Corporation's planning department at the time decreed that many of Glasgow's world-class buildings should be torn down and replaced with job lots of concrete bunkers that leaked, cracked and drove their residents doolally until, a few short years after they went up, they in their turn were torn down and replaced.

the tails of their jackets, was a third lad. Sitting astride his back, the fourth member of the team was cracking an imaginary whip and spurring the front pair onwards. I noticed one of my classmates running alongside them and cheering. I caught up with him and asked what was going on. 'We're daein' a Roman Picture,' he told me excitedly. 'They two are the horses, he's the chariot, and the wan wi' the whip's Ben Hur.'

'And what are you?' I asked.

'Ah'm the perzoosher,' he explained.

Now, here's a thing – despite having worked in quite a few pictures during the course of my career, I've yet to discover what a perzoosher is, or does. My best guess is that a perzoosher is the character in a movie whose function is to explain complicated stuff for the benefit of the audience – Jeff Goldblum, for example. Fine actor though he is, I suspect he's hired primarily for his unique skill at perzooshing, since in most of the films I've seen him in, he seems to spends most of his screen time explaining hard-to-grasp concepts such as transmutation of matter in *The Fly*, chaos theory in *Jurassic Park* or the fundamental principles of alien communication in *Independence Day*.[2]

My teacher, Mrs Dow, seemed to take a bit of a shine to me, because I usually came first or second in the class exams. I certainly wasn't a swot by any means. I think the reason I never really had to try that hard was thanks to 'The World of the Children', a set of encyclopaedias I loved to read each time I stayed at my granny's house. I was an avid reader and Pollokshaws had a wonderful lending library. To reach it, you had to go through a close in the middle of Shawbridge Street. Once up the steps and through the big swing doors, its dark and polished interior was a wonderful oasis of quiet and tranquillity where time seemed to be on hold as I worked my way through the shelves of immaculately kept books in the children's section. Inspired by the tales in *Classics Illustrated*, a

---

[2] Here's a handy hint – you can usually spot a movie's perzoosher if he starts a lengthy monologue with the words 'OK, so what you're trying to tell me is . . .'

brilliant series of American comics that I used to collect along with all the usual superhero comics (why oh why didn't anyone tell me they'd be worth a fortune one day?) I found my way into the novels of Mark Twain, Charles Dickens, Herman Melville, Jack London, H.G. Wells, Jules Verne, Robert Louis Stephenson, as well as the collections of European folk tales by Hans Andersen and the brothers Grimm. Between the encyclopaedias and the library books, class work was a scoosh. Whenever we were given a new reading book at school, I'd take it home and finish it in a few hours, spending English lessons daydreaming while the majority of my classmates trailed their index fingers along the page, silently moving their lips as they read the awkward and unfamiliar sentences. I could never begin to repay the debt I owe to the enlightened souls who provided free public libraries for kids like me – their foresight and benevolence enriched my life beyond measure.

In fact, it was in the library that I came across a book that was to change my life completely. Under the stage name 'Al Koran', Edward Doe was a popular stage and TV mentalist who regularly baffled his audience by predicting the results of a horse race, or knowing the very word a volunteer from the audience would pick out at random from a dictionary. So was it really by chance that I came across his book *Bring Out the Magic in Your Mind* in the Pollokshaws library one day? There's an old Zen saying – 'When the pupil is ready, the teacher will appear'. As I entered my early teens, I began to feel a creeping sense of unease about what was waiting for me when I left school. My qualms probably started the Saturday morning my dad took me with him to his work. Although his mates were a cheery bunch of souls who gave me a few bob for brewing tea for them, the thought of labouring day after day on a muddy building site in all weathers seemed like a terrible curse hanging over my head like the sword of Damocles. The heroes in the storybooks I loved to read hadn't settled for the ordinary life. They packed their belongings in a hanky, tied it to a stick slung over their shoulders and set out to slay dragons and win the hearts of beautiful princesses. Even though I knew dragons and princesses were fairly thin on the ground in Pollokshaws, I was unconsciously searching for the hidden door that would lead to a different future from the one that was being pencilled in for me. Edward Doe's remarkable book showed me where to find the door, and quietly slipped me the key to the lock. To this day I still keep a tattered old copy on my bookshelf.

'The Quali' was the name given to the eleven-plus (qualifying) exam that determined your academic future. At Pollok Primary, if you passed, you went to Shawlands Academy. If you failed, you went back to Sir Jake's to learn a trade. Despite having done little or no preparation, I sailed through the exam and got ready to start a new chapter in my life.

Apart from a perpetual sense of boredom, the only major trauma that blighted my time at Wee Pollok was the day Mrs Dow ordered me to report to the headmaster at once. I could tell from her tone that this was something serious, but what? She hadn't said. My mind was racing as I took the long walk to the heidie's office. I knew I hadn't done anything bad – I was top of the class, for God's sake! So what could this possibly be about? I found out soon enough as I stood anxiously in front of Mr Wood's desk.

'Do you know why you're here?' he asked.

'No, Sir,' I answered truthfully.

'Yes you do,' he insisted.

'Please, Sir, I don't.'

'It's been brought to my attention that you've been saying certain things and behaving in a certain way. Is that correct?' Is *what* correct? I wondered. I still didn't have a clue what this was all about.

'Sir, I don't know what—'

'Two girls in your class said that you told them filthy stories. Is this true?'

Oh shit. I knew instantly who he meant: Anne and her pal Carol. They had called me over to the railings and asked me if I knew any rude jokes. Being an averagely dirty wee bugger, I had a fair repertoire and was more than happy to share a few of my favourites. They had both sniggered gratifyingly at the one which involved pointing at your naughty bits and chanting, 'Milk, milk, lemonade – round the corner chocolate's made.' Then the sleekit wee pair must have clyped on me.

'I asked you if it's true?' Mr Wood repeated.

'Yes, Sir,' I whispered.

'They also said that you had stood on top of a desk when your teacher was out of the room and exposed yourself to the rest of the class.'

A trapdoor opened beneath my feet and I plunged into it. I could scarcely comprehend what was being said as I felt the blood drain from my face and an iron band tighten around my chest.

'No, Sir, I didn't.'

'Yes you did.'

'Please, Sir, I did not.'

Mr Wood thrust his angry red face close to mine. 'You did, boy. Don't lie to me. You stood on your desk and took down your trousers and exposed yourself to the entire class, didn't you? *Didn't you!*'

Why was this happening? I hadn't done anything of the kind. Why was the headmaster yelling at me and saying that I had. He seemed so certain that I started to believe he was right and I was wrong – I must have done this shameful thing and somehow blanked out the memory. In my fear and confusion, I could only think of one way to end the nightmare.

'Tell the truth!' Mr Wood shrieked as flecks of spittle hit my face. 'You did. *Didn't you?'*

'Yes, Sir,' I whispered.

I walked home that day with legs that threatened to give way under me at every step. In my schoolbag was a sealed letter asking my parents to attend an urgent meeting with the School Board. Never again in my life have I felt as wretched as I did that day. Guilt and shame hung on my heart like lead weights. Why would two lassies make such an outrageous accusation against me? Why would the headmaster browbeat me into a false confession? I burst into tears the moment my mother opened the door to me. All I could manage to choke out, over and over again, was, 'I didny do it mammy. I didny do it.'

You might wonder why I've gone on at length about this incident, since it's fairly minor stuff compared to the hair-raising tales of childhood abuse that have become so popular they now have their very own section in bookshops. The truth is that the feeling of hurt and betrayal left me with a deep wound that never quite healed over. However, I believe that you can always learn a positive lesson from a negative experience, and from that incident, I now know just how easy it is to browbeat a vulnerable person into making a false confession – another five minutes of Mr Wood screaming at me and I'd have owned up to being Jack the Ripper. The other reason I mention it is this: if you're at all interested in seeing an actor get in touch with his own emotions in an attempt to play for truth, then look no further than my performance in Peter McDougall's *A Sense of Freedom*. In the scene where my character, Malkie, has to face the consequences of not being able to pay back his loan to Jimmy Boyle, I used my memory of that day in the headmaster's office to portray his terror and despair. When the drama was transmitted, many of the reviews singled out my performance for special mention.

I assume you've gone to the big staffroom in the sky by now, Mr Wood, but if by chance I ever come across your final resting place, as a token of my respect I'll place a bouquet of flowers on your grave. I'll even sprinkle a little water over them – although I hope you won't mind if I pass it through my kidneys first.

As my primary school days drew to a close, our little family increased by one when, to my absolute delight, Dougie, my brand-new baby brother, made a welcome appearance. And by the time I was about to start the Big School in Shawlands, the plan to obliterate Pollokshaws had begun in earnest.

To my pals and me it was all hugely exciting. Tenements seemed to vanish overnight and big deep trenches appeared in their place.

After the workmen had finished for the day, the building sites were great places to restage battle scenes. Defending my trench one particular evening, after all my squad had been wiped out by the dastardly Hun, I was about to mount a heroic and solitary sortie across no man's land to 'tig' the poor blighters back to life when I heard an ominous groaning sound. A shower of dirt and stones began to rain down on me with increasing ferocity. Blind instinct took over – I dropped my tommy gun and ran like hell, just managing to scramble out the far end of the trench as its walls collapsed with a noise like thunder. When I looked back, the spot where I had just been standing was now buried under about six feet of rubble and heavy clay. I never played in the trenches again, and soon afterwards they were filled in with concrete to form the foundations of the new high-rise flats that would change the face of the Shaws forever, and beneath one of them, like a metaphor for the end of childhood, is the plastic tommy gun I left behind on a day that might have been the last of my life.

6

Act One – Beginners

For as long as I can remember, I wanted to learn to play the piano. There was an old piano in my granny's house and I would plonk out popular tunes like 'Scotland the Brave' for hours on end, using the first two fingers on my left hand to provide a rhythmic drone. I was always frustrated, knowing I couldn't improve without someone who could really play showing me how. Each time I travelled into the town on the tram, I noticed a sign in a window in Shawlands that read: 'Grace Binnie, Piano Teacher'. I pleaded with my mother to send me there for lessons. Although she was sympathetic, the answer was always the same: we couldn't afford it.[1] I was determined to play *something*, though, and if I stumbled across an old instrument at the jumble sales I regularly went to with my granny, I would wheedle her into buying it for me. At one time or another, and in no particular order, I was the proud possessor of a violin, a clarinet, a flute, a banjo, a zither, a Neapolitan mandolin and a xylophone, none of which cost more than a couple of bob, and all of which, in the absence of even the most basic instruction, were utterly useless. In my desperation to learn an instrument, I signed up for trumpet lessons at the Salvation Army. I even went to weekly meetings of the local Orange Lodge in hopes

---

[1] I subsequently discovered the real reason had nothing to do with the cost – it was because my dad thought piano lessons were for sissies.

of learning the accordion. But ultimately, it was the drum lessons at the Boys' Brigade that made the crucial difference to my future.

Not long after starting my first year at Shawlands Academy, I became aware of a lad in my class named Ronnie Christie who had won a talent contest in Lewis's department store for singing and playing the guitar. As luck – or fate – would have it, my talented classmate turned out to be a fellow B.B. boy and somehow word reached him that I was taking drum lessons. He approached me one day in the playground with a proposition – he had netted fifty pounds' prize money in the Lewis's talent competition and spent some of it on a snare drum and a hi-hat cymbal. There was a school concert coming up that he would be playing in, and asked would I be interested in backing him on the drums. I thought it was a great idea, so after school I went back to his house in Eastwood and gave him a taste of my prowess. Of course, all I knew were military rhythms – two-fours, four-fours and paradiddles – none of which sat too comfortably with the pop hits of the day, but at least I was able to keep time. As a born musician, Ronnie showed me how to do a simple beat on the snare while keeping a steady rhythm on the cymbal.

With the date for the end-of-term concert rapidly approaching, Ronnie and I practised regularly. The sessions were always held at his house for the shameful reason that since starting classes at Shawlands Academy, I had become terribly aware of my working-class background and didn't want my posh new friends to see where I came from or how I lived. When I first started to visit the two- (or even three-) bedroomed homes of my middle-class school friends, with their neat little kitchenettes and indoor toilets, I began to see my own home from a different perspective. The wee room and kitchen I had so loved when we first moved to the Shaws I now viewed as a dingy hovel in an impoverished neighbourhood. I'm ashamed to admit that my background had become a major source of embarrassment to me. The lack of money for stylish clothes to keep up with my smartly dressed friends was a constant humiliation. In fact, for my debut at the school concert

I resorted to borrowing some of my long-suffering uncle Willie's clothes, even though I had to roll up the sleeves of his cardigan to stop them hanging over my hands, while his two-sizes-too-big shoes must have made me look like one of the Keystone Kops. Still, all things considered, our performance was an unqualified success. We were even encouraged to play an encore, which Ronnie, the seasoned performer, had anticipated – belting out Joe Brown's 'A Picture of You' to rousing cheers and prolonged applause. Even though the acclaim was mainly for Ronnie's precocious talent, I think I can honestly say if ever there was a defining moment in my life when I caught a glimpse of the way forward, that was it. As our repertoire grew, Ronnie and I began to play gigs in pensioners' clubs and old folks' homes. They loved us (especially when Ronnie launched into a medley of George Formby hits on the ukulele) and we usually pocketed five or ten bob each for our efforts. I knew then I wanted nothing other than to make a life for myself in this heady world of show business. I realised it might be a difficult road to navigate, but of all the obstacles I had to overcome, the first and by far the hardest was trying to gain my dad's approval for my newfound ambition.

I didn't really know my dad terribly well – like most kids of my background and generation I was closer to my mother than my father, for the simple reason that I saw a lot more of her. On weekdays my dad would leave for work a few hours before I got up for school and I would see him briefly at teatime, when he came home exhausted after humping cast-iron baths and hefty china lavvy pans up three or four flights of stairs all day. After supper, he would doze off in his chair in front of the telly for an hour before heading off to the Maxwell Arms or the Cabin Bar, returning to the house after last orders had been called. By the time he got back, I would be in bed, asleep.

I saw a bit more of him at the weekends. Most Saturdays I'd travel on the coach with him and his fellow members of the Pollokshaws Rangers Supporters Club to wherever the team happened to be playing that day. Although I sang 'Follow Follow' and 'The Billy Boys' along with the rest of the coach party, in truth I didn't really give a toss about football in general or Rangers in particular. For one thing, being a bit on the short side, the only view I got from the terrace was my own reflection in the shiny arse on the trousers of the guy standing in front of me. No, for me the highlight of the trip was after the game ended, when I would pick up the empty beer bottles to collect the threepenny deposit when I handed them in at the Maxwell Arms in Pollokshaws. Actually, it's not quite true to say they were empty, as, rather than risk missing the action by going to the lavatories, the fans would simply pee in their beer bottles and leave them for lads like me to empty out the lukewarm contents and cash in on the bonanza. My heady days as an empty-bottle entrepreneur came to an abrupt end when my dad's fellow supporters told him they had had enough of the stink from my pee-soaked duffel bag on the coach home. Since collecting the empties was the only reason I went to the matches, I had to seek an alternative source of funds in order to continue living in the style to which I'd become accustomed, so I got an early-morning milk round. Then, after popping back home for breakfast, I would deliver orders of butcher meat for the Co-op in Shawbridge Street. Finally, I became a Saturday morning van boy for the local bakery, spending my Saturday afternoons in the relative comfort of the Pollok Picture House, rather than the rain-swept terraces of Ibrox. Still, my dad didn't *entirely* despair at my lack of interest in fitba, since I was still very keen on his other favourite sport – the gowf.

Golf is a much more egalitarian game in Scotland than just about everywhere else in the world, and my dad was a keen amateur golfer. On Sunday mornings I would regularly tag along with him and his mates as they played for a tanner a hole at Deaconsbank, our nearest public course – in fact, it was at Deaconsbank one fresh spring morning that I experienced my first Zen moment. In traditional Japanese archery, the Zen moment is where the archer is one with the bow, the arrow and the target. In such a moment, no outcome is possible other than the one intended by the archer, since all three elements are spiritually united. My initiation into the art and practice of Zen began as my dad and his pals walked on towards the green, leaving me behind to take my next shot from the edge of the rough. Instead of my usual shanking or clipping, I executed a well-nigh perfect swing, and from the second the ball left my club head, I knew with every atom of my being exactly where it was going to land. In that eternal moment, I was one with the club, one with the ball and one with the back of my dad's head. I tried to yell 'fore' but my senses had temporarily deserted me and all I managed to stammer out was 'ehhh – thingmy!' as the ball arced gracefully through the crisp morning air and smacked him squarely on the napper. With a yelp, he dropped his golf bag and launched into a lively hopping routine that would have stood him in good stead at the *Riverdance* auditions. From his expletives, it was clear he didn't find the incident quite as amusing as his mates, who were literally rolling around the fairway, helpless with laughter. From that day on, I have no memory of ever going golfing with him again.

I think my relationship with my dad began to founder around the age of eight or nine, when I'd be woken up yet again by the sound of my parents arguing in the kitchen, my father's voice loud and angry, my mother's tearful and defensive. I have no idea what they fought about. All I remember is lying in bed with the blankets pulled over my head, shivering with fear and hoping it was a bad dream but knowing it wasn't. Some nights, when the angry words were accompanied by the sounds of crockery smashing, my mother would throw open my bedroom door and yank me out of bed. 'Get your claes on, son,' she would sob. 'We're leavin'.'

'Aye, go!' my dad would yell as my Ma dragged me out the front door. 'And don't bother yer arse comin' back.' Tripping over my shoelaces I'd be hurried down the stairs and out into the night. My mother worked as a cleaner for our local doctor and had a set of keys for his surgery. If it was raining when we fled the house, she would unlock the front door and sit in the semi-darkness of the empty waiting room, weeping quietly and telling me she would go and find us somewhere else to live in the morning. She never did, of course. After an hour or so she would invariably return to the devil she knew.

Of course, these angry scenes didn't happen every night, or even every week – just often enough to turn me into a classic example of an anxiety-ridden pee-the-bed. Until I was about fourteen or so, I didn't dare risk a sleepover at any of my posh new friends' houses for fear of leaving their mothers with a couple of sheets that smelled like my old Rangers Club duffel bag.

By now, Ronnie and I were best pals, and I spent much more time at his house than my own. His two elder brothers, Norman and Peter, were great lads, and his parents were the soul of generosity, his mother uncomplainingly setting a place for me at the table along with her own family.

The Big Bang that was the Beatles had recently exploded and Ronnie and I began to work their songs into our repertoire. Thanks to my three part-time jobs, I had managed to scrape enough money together to buy a second-hand guitar and Ronnie showed me how to tune it and strum a few basic chords. I had finally found the teacher I had been searching for, and the drums took second place as I spent most of my spare time practising the guitar – the instrument I fell in love with and still play to this day.

Despite heartfelt pleas from my Captain to stay with my local B.B. company, the 9th, I transferred to the 145 Company in Eastwood, where Ronnie and some of my new friends were members. At the time I didn't really know why, I was perfectly happy with my old company, but somehow it just seemed the right thing to do. (I'm sure that in his book, Al Koran would have pointed out that my subconscious mind was taking the next step necessary to achieve my goal.) As it was, attending the Friday evening parade at Eastwood Parish church hall marked the point where I took the first step on the path I was to follow for the rest of my life.

The church had its own amateur drama group – the excitingly named Eastwood Parish Church Dramatic Society. An officer in my new B.B. company was one of the Dramatic Society's regular players, and one evening I went with a few pals to see him in their latest production. A quietly spoken and fairly diffident person in everyday life, I was struck by the change in his personality as he portrayed a strong, confident character on stage. I remember thinking that if he could do it, maybe I could too. After the play ended, I timidly asked him to ask Margaret, their director, whether I could join her little company. Despite her initial misgivings (she told me, when I interviewed her years later for my episode of the BBC Scotland series *I Belong to Glasgow*, that she thought I was far too young) she agreed to accept me as a member, and a few weeks later I started rehearsals for their next production.

Spring Madness was something of a departure for the Eastwood Parish Church Dramatic Society. Instead of the usual am-dram fare – a French's Acting Edition[2] of some creaky old whodunit for instance – Margaret had decided to play a wild card and stage a revue, complete with songs, sketches and dance routines. Wednesday evening became the highlight of my week, when I would take the bus to the church hall and throw myself whole-heartedly into the rehearsals. I loved it.

I vividly remember the knot in my stomach on our first night, as I waited for the curtain to rise on our opening number, but once the show got under way the nerves were soon dissipated by the incredible buzz of performing in front of a live audience. I got my first delicious taste of laughter in one of our big musical numbers – a Charleston routine, with all the male members of the company dressed as 1920s flappers. The fringed dresses came courtesy of the Women's Guild, but Margaret had asked us all to provide our own stockings. My mother must have wondered what her changeling child was getting himself into, as she loaned me her best pair of nylons, neglecting to tell me that they needed garters to hold them up. The Charleston number was in full swing when I became aware the audience were cracking up. Although the laughter was gratifying, I didn't think the routine was *that* funny. A furtive glance

---

[2] French's Acting Editions are a collection of plays published for amateur companies by Samuel French & Co. with all the stage directions laid out alongside the text.

down revealed the reason for the hilarity. Without anything to hold them up, my maw's nylons were now flapping round my ankles in time to the music. I thought it was a great comic touch, but back in the dressing room a few of my fellow flappers gave me a roasting for screwing up their carefully rehearsed choreography. Oh yeah? Thanks to me, the audience were in stitches, so how was that a bad thing exactly? Somewhere in the distance, I heard the sound of a penny dropping.

Since spending most of my free time in and around Ronnie's home turf, I had joined a local youth club. Although it was a bit of a hike from the Shaws, it appealed to me for the table tennis and the group of attractive lassies who frequented the place. One evening a blonde vision appeared in our midst, instantly making all the other girls in the club look like something out of a Breughel painting. The vision in the fringed suede jacket and Robin Hood boots introduced herself as Jane Peebles and told us she was a student at the Royal Scottish Academy of Music and Drama. She said she was starting up a drama group in the club, and when she asked if anyone was interested in joining, I was the first to put my hand up. Simply to be in her presence I would have volunteered if she'd been recruiting for the West of Scotland junior hara-kiri society.

The following week, we gathered for the first rehearsal of *The Insect Play*, a surprising and radical choice for an untried junior drama group. Written in 1920 by two Czechoslovakian brothers, Josef and Karel Čapek, the play is a surreal satire on the human condition. Set in a wood, it begins with an old tramp with a serious bout of the DTs. In his alcohol-induced visions, he sees all the insects at his eye level behaving very much like his fellow human beings. Jane cast me as Mister Cricket, an optimistic young chap whose wife is just about to give birth to their first child. I thought the part was OK, but I secretly coveted the main role of the tramp. Unfortunately, that part had been given to Billy Colville, the only other male in the company. Still, I gave Mister Cricket my all, even coming up with an original tune for the little crickety song he sings to his darling wife. We were a few weeks into rehearsals when we discovered that Billy had bottled out and done a runner. We were due to perform the piece at a youth club drama festival in about six weeks' time, so Jane suggested we carry on rehearsing until a replacement could be found. Taking a big deep breath and summoning up courage from God knows where, I told her I would very much like to take over the role of the tramp. My earnestness must have convinced her. One of the small-part players took over as Mister Cricket and I started rehearsing the tramp that evening. I already had a notion that the character shouldn't be Scottish. I wanted him to be an outsider, someone completely different from myself, and with Jane's help and encouragement I began to inhabit the Čapek brothers' drunken, ragged narrator – cockney accent and all.

At a school hall in Knightswood, there were about half a dozen youth club drama groups competing for the winner's trophy. Shortly before we were due to go on, Jane's fellow student John Murtagh, who had been pressed into service as our stage manager, frowned at my make-up and drew his fingers along the dust on the top of a door. 'You canny beat the real thing,' he said, rubbing the grime on my face.

I stood behind the curtains with my stomach churning as I listened to the hum of chatter from out front. The hall became deathly quiet as the tabs squeaked open and I launched into my opening monologue. Halfway through it, there was a gasp from the audience as I toppled forward and crashed, face first, on to the stage. John Murtagh had shown me how to execute a pratfall by putting my hands out at the last minute to absorb the impact. I waited till the audience were silent again before delivering my next line. 'You thought I hurt meself there, didn'tcha?' There was a huge laugh followed by a round of applause – we were off to the races.

Thirty minutes later, we took our curtain call to a riot of applause, whistles and cheers. It had all gone better than we could have dreamed and, in high spirits, we sat at the back of the hall to watch the rest of the competitors. One of the plays was an 'Anyone for tennis?' type of light comedy. The cast all seemed terribly assured and I thought the leading man gave a wonderfully comic performance. I leaned over to Jane and whispered that I thought they would take the first prize. She gave an enigmatic smile and said nothing.

Amateur drama competitions generally have an adjudicator. Usually, this is someone with a connection to the professional (or semi-professional) stage who will give a thoughtful and constructive critique of the productions and decide the overall winner. Our adjudicator was a tall, elegant man named Cecil Williams, a name that meant nothing to me until many years later, when I discovered his extraordinary life story. Apart from his bow tie (unusual in Glasgow) and his slightly odd-sounding accent, all I remember of him from that night was the jolt of electricity that shot through me when he announced that our youth club had won the competition. The applause was rapturous as our company trooped up to the stage to receive the trophy. Then Cecil said something about the Award for the Best Actor of the Festival. This was news to me – I hadn't heard of any 'best actor' prize. I thought of the lad who had played the silly ass role in the light comedy would walk off with it. Ah well, our club had won the drama prize and that was all that really mattered. Then I heard my name being announced. Jane beamed as I was cheered on to the stage and presented with a silver cup. As the audience rose to give me a standing ovation, I remember being terribly self-conscious about my slightly too-short school trousers I had outgrown and my cheap shoes that had started to come apart at the sole. Nevertheless, I was overwhelmed – nothing remotely like this had ever happened to me before. I was particularly pleased for Jane; her decision to let me play the tramp had paid off in spades. Afterwards, the lad who I thought would take the prize came up to offer his congratulations. That was the first time I met Sandy Morton, a working-class lad like myself, and one of the few young actors from that period who would stay the course and turn professional, making a well-deserved splash some years ago as Golly Mackenzie in BBC Scotland's long-running series *Monarch of the Glen*.

At the next meeting of our group, Jane told me that Phil Douglas, the secretary of the Royal Scottish Academy of Music and Drama, had seen me that night in *The Insect Play* and wondered if I would be interested in joining the junior course. I said that I would love to. Then Jane dropped the big one.

The junior course was the first port of call for any TV or theatre companies who needed kids for their productions, and Jane told me that Phil had put me up for an episode of *Dr. Finlay's Casebook*, a long-running BBC series that was blanket viewing throughout the country. She said that, strictly speaking, Phil wasn't supposed to cast anyone who wasn't a student, but had been so impressed with my performance in *The Insect Play* that she decided to jump the gun, but only on condition that I agreed to join the junior course. As I ran home that night high as a kite, I felt the hidden door had swung wide open and the wind of fortune was blowing me through.

My mother was dumbstruck when I told her the news – *Dr. Finlay's Casebook* was her favourite programme. She said that when my dad got back from the pub she would talk to him about finding a way to pay the cost of the course. We were both much too excited to see the train wreck that was barrelling down the tracks towards us. 'We should let him go to the drama college,' said my mother, as my father stood swaying unsteadily in the middle of the room. 'It's what he wants to do wi' his life.'

'Aw for Christ Almighty's sake!' he roared. 'Will you stop fillin' the boy's head wi' stupid bloody notions.'

'It's no' stupid, John. I think he's got it.'

'What the hell are ye talkin' aboot? He's no' "got it", or anythin' like it. Ye want tae turn him intae a jessie? Is that whit ye want? Paradin' aboot in make-up like a bloody oddity? He'll leave the school when he's fifteen an' get an apprenticeship as a plumber. That's whit he'll dae wi' his life, an' nae mair o' this God's-cursed actin' nonsense.' The following morning, as I was leaving for school, my mother told me she would take on another cleaning job to raise the money for the fee, and to tell Jane I would join the junior course at the start of the next term.

As soon as my registration at the drama college was confirmed, I was offered the part of 'A Boy' in an episode of *Dr. Finlay's Casebook* called 'The Devil's Dozen'. The series was recorded in London and I was to be flown down and put up at a hotel for a fortnight. Being under sixteen, BBC regulations required I had to have a chaperone. In the absence of anyone else, my mother volunteered for the job and had her second-hand fur coat dry-cleaned for the occasion. My fee amounted to the princely sum of twelve guineas – not that I ever saw a penny of it.

7

Over the Hills and Far Away

I think my mother's nervousness matched my level of excitement as we took our seats aboard the BEA Comet at Abbotsinch airport. Neither of us had ever flown before and as the plane sped down the runway, she gripped my hand tightly as we lifted off towards a new horizon.

A BBC car met us at Heathrow and took us to South Kensington, where we stepped through the revolving door of the Onslow Court Hotel and into a world of polished brass and dark mahogany that I had only ever seen in old British pictures. After we had checked in, a liveried bellboy, like the one who grinned cheekily every week from the front cover of *The Dandy*, picked up our shabby Fair Fortnight suitcase and led the way to the ancient lift. Finally realising why he was hanging about after having shown us into our suite, my Ma graciously slipped him a shilling. His cheeky *Dandy*-style grin vanished as he sullenly shut the door behind him.

I had a few days free before I was due to start rehearsals and, with the help of a guide book I had borrowed from the library, I dragged my mother round most of London's principal tourist attractions. I've always loved museums, and the Science Museum, the Natural History Museum and the Victoria and Albert Museum were right on our doorstep, with the British Museum a short hop away on the tube – but my number one destination was Madame Tussaud's. My ma wasn't all that happy about visiting its famous chamber of horrors – even less so when she discovered that John George Haig, the 'Brides in the Bath' multiple murderer (they hadn't invented the term 'serial killer' back then), had committed some of his grisly crimes while he was a resident of the Onslow Court Hotel. I think from that moment on the place lost something of its charm as my mother became convinced that the murders had probably been carried out in our en-suite bathroom.

On my first day of rehearsals, it came as a bit of a surprise when, instead of taking us to the BBC studios in Lime Grove, the car dropped us off at a Territorial Army drill hall in Horseferry Road. I was to discover that rehearsals for a TV drama seldom took place in the actual studio; they were usually held in a hall specially rented for the purpose. In the *Dr. Finlay* rehearsal hall, the various sets were simply outlined on the floor with coloured tape while a couple of broom handles stuck into wooden bases marked the doorways. The furniture and props looked as if they had been picked up at Paddy's Market. It wasn't quite the introduction to the glamorous world of television I had anticipated, and I was still wondering whether it was all just a dream when the stars of the series, Bill Simpson, Andrew Cruikshank and Barbara Mullen, came over to welcome my mother and me to the behind-the-scenes world of Tannochbrae.

The highlight of my first day as a professional actor was rehearsing my short scene with Roddy McMillan – an actor I admired tremendously. The plot of 'The Devil's Dozen' was about an outbreak of food poisoning in Tannochbrae. Roddy played Murchie, an alcoholic baker, in whose kitchen an infestation of cockroaches is discovered. At first it appears his lack of basic hygiene seems to be responsible for half the village turning up in Finlay's surgery with gastroenteritis. Our scene went something like this:

INTERIOR: MURCHIE'S BAKERS SHOP. DAY.

As Murchie stacks a fresh batch of meat pies on the shelves, the door opens and a scruffy boy enters.

MURCHIE

Aye? What can ah do for ye?

BOY

(*Nervously*) Eh, some men sent me, mister. They said ah was tae ask ye somethin'.

MURCHIE

Ask me what?

BOY

They said ah was tae ask ye if ye've any beetles ye don't want. They want to race them.

The boy runs laughing out of the shop before a furious Murchie can grab him.

That was it. That was the sum and substance of my very first professional engagement. I remember it vividly. Finlay was recorded like a stage play – starting at the beginning and carrying on in real time to the end. The recording began with the floor assistant calling out, 'Good luck, studio, and going in – 5, 4, 3 . . .' – the final two numbers being indicated in sign language in case the microphones accidentally picked up his voice. The programme was recorded by a process known as telerecording, which basically involved pointing a cine camera at a studio monitor and recording the image on the screen. Editing facilities were virtually non-existent. Only if you fainted – or even worse, swore (in which case you could kiss goodbye to the prospect of any further work from the BBC) – would they consider the possibility of a retake. If the unthinkable happened and you forgot your lines, the floor manager would press a button that would blank out the screen momentarily while he gave you a prompt – not something you would wish to happen on any kind of regular basis. This dread of drying on screen led Eric Woodburn, the elderly character actor who played Dr Snoddie, to write his dialogue on little bits of paper which he concealed at strategic points around the set. (If you ever get the chance to watch an old episode, note how often during one of his scenes Dr Snoddie examines the ornaments on the mantelpiece, or the large bowl of flowers on the table.) Apparently there was a legendary moment where Dr Snoddie entered the drawing room in Arden House, politely removed his hat and greeted Bill Simpson with the words, "Ah. Good morning, Doctor, er, umm . . ." Then, after a glance into his upturned bowler: ". . . Finlay."

My most precious memory of that whole magical, life-changing experience was the time I spent in the company of Roddy McMillan, who generously gave of his time to chat with my mother and me during the coffee breaks. Like me, Roddy hailed from a tenement background, and one of his many achievements was being a founder member of Unity Theatre, a left-wing stage company that was formed in the 1940s and toured working-class communities with a series of controversial plays like *Men Should Weep* and *The Gorbals Story* – contemporary plays that portrayed working people's lives in a way the stuffy middle-class theatre of the period conspicuously avoided. It was a heritage the 7:84 Company would revive to great acclaim thirty-odd years later.

Roddy's prodigious talent also encompassed playwriting, directing and composing folk songs. He was the genuine article – a working-class Glaswegian who, despite his many achievements, never lost touch with his roots. Whether consciously or not, my own life seems to have followed a similar path and some fellow actors have likened my career to his. Roddy said in an interview once that he thought of himself as a 'useful' actor. Well, if I've been anywhere near as useful an actor as Roddy McMillan, that'll do me fine, thanks.

A few weeks after we had returned to Glasgow, my mother was taken into hospital suffering with renal problems. In the selfish way of teenagers who are so wrapped up in their own life experiences, I hardly gave it a moment's serious thought. I mean, hospitals are places where you go to get better – right? I simply refused to accept that my mother's illness might be terminal. Even now, I find it almost impossible to write objectively about that period of my life. Looking back, I think as my mother's health slowly worsened, I began to drift into a kind of alternative reality, becoming oddly detached from the rising tide of anxiety that constantly threatened to overwhelm me.

My mother, along with hundreds of other Glasgow women in the 1960s, was paying the piper for her years of self-dosing with Askit powders, as their 'pick me up' ingredient, phenacetin, had finally taken its toll and destroyed most of her kidneys.[1] Years later, when I asked her about the circumstances of my mother's death, my auntie Betty told me that she had begged the specialist who was treating her to consider giving her a kidney transplant. 'She's got two wee boys,' she told him. Almost fifty years later, her eyes still blazed with anger when she told me his curt reply: 'Don't be ridiculous. She's far too old to be considered for a transplant.' At the time, my mother was in her late thirties.

Since there was nothing more medical science could, or would, do for her, my mother was discharged from the hospital to spend the little that remained of her life at home. By not allowing myself to acknowledge how grave her condition had become, I was probably deep in what psychiatrists would term a state of denial. Still, each day when I came home from school I would glance up at the window to see if the curtains had been drawn – the traditional sign in Scottish households that someone has just died. Despite knowing deep in my heart that my mother had no hope of recovery,

---

[1] Despite the fact that phenacetin's lethal effects had been documented since the early fifties, it wasn't until 1968 that the Askit Company finally removed the deadly ingredient from their highly profitable product.

I carried on with my life as if everything was perfectly normal and I hadn't a worry in the world, despite John Lennon's song 'I'm a Loser' constantly running through my mind – in particular the lyrics about laughing and acting like a clown while wearing a mask that conceals the unhappy frown beneath.

I lived for the twice-weekly classes at the drama college, perhaps trying a bit too hard and shining a little too brightly in an effort to stifle the feelings of impending disaster. Difficult as things were, I clung to the thought that acting was somehow the lifeline that would lead to a brighter future and I threw myself into the lessons with a passion. My tutors seemed pleased with me, and my first-term reports praised my performance skills and my character work – although I doubt if any of them realised it was in the character of a carefree fourteen-year-old that I was giving the performance of a lifetime.

Among my fellow students at the college was a lad I had seen giving an outstanding performance in an episode of Dr. Finlay as a geeky misfit whose peculiarities included eating worms. Despite being less than a year older than me, Brian Pettifer seemed somehow to have the bearing of an old pro. He had a great sense of humour and we soon became firm friends. When I was introduced to his family, I realised that I had met Linda, his strikingly attractive older sister, once before – she had been one of the actresses in the Youth Club Drama Festival where I had appeared in *The Insect Play*. As I became a regular visitor at Brian's house, I began to meet Linda's sophisticated (well, they seemed terribly sophisticated to me) circle of friends and admirers. Among them was Siggy, a tall, reedy, bespectacled intellectual with the air of an impoverished Russian émigré, and who looked as if he had stepped straight out of a Tolstoy novel. Siggy played acoustic guitar beautifully and was Linda's accompanist as she sang in the folk clubs that had recently started to spring up around the city.

Through Linda and her bohemian friends, my awareness of the world that lay beyond the narrow boundaries of my upbringing expanded at a dizzying rate. Thanks to them I became an avid reader of publications like the *Evergreen Review*, an American periodical so daring and scandalous it had to be printed in Paris, as no mainstream publisher would touch it. The *Evergreen Review* was a great hurrah for artists, writers and free thinkers of the American avant garde – literary iconoclasts like Jack Kerouac, and 'beat' poets like Alan Ginsberg and Lawrence Ferlinghetti, whose dazzling use of language was like nothing I had ever known before. Then of course there was the erotic content – humorous tales of sex and seduction by the likes of Terry Southern sat alongside graphic comic strips like Barbarella (later made into a crap film by Roger Vadim) and the thrillingly fetishistic Adventures of Phoebe Zeit-Geist. After that heady brew of sophisticated titillation, the dog-eared and crinkly copies of Parade that were furtively passed around in the school lavatories were never quite the same again.

Before my fifteenth birthday, I had appeared in quite a few productions, both amateur and professional, including playing Puck in an open-air production of *A Midsummer Night's Dream* that Cecil Williams, the adjudicator of *The Insect Play*, was producing and directing as part of Glasgow's contribution to the nationwide Shakespeare quatercentenary celebrations.[2] I loved the experience of playing Shakespeare's mischievous sprite, stealing the show and falling madly for the 'First Fairy' – a beautiful girl named Ishbel Miller. It was during rehearsals that I learned of Cecil's previous life. Cecil Williams was a white South African who had been an important theatre director in Johannesburg. While there, he led a doubly secret life – the first was being gay in a rabidly homophobic society; the second was being a committed communist and active member of Nelson Mandela's African National Congress party. He had fled to Scotland in 1962, after the security forces issued an

---

[2] Although I didn't know it then, one of the fairies was a wee lassie named Lesley, who I would come to know well in later life when she married one of my dearest friends, the film composer Patrick Doyle. Lesley still takes a wicked delight in reminding me how all the wee fairies fancied me in my green make-up and skimpy off-the-shoulder costume of twigs and leaves.

arrest warrant for him when they discovered he had been ferrying Nelson Mandela to secret ANC meetings around the country. Cecil had managed to get the country's future president past the frequent roadside security checks, by the simple but brilliantly theatrical trick of having Mandela pose as his chauffeur while he played the white master in the rear passenger seat. I was delighted when Royal Exchange Square, the site of the old Glasgow Drama College where Cecil found a job teaching, was renamed in honour of Nelson Mandela – although I can't help thinking that Cecil Williams Square might have made a fitting tribute to the man without whose bravery and daring Mandela might never have become South Africa's greatest statesman.

In 1964, BBC2 was just kicking off. With few productions other than the news and *The White Heather Club* to keep them busy, the BBC's Glasgow studios in Queen Margaret Drive had been pressed into service as a production facility for the new channel's increased drama output. Whenever kids were required for small parts, the directors would invariably cast from the junior course at the Drama College. I played a couple of small roles in long-forgotten BBC drama productions, but the one I'll never forget was *Liza of Lambeth*. Adapted from Somerset Maugham's novel of life in London's East End during the Victorian era, it starred Jo Rowbottom and Patrick Allen. In one of the scenes I was supposed to charge into a pub crammed with costumed extras, snatch a bottle of beer from the bar and run out again. All went well until the take. When my cue came, I fought my way through the crowd towards the bar as I had been directed. Next thing I knew, I was lying on the floor surrounded by broken glass and looking up at the contorted face of Rita Webb, the well-known cockney character actress, who seemed to be literally frothing with rage. 'You fahkkin' little cahnnt!' she screamed through the foam that streamed from her nose and mouth. 'You fahkked me fahkkin' close-up!' It seemed that on my way to the bar I had inadvertently bumped into Rita's ample bosoms as the camera zoomed in on her glugging ale from a big glass tankard. My

49

accidental dunt had caused her to inhale sharply, which resulted in most of the beer shooting up her nostrils. Her outraged reaction had been to bring the tankard down on my head, shattering it and momentarily knocking me out. As the cameras were being repositioned to start the scene again, I was helped off the set, patched up with an Elastoplast and given a reviving cup of tea. To her credit, Rita came to my dressing room later to offer profuse apologies and slip me a ten-bob note, which was big of her – but where were fahkkin' Claims Direct when I needed them?

Each job I did gave me the chance to work with professional actors and directors, and I gave every part, no matter how small, my best shot, knowing it was a unique learning opportunity. I knew instinctively this was the education I really needed, and as a result my schoolwork took a back seat. At Wee Pollok Primary I'd known I was smarter than average, but here at 'the Big School' I was failing miserably. Despite Mr Dickie's well-meaning attempt to increase my understanding of fulcrum points and load-bearing trusses by frequent applications of the Belt of Knowledge, I found the theory of mechanics completely incomprehensible. And, since science class didn't involve inventing death-rays or perpetual-motion machines, the importance of the periodic table somehow escaped me. Algebra? They might as well have tried to explain it to me in Urdu. I'm sure Mr McIver was a passionate and committed geometry teacher, but to this day I couldn't tell you what the hell tangents and cosines are, or when my sketchy knowledge of trigonometry is ever likely to come in handy. In my own defence, I can only say that I knew without doubt that I wanted nothing other than to become an actor – something I was unlikely to learn at Shawlands Academy. Not only that, but my pal Ronnie and I had a bitter falling out. I can only guess that as I started to move along my new life path, he felt I had rejected his friendship and was leaving him behind. Although it pains me to admit it, I can see he wasn't mistaken.

As if trying to cope with my mother's illness wasn't difficult enough, I began to be targeted by a couple of bullies who contrived to make my schooldays as miserable as possible. As I wasn't too strapping when I was a kid, it wasn't the first time I'd had to deal with being bullied – when I was nine, in a desperate attempt to stop having sand kicked in my face, I sent off for the Charles Atlas bodybuilding course. The wording of the advert inside the back cover of my Superman comic (Mr Atlas certainly knew his market) duped me into thinking the course was free, gratis and for nothing, until the morning when a thick buff envelope with my name on it clattered through the letterbox. Inside were sheaves of promotional literature extolling the benefits of DYNAMIC TENSION, with photos of the mighty man himself performing feats of almost superhuman strength, like pulling a locomotive with his teeth. From the flapper dresses and the straw boaters of the cheering onlookers, I guessed the snaps weren't taken yesterday. Along with all this was a letter that began 'Dear friend' and ended by requesting an impossibly huge sum of cash in exchange for the secrets of Mr Atlas's DYNAMIC TENSION. My regular tension increased dramatically, as the tone of the letter seemed to imply that having sent in the coupon I was now obligated to cough up (in easy instalments if I preferred) thirty-odd quid. Since the weekly income from my butcher's round amounted to precisely ten and sixpence, I decided to ignore the letter and hope good old Charlie boy would forget all about our little misunderstanding. Not a chance – week after week, the hefty envelopes kept right on a-comin' while, surprisingly, the cost of the course dropped lower and lower, until finally I could learn how to be the Hero of the Beach for around seven pounds ten shillings, including postage and packing. After nervously skimming through each envelope to see if my act of criminal deception had become a police matter, I would burn them in the grate in case my dad found out and made me honour the debt. For months I lived in constant terror of hearing a thunderous knock at the door one morning and opening it to find Charles Atlas standing there in his Tarzan-style leopard skin, arms akimbo, muscles quivering with DYNAMIC TENSION and demanding the seven and a half quid I owed him.

The bullying I faced on an almost daily basis at Shawlands Academy finally ended after I took the simple but effective solution of leaving at the earliest possible opportunity. No O levels, no A levels, no GCSEs and no graduation ceremony. After classes had finished one day, I caught the bus home and never went back. I had just turned fifteen, and although my schooldays were over, my education was just beginning.

8

Final Act

Like most actors have to do at some point in their careers, I went to sign on at the nearest Labour Exchange, which in my case was at Eglinton Toll. After sitting around for about an hour in a waiting room that looked like it had been designed by someone who was a big fan of Eastern European bus stations, I was called into one of the dingy cubicles to be issued with a National Insurance number and a booklet to collect my weekly stamps in. Next came the in-depth career interview. It went like this:

CLERK
So, what kind of work is it is ye're after?

ALEX
I want to be an actor.

CLERK
Ye want to what?

ALEX
Be an actor.

There is a long, Pinteresque pause as the clerk takes this in.

CLERK

An actor. Right. Just hang on a minute, would ye?

He disappears for several minutes and returns bearing a large, dusty ring binder. He sets it on the counter and starts to search through it, stopping at a faded and yellowing page.

Armature winder . . . Agricultural labourer . . . Ah yes, here we are – Actor.

He scrutinises the page closely.

So . . . whit kinna actin' is it ye do exactly?

ALEX

Well – anything really. You know, whatever comes along.

The clerk seems slightly perplexed by Alex's reply. He consults the big book again.

CLERK

Are ye a stage actor, a radio actor, a television actor or a film actor?

ALEX

All of them I suppose. I'll be happy to take whatever I'm offered.

CLERK

(*Exasperated*) Aye, well that's nae use tae me. Nae use at all. See, I have to put down a different code for each individual category. So whit category of actor d'ye want me to put ye doon as – stage, radio, television or film?

Realising the futility of a debate, Alex makes a rapid decision.

ALEX

Umm . . . Film actor.

CLERK

Film actor. Right, now we're gettin' somewhere. That wid be, eh, let me see now . . . aye, here we are – 0486 dash 10 oblique 337.

He enters the relevant code in Alex's file.

OK. That's you done. There's yer registration card. Ye sign on at box twelve every Tuesday at quarter past eleven.

As Alex starts to leave, the clerk leans in confidentially.

Listen, son. Ah have tae be honest wi' ye – we don't get a lot o' call for film actors in here.

As I stood waiting for my bus home, I couldn't help smiling at the wee clerk's genuinely well-meaning attempt to let me down gently. 'We don't get a lot o' call for film actors' – as if the Eglinton Toll branch of the buroo got *any* call for film actors. Like Bob Newhart's 'Walter Raleigh on the Phone' routine, I pictured the wee clerk fielding a call from Hollywood – 'So what ye're sayin' is that ye're lookin' for a film actor to take ower fae Sean Connery in the next Bond picture? Well, it's lucky ye phoned here, Mr Broccoli, cos we've jist had a film actor register wi' us this mornin' – Alec Norton. So, let's get straight doon tae the nitty gritty – first ot all, will Mr Norton be expected tae provide his ain Aston Martin? Secondly – an' this is the deal breaker – are we are talkin' class one N.I. contributions here?'

While waiting for the film industry to call, the buroo sent me for a job as an office boy with Craig and Rose Ltd, a paint company located on the site of the old Dixon's Blazes ironworks where just ten years earlier I'd sat on my dad's shoulders in Moffat Street, fearfully watching the red glow from Dixon's blast furnace and thinking it was a fiery portal to Hell. Now the place looked more like limbo, a featureless wasteland where lost souls drift around aimlessly for the rest of eternity. You'd think being a company who made paint, Craig and Rose might have taken the initiative and used a few tins of their product to brighten up their warehouse. But no, their premises were as bleak and charmless as the rest of the jerry-built warehouses that had been hastily erected on the acres of compressed slag left behind by the old foundry.

The boss, Mr Davis, took me on a brief guided tour of the premises, proudly informing me of the company's main claim to fame – that they manufactured the red, lead-based paint used on the Forth Bridge. Sitting behind his wood-veneered desk and leaning back on his squeaky leatherette chair, he said, 'If you stick in and carry out your duties satisfactorily, who knows – maybe one day you could be sitting where I am.' I remember thinking at that moment I hadn't been far off the mark in my assessment of Dixon's Blazes when I first viewed it as a kid: despite its change of purpose, it was still the gateway to Hell.

Fortunately, after only a few months of bum-numbing paper shuffling, the cavalry, in the shape of the BBC, rode to my rescue by offering me another episode of Dr. Finlay's Casebook. I approached Mr Davis as he nibbled on his lunchtime Spamwiches, and asked him if I could possibly take my two weeks' summer holiday in advance.

'And when would you want to take them?' he asked.

'Starting next Monday,' I answered.

I think it was probably at that moment he realised that his assessment of me as a potential heir to his leatherette throne may have been misplaced.

'I'm afraid that's out of the question,' was his terse reply.

The following Monday, as my plane took off for London, I wondered for a brief moment how Craig and Rose were coping without their number-one office boy. Like my final day of school, I simply turned and walked away without asking if that would be OK with everyone else. When Mr Davis didn't report me to the polis, or chase after me and drag me back to my desk, I began to grasp one of life's fundamental principles: no one but you has either the right, or the power, to decide your destiny.

When I got back to Glasgow, I was struck by the rapid decline in my mother's condition. My dad had moved her bed into the front room so she could still have some semblance of family life around her. I finally had to face the truth that there was no hope and, short of a miracle, no possibility of a reprieve. Her suffering was such that I found myself guiltily wishing it would all be over sooner rather than later.

One evening, my friend Brian and his sister Linda invited me out to see the great Matt McGinn in concert. I needed a bit of cheering up, so I agreed to go. As we sat through Matt's concert I began to be aware of a sense of unease. From somewhere deep inside me I heard a deep, sonorous note, as if someone was bowing a double bass. Linda had arranged for us all to meet Matt afterwards (Linda knew everybody), but something told me I had to get back home as quickly as possible. As soon as I walked through our living-room door I could see it was my mother's final night. Our family doctor was in attendance and I looked on helplessly as she gave up her struggle to live and sank silently back on to the pillow. Even at that point I was still hoping she had just fainted or fallen asleep – but when the doctor gently closed her eyes and pulled the blanket up over her face, my sense of reality deserted me. The low drone from the double bass in my head grew ever more sonorous and I felt as if I was standing outside my physical body, silently observing myself as the juvenile lead in the final scene of a stage play. My dad delivered the final line: 'That's yer mother away, son.' There was no applause as he closed the curtains. That was because it wasn't a play, and I wasn't the juvenile lead. I was a small-part player in something called Real Life – and I wanted to run away from it as far and as fast as I could.

9

'Keep it Bright!'

Life carried on as near to normal as it could in the weirdly disjointed days and months after my mother's funeral. My dad
went back to work and my wee brother Dougie went back to
school, while I sat alone day after day, writing melancholy songs
and picking listlessly at my guitar in a house where the silence
was a constant reminder of my loss. I knew I needed to get out
and work, and decided that I should try to get some more
theatre experience by getting a job backstage and learning the
business from the ground up, so one morning I took a bus into
town and got off at the top of Renfield Street. Directly opposite
the stop was the Pavilion Theatre. Of course, my first port of
call should have been the Citz, where they were doing proper
plays, but looking back, I don't think my choice of the Pavilion
as a training ground could have been any more serendipitous –
even though at the time I wasn't aware I'd made any sort of
choice at all. At the side of the theatre's main entrance, a hand-
painted sign said 'Stage Door'. Oh well, nothing ventured, nothing
gained, I thought to myself as I screwed up my courage and gave
a tentative knock.

After a few louder knocks, a plooky-faced guy in his early
twenties with a teddy boy haircut and a fag clamped in the side of
his mouth opened the door an inch or two.

'Aye?' he asked suspiciously.

'Emm . . . I was just wondering if you were needin' anybody for backstage work,' I said. He gave me a quick once-over.

'Any experience?'

'I've done a few acting jobs for the BBC and I'm hoping to go to drama school in a year or so.'

'Is that right?' he said. 'Well ah could dae wi' an assistant – know anythin' aboot electrics?'

'Not really, no.'

'Ach well, ah could soon huv ye trained up. Ah'm Fergie, by the way – chief electrician. Ye'd better come in an' huv a word wi' the heid bummer."

As Fergie ushered me in the stage door, I walked into a world that would influence my life in more ways than I could have imagined.

The golden age of the Glasgow variety theatre stretched roughly from the early twenties to the late fifties. Before that was the music hall, peopled with characters like W.F. Frame (The Man 'U' Know), Harry Lauder and the great Will Fyffe. What was the difference between music hall and variety? Basically, music hall consisted of a series of individual acts or 'turns' that were performed in halls attached to established pubs or hotels. Realising the fortunes that were to be made from this hugely popular form of entertainment, impresarios began to commission new purpose-built 'Palace of Variety' theatres, such as the Pavilion. Variety was more of a structured show with a regular company of singers, dancers and speciality ('spesh') acts, generally led by a principal comedian. Up until the fifties, there were around half a dozen variety theatres in Glasgow's city centre, including architectural gems like the Metropole, the Alhambra and the legendary Glasgow Empire. Of them all, only the Pavilion and the King's are still standing – although hopefully, the old Panopticon may come back to life if the dedicated group of enthusiasts who have taken on the task of looking after the place can raise the cash to complete the restoration.

The variety period was a unique era in popular entertainment that brought a welcome few hours of gaiety into what were, for most folk, arduous and difficult lives. The turns who graced the variety stage were, almost without exception, outstanding performers – they had to be, otherwise they wouldn't have lasted five minutes in front of a Glasgow audience. Variety was a big part of what gave Glasgow its unique identity, along with many of its once popular catchphrases like 'Sausages is the boys', 'Way up a kye', and 'clairty, clairty' as well as the song that captured the very essence of the city's character: Will Fyffe's immortal 'I Belong to Glasgow'. The characters who fleshed out typical variety sketches – nagging wives, henpecked husbands, dodgy doctors, battleaxe mothers-in-law and of course the auld enemy – the polis – were universal archetypes that would have been as familiar to the patrons of the Commedia Dell'arte during the Italian Renaissance as to a Scottish audience in the 1930s. Purpose-built variety theatres began to spring up in every major Scottish city, providing a circuit that enabled companies to tour their shows the length and breadth of Scotland. In fact, there's a strong argument for saying that variety was the original National Theatre of Scotland.

After a brief interview with the 'heid bummer' (in reality the Pavilion's front-of-house manager) I was taken on as Fergie's assistant, starting immediately. This meant working on general maintenance – including sweeping the stage daily – from nine in the morning till one, then having the afternoon free before starting again at five thirty until the second show ended around ten o'clock – and all for a wage of four pounds ten a week. After I shook hands with the manager, I was handed back to Fergie, who led me into the wings where a rickety iron ladder led up to a small platform attached to a gigantic apparatus that looked like it had first seen service in Fritz Lang's Metropolis. It was covered in dials, gauges and switches, beneath which dozens of things called 'faders' were arranged in parallel ranks. In the centre, resembling something you might find in the driver's cab of the Flying Scotsman, was a big spoked wheel with a brass handle. This prime example of the electrical engineer's art, Fergie proudly told me, was the master control panel for the entire theatre's lighting system. 'Ah'll show ye the ropes for the furst week,' he said. 'Then ah'll leave ye tae run it on yer ain.' An icy chill ran up my spine at the thought of being left in control of this scary and incomprehensible contraption. Fergie's demonstration began with him throwing the main switch to ON, which brought the ancient mechanism to crackling and sparking life, and immediately brought to mind an H.G. Wells story I read once, about a dull-witted and supersti-tious worker at a power station who begins to worship the huge electrical dynamo that he is being paid a pittance to maintain. The saga ended with the (literally) shocking sacrifice of his boss to the dark god of the machine. As Fergie leapt around the platform, locking off the worn banks of faders with bits of string, and energetically spinning the big iron wheel to apply the cross-fades, I crossed my fingers and hoped that I wouldn't, at some point in the future, feel the urge to offer up his still-beating heart as a token of my obeisance.

My introduction to the theory and practice of stage lighting over for the day, Fergie handed me a brush and a tin of white emulsion and told me to get started smartening up the ladies' lavatories at the back of the dress circle. As I was painting over the eye-opening graffiti on the grimy cubicle walls, I thought of the story I once heard about a man telling a friend about his recent job in a circus: 'Basically,' he says, 'ah'm the guy that goes roon' efter the elephants and clears up a' their shite. Hauf the time, if ah'm no' quick enough off the mark, Ah end up plastered wi' the bloody stuff.'

'That's terrible,' says his mate. 'Surely ye can get yersel' a better job somewhere else.'

'Whit?' he replies. 'An' leave showbusiness?'

That night, under Fergie's watchful eye, I was allowed to crank the big wheel that changed the lighting states, and in the brief moments when I wasn't trying to make sense of all the complex levers and faders, I caught my first sight of one of Scotland's greatest variety legends – Lex McLean.

Like many Glasgow comedy heroes – Billy Connolly being a prime example – Alexander McLean Cameron had emerged from the traditional comic's breeding ground of the Clyde shipyards. Lex's material was what was euphemistically termed 'risqué', and in that sense was directly descended from Aristophanes and Plautus, who were both aware that a healthy measure of good honest vulgarity was the way to keep an audience coming back for more.

Lex's show would always begin with the full company on stage, doing a simple time step in front of a glittery set while belting out some up-tempo show tune like 'There's No Business Like Showbusiness' or 'Everything's Coming up Roses'. The basic rule seemed to be that any show tune good enough for Ethel Merman was good enough for Lex McLean. As the opening number neared its climax, a grim-faced figure would pass silently under my gantry and take up a position at the rear of the stage. When the opening number ended, a pair of sliding doors would open to reveal McLean, instantaneously transformed from the dead-eyed golem of a moment before into the one and only 'Sexy Lexy'. It was as though he was wired to a high-voltage charge that was only activated when hit by the beam of a follow spot. Like his comedy hero, Max Miller, McLean sported outrageously gaudy outfits to grab the audience's attention. As he strolled downstage to start his opening patter, the punters would cheer and wolf whistle at his camp appearance. Putting a hand on his hip he would lisp, 'Well? And what if I am?'[1]

It was an unforgettable experience to watch him walk on to that stage twice a night, week in, week out, and have the audience

---

[1] A wonderful, if unlikely, story I heard about Lex was the time he supposedly shared the bill with the great African-American singer Paul Robeson. A deeply committed communist and civil rights campaigner, Robeson played a number of engagements in Britain in the late fifties. For his sell-out concert at St Andrews Hall, some bright spark had decided to engage McLean as the opening act. The majority of Robeson's audience were serious lefties and intellectuals, and Lex's red-nose patter went down like a lead balloon. As he walked offstage to the sound of his own footsteps, he passed Robeson on his way to the stage. 'Forget it, son,' he muttered ruefully, 'they're no' worth blackin' up for . . .'

eating out of his hand. You strayed in late to a Lex McLean show at your peril. 'What happened?' he would ask a luckless couple as they tried to find their way down the aisle in the dark. 'Did yer bus break doon?' Any gent who had taken the trouble to dress smartly for their night out faced cracks like, 'Lovely suit, sir – are ye wearin' it for a bet?' Or, if he was accompanied by a female companion, 'Is that yer girlfriend with you, sir, or are ye jist breakin' her in for a pal?' After I'd been there for a few weeks, I noticed that Lex would always scan the auditorium through a gap in the curtains before making his entrance. I asked Fergie if he knew why. 'He's countin' the hoose,' he said. 'He's on a percentage o' the takin's and doesny trust the thievin' bastards that run the box office.'

One of Lex's turns was a Sinatra-style crooner named Billy. One night as I was watching the show from my gantry, Billy, perched on a bar stool in the centre of the stage, whisky glass in hand and sports jacket casually slung over his shoulder, was serenading the audience with some of Old Blue Eyes' greatest hits. In the wing opposite me, wee Tommy the fly operator was climbing up the rusty iron ladder that led to a walkway high above the stage when, to his horror, it pulled free from the crumbling masonry and began to topple backwards. As it fell, it hit a horizontal beam, which, although it stopped the ladder falling further, had the effect of catapulting wee Tommy towards the stage. Picture the Glasgow Sinatra's surprise when his act was interrupted by a howling banshee who came cartwheeling out of nowhere and landed at his feet in a crumpled heap before crawling round the stage screaming, 'Mah legs! Mah legs! Oh Jesus Christ Ah've broke mah fuckin' legs!' Like the seasoned trouper he was, Billy never missed a beat, carrying on with his song as if nothing out of the ordinary had happened. As wee Tommy was dragged wailing into the wings by a couple of stagehands, I guessed from the audience's applause that most of them thought they were watching the surprise climax of an avant-garde comedy act.

Although I wasn't really aware of it then, I appreciate now just how privileged I was to have caught the tail end of Glasgow's great variety era. John Osborne, in his play The Entertainer, used variety's fading glory as a metaphor for the state of post-war Britain. Clearly, even back in 1957, Osborne could see its days were numbered.

Let me tell you a little story that, for me, sums up the role that variety played in people's lives. Through my friendship with his son Jake, I have the great fortune to be acquainted with one of the world's greatest living modern artists, Frank Auerbach. The first time I met Frank was at his birthday party. I found myself sitting next to him and felt slightly awkward, wondering what I could possibly talk about to this exceptional man. I needn't have worried. As soon as he discovered I was from Glasgow, he asked me if had ever heard of Chic Murray. Frank was delighted when I told him that not only had I heard of Chic, but that I had worked with him on a number of occasions. That was it – the ice was broken and we chatted for most of the evening about our mutual love of variety. Frank told me that his mother and father had managed to get him out of Germany shortly before the war, sending him to the safety of friends in England. He never saw them again. When he was seventeen, as a special treat he was taken to the Metropolitan Theatre of Varieties in London's Edgeware Road. He said he watched spellbound as a collection of top-class performers brought the house down and for a few hours made everyone, including Frank, forget about their troubles. From that night on, he became a passionate variety fan, visiting as many shows as he could afford. The lights, the atmosphere, the sheer life-enhancing exuberance of the turns and the audience alike lifted his spirits and helped give him the will to rise above his desperate situation and make a new life for himself in a strange and foreign city. As we talked, I discovered there was scarcely a speciality act or comic turn that Frank hadn't seen in the flesh – Max Miller, Jimmy James, Norman Evans, Rob Wilton and of course the eccentric dancers sans pareil, Wilson, Keppel and Betty. But of all the stars Frank saw from the thirties onwards, he said his favourite without question was the incomparable Chic Murray. I didn't feel I knew Frank well enough at that point to tell him one of my favourite stories that I got from the Tall Droll himself. According to Chic, one of the greatest stars of the music hall era, Eugene Stratton, had been engaged at great expense to head the bill at the Pavilion Theatre. Stratton was one of the earliest of the blackface performers and his act would begin with a surprise opening – there would be a dramatic drum roll and a single small circle of light would appear on the tabs. Suddenly, Stratton's cork-blackened face with white-ringed eyes and lips would appear in the spotlight, and with a dazzling grin he would say, 'Hello, I's a coon!' Then the tabs would open as the band struck up his signature tune – 'Lily of Laguna'. On his debut night at the Pavilion, however, his opening was more of a surprise than usual. As he stuck his head through the tabs and called, 'Hello, I's a coon!' a voice called back, 'Ye're a cunt!' The black face vanished instantly as a furious Stratton stormed back to his dressing room, wiping off the burnt cork and vowing never again to return to Glasgow. The Pavilion management did their best to calm the great star down, assuring him that the incident was an exceptional occurrence, that the heckler had been dealt with and besides, they didn't want such a great artiste to leave their theatre with a bad impression of a Glasgow audience. Finally, after much grovelling and pleading, Stratton seemed mollified and agreed to go back on after the interval. As the audience settled back in their seats at the start of the second half, the drums rolled and the lights went down to a single small spot. Once again Stratton stuck his face through the curtains and called out, 'Hello, I's a coon!' and a voice called back, 'Ye're still a cunt!'

10

The Secret Agent

Fascinating as my time as Fergie's assistant electrician had been, I wanted to follow my dream of being an actor and quit my job at the Pavilion not long after Lex's summer show ended. It seemed the right decision to take, as BBC Scotland were casting for a new series called *Tomorrow's People*. Devised by George Byatt and Sinclair Aitken, two ex-teachers who worked in the BBC's schools department, the main focus of the series was to be the everyday lives of the teenage pupils in a Glasgow comprehensive. I auditioned for the part of the English teacher's son and thought it was mine for the taking, until I went to the final recall and bumped into my pal Brian Pettifer. I hadn't seen Brian for some time, as working at the Pavilion each night had put the tin lid on any kind of social life. He told me he had just finished working on *If* – Lindsay Anderson's iconic film about a public school. In my head, I heard the steady tolling of a distant warning bell. Sure enough, as we were walking through the reception area after the meeting was over, Peter Graham Scott, the series producer, came after us. 'Brian,' he said, as my heart sank, 'would you mind coming back in for a minute?'

The warning bell I had heard earlier was no delusion. My hope of imminent fame and fortune vanished like snow off a dyke as Brian snatched the part from under my nose. It was an early and bitter lesson in coping with disappointment – something actors have to learn to deal with on a regular basis. I waited for him, and as we walked down Byres Road together, I have to confess I wished my old pal would miraculously fall under a bus. Thankfully my wish wasn't granted and our friendship continues to flourish to this day.

Although I didn't get the part I so badly wanted – or, equally importantly, the regular income that went along with it – I did get to play some meaty roles during the run of the series, which, since the casting of John Cairney as the school's dashing English teacher, was now called *This Man Craig*. I tended to play troubled teenagers, and must have made something of an impression on John Cairney, as he and Jack Gerson co-wrote an episode expressly for me called 'The Parasite'. In it, I played a bitter, disabled lad in a wheelchair who forms a destructive relationship with a shy young loner from the Hebrides. When the episode was screened, I got some of the best reviews of my life. It was exactly the spur I needed to convince me I was on the right path after all.

Thanks largely to his mates at work telling him how good they thought I was in the series, I sensed a change in my father's attitude towards me. I think he had begun to realise I was serious about my calling, and that being an actor didn't necessarily mean poncing about in tights and a frilly shirt. 'There's always work for good tradesmen,' he would say to me. 'If the actin' game doesny work out, you should have a trade to fall back on.' Now, as a father myself, I completely understand his reasoning – I mean, when have you ever heard anyone say, 'Jesus – we've got a real emergency here. Quick, somebody call an actor.'?

My performance as the bitter young misfit in John's episode of *This Man Craig* got me my first agent – Campbell Godley, a name that never fails to raise a wry chuckle from anyone who ever knew him. Campbell had once been an actor, whose measure of success can probably be guessed by one of the many stories told about him: at the Citizens Theatre he had been cast in the tiny but crucial role of a herald in a Shakespearian drama. On the opening night, he ran on to deliver his single line with such nervous energy that he overshot the stage and plunged headlong into the orchestra pit. Since the rest of the plot hinged on the herald delivering his message, there was a terrible silence as the king and his retinue wondered what the hell to do next. In desperation one of the actors began to launch into an improvised summary of what the herald might have told them if not for his sudden disappearance. His valiant soliloquy was interrupted by a pair of hands appearing over the edge of the stage, followed by Campbell's voice, still in character, saying, 'Helpeth me up, my noble Lords, for I have fell . . .'

Nobody ever believes me when I tell them that my first agent didn't have a phone, but it's absolutely true: Campbell lived with his mother in a council house in Cumbernauld and ran his business empire using his next-door neighbour's phone. Here's an example of the sort of exchange that would take place when someone rang Campbell Godley Associates (quite who the associates were, I never did find out) to enquire about one of his clients:

CALLER

Good morning. I am a Very Important Producer with the BBC. May I speak with Campbell Godley please?

WOMAN NEXT DOOR

Oh aye, right – if ye jist hing on a minute Ah'll see if he's in.

The Very Important Producer grimaces and holds the phone away from his ear as he hears a deafening series of thumps. Cut back to the WOMAN NEXT DOOR, who is banging on her living-room wall.

WOMAN NEXT DOOR

(*Shouting*) Campbell? Are ye there, Campbell? It's the BBC on the phone for ye.

There is a muffled reply from the other side of the wall. The
WOMAN NEXT DOOR returns and picks up the phone.

WOMAN NEXT DOOR
Ah'm awfy sorry, but Mr Godley's mother says he's no'
in the now. She says he had tae go oot for the messages
seein' as how the Cooperative shuts early the day, and
could ye maybe call back later?

I hadn't been with Campbell for very long when I was offered a leading
part in *The Borderers*, a historical drama series that the BBC was about
to start shooting. Set in the fifteenth century, it followed the fortunes of
the Kerrs, a warring family in the lawless border country between
Scotland and England. Ian Halliburton, a handsome young actor fresh
out of the Glasgow Drama College, had been cast in the leading role
with Nell Brennan as his wife. I was cast as his younger brother while
my hero, Roddy McMillan, was set to play the Warden of the Marches.
All the location scenes were to be filmed in Scotland, while the interiors
would be recorded at the BBC's new Television Centre in London. I
was thrilled beyond measure. It meant I would be able to break away
from the depressing housing scheme I was stuck in and start living the
life I wanted. In anticipation of my big break, I persuaded two
acquaintances, Phil McCall and Paul Young, to sponsor me as a
probationary member of the British Actors' Equity Association.

I'll never forget the day I got my Equity card. I was so proud to
be a member of the actors' union, feeling it gave a stamp of legiti-
macy to my dreams of being an actor. How things have changed.
The legacy of Margaret Thatcher's union bashing means that Equity
can no longer protect its members from the worst kind of exploitation. This means that any dodgy bastard can set themselves up as
an agent and charge a hefty 'registration fee' for the thousands of
wannabes who naively think that being on their books will be the
first step towards a celebrity lifestyle. To anyone tempted by this
notion, I wish you lots of luck, because believe me, you're going to
need as much of it as you can get.

I was all set to start my new job when a telegram from Campbell arrived saying that *The Borderers* had been temporarily postponed due to script problems. Oh well, I thought, a slight setback, nothing more. How wrong I was. At the same time they were rewriting the scripts, the original producer who had cast me had been replaced with Peter Graham-Scott – the same man who had knocked me back as John Cairney's son in *This Man Craig*. I sensed impending disaster, and I was right. Graham-Scott's first executive decision was to replace the previous cast with actors of his own choosing. So, along with Roddy McMillan, Nell Brennan and Ian Halliburton, I was back in the dole queue again

Since most of the mainly young, mainly male actors on my agent Campbell's books weren't exactly making him rich, his next business scam – sorry, *scheme* – was to lay on medieval banquets for coach parties of American tourists. To that end, he had somehow managed to finagle a lease on Kilbryde Castle – a run-down pile a few miles south of Dunblane. Campbell himself, in full Actor Laddie mode, would play the role of the tartan-bedecked Laird O' Kilbryde, while the entertainment (and the waiting staff) would be provided by anyone on his client list who happened to be out of work at the time – i.e. most of them.

In order to bring in some ready cash to cover his expenses until the tourists started arriving, Campbell offered some of his clients the opportunity to rent rooms in the servants' quarters at the top of the castle for a couple of quid a week. Reasoning that 'Fancy coming back to my bachelor pad in a castle?' might be a novel chat-up line, I started taking driving lessons and bought a used Mini so I could drive out to Kilbryde, hopefully with a glamorous dolly bird in the passenger seat. Unfortunately, the swinging sixties hadn't quite reached Carnwadric yet and dolly birds weren't exactly thick on the ground. There were lots of them in London, though, and Pettifer and I would often get a cheap standby ticket on the late-night BEA flight to Heathrow, where we would stay over with one of his sister's ex-boyfriends in a basement flat in West Kensington. On one of our trips, we decided to score some trendy threads and headed along to a famous boutique in the Portobello Road called I Was Lord Kitchener's Valet. It specialised in selling old military uniforms, and we left with a couple of outfits that Lord Kitchener would probably have been quite glad to see the back of. Brian bought a dark-blue Adam Adamant (remember Adam Adamant?) style cape while I came away sporting a scarlet military jacket with brass buttons and gold braid. In Swinging London, no one turned a hair as we strolled along the Kings Road looking like a couple of extras from the Charge of the Light Brigade. However, back in Not-So-Swinging Glasgow it was another story altogether. As we swanned around in our finery, people's reactions ranged from open-mouthed incredulity to verbal abuse – and this in a city where a sizeable percentage of the population wouldn't think twice about parading through the streets in orange sashes, white gloves and bowler hats!

Here's an example of the sort of attitude we two dedicated followers of fashion had to deal with. We were crossing George Square one Saturday afternoon in all our Portobello Road finery, when we suddenly found ourselves surrounded by a team of scowling neds. 'Where did yez get them claes, boys?' asked their leader, a lad so riddled with acne his face looked like a relief map of one of Jupiter's moons.

'We got them in London,' answered Brian.

'Izzat right?' said the plookmeister with a malevolent grin. 'Well, we're the Calton Tongs, an' it jist so happens that cape an' that jaiket wiz stole aff us at a party last night, so get them aff!'

'Have you any proof they're yours?' asked Brian.

Their leader grinned menacingly. 'Proof? Aye, sure – here's wur proof.' Unbuttoning his Crombie coat, he revealed the ornate hilt of a cavalry sword, its long, curved blade concealed down the leg of his trousers. Glancing round, I spotted a big polisman at the far end of the square.

'Run Brian!' I yelled, grabbing his arm and hauling him away from the killing zone. The gang of neds must have clocked the cop too, since, instead of giving chase, they stood where they were,

71

glowering after us. 'Those boys,' I gasped breathlessly as we reached the safety of the law. 'That gang over there – they've got swords and knives. They were going to stab us.' The big polis looked us up and down disdainfully.

'Well,' he growled, 'what the fuck dae youse expect, dressed like that?' And turning on his heel, he marched off, leaving Brian and me to the fate he clearly felt we deserved.

11

Stable Relationships

There's no such thing as an actor who can't ride a horse. Or, for the sake of honesty, perhaps I should say there isn't an actor prepared to risk the possibility of losing a job by admitting their only experience of equestrianism has been a couple of donkey rides at the seaside. My cousin Margaret was a part-time instructor at Dumbreck stables, over the Pollok Estate, and the reason I took a series of riding lessons when I was sixteen was because instinct told me it was a skill that would pay dividends one day. As it turned out, I was absolutely right. Over the course of my career I've ridden in quite a few productions, and although there have been a couple of times when I've almost come a cropper, my riding lessons all those years ago have stood me in pretty good stead – although an even more compelling reason for spending my Saturday morning trotting round a paddock was the number of attractive lassies among Margaret's horse-daft friends.

Here's how it generally goes with actors and horses. If, after lying through your teeth about your riding skills at the interview, you're lucky enough to be offered the part, the film company's horse master will arrange a day for you to come out to a riding school and demonstrate your level of competence. This usually isn't too taxing, as the horse you'll be given will be a placid and docile creature named Buttercup, who, after years of dealing with tiny pigtailed girls from the pony club, will respond meekly to your tugs and nudges. Walking? Fine. Trotting? No bother, apart from getting a bit uncoordinated with that bloody 'posting' thing where you raise and lower your backside in time to the horse's gait. Cantering while holding the reins with one hand? Yep, can do. Bit of a gallop? Delighted to oblige. Thank you very much for a lovely day out – see you on location.

It's only when you turn up for your first day's filming you discover that instead of the docile gelding from the riding stables, the creature you've been allocated is a huge, pitch-black beast named Satan, who fixes you with a wild and bloodshot eye while thinking to himself, 'Right, you pathetic little ponce. I'm the boss here, and to prove it, you're for the heave-ho at the first fucking opportunity!' Next thing you know, rather than a genteel trot round a sun-dappled paddock, you find yourself with one hand clinging to the reins for dear life, the other waving a sword or battleaxe (now you realise why the horse master wanted to see you ride one-handed) as you charge full tilt through a dense forest with low hanging branches that Satan keeps swerving towards in the hope that one of them will knock you clean out of the saddle and leave you to be trampled into pulp by the hooves of the foam-flecked Clydesdales bringing up the rear. Believe me, I know whereof I speak. No amount of riding lessons can ever prepare you for the kind of terror I went through during the filming of Rowan Atkinson's *Blackadder* – but I'll save *that* little tale for a later chapter . . .

At Dumbreck stables, a heart-stoppingly beautiful girl named Jill took me for my first lessons. Too tongue-tied and awkward to ask her out, I dreamed up a brilliantly clever ploy that I felt was sure to do the trick. Jill and I would be cantering through the bluebell woods one golden summer evening, when I would 'accidentally' fall off my horse. As I lay there, Jill would dismount and lean anxiously over me to see if I was hurt. That would be the Mills & Boon moment when, gazing into her eyes, I would slip my hand round the back of her swan-like neck and draw her trembling lips gently but firmly towards mine.

I never put my cunning plan into action, thank God – if I had actually been so stupid as to fake falling off a cantering horse, instead of tumbling romantically in fields of gold, Jill would probably have been busy tumbling a comatose quadriplegic into a wheelbarrow.

Flash forward to 2003 and Billy Connolly is appearing on film from his home in LA as his contribution to my episode of *This Is Your Life*. 'Hello Alec,' he begins. 'The first time I met you, you were chasin' after a load of lassies at a ridin' school over the Pollok Estate!'

Until that moment, I had completely forgotten that my long acquaintance with Billy Connolly began at a party in Dumbreck stables the night he and Tam Harvey (they were a folk duo called the Humblebums at that point) turned up, having been invited by a big jodhpur-wearing Amazon who, I seem to recall, was giving Billy riding lessons of a rather different nature to the ones I got. A long-forgotten image came to mind, of Billy playing his banjo in the old tack room while Tam backed him up on guitar, and I realised the reason I had forgotten our first meeting was because something of far greater significance happened to me that night. As the moonlight shone through the dusty old dormer window of the hayloft, a stable hand named Beryl initiated me into life's great mystery. It was a beautiful moment, only slightly sullied by Scruff, the wee stables collie dog who had been woken up from his sleeping place in the corner and decided to investigate the strange noises by padding silently across the floor and sticking his cold wet nose up my jacksie, resulting in a yelp of surprise from me and a whoop of delight from Beryl. So, Billy, with everything that happened to me on that memorable night, I'm sure you'll forgive me for not remembering our first meeting.

But I'll always remember you, Beryl.

And I'm bloody sure I'll never forget you, Scruff . . .

12

Monkey Business

Campbell sent me for an interview with Jimmy Logan, who was looking for someone to play his son in a new comedy he was about to produce and star in. I had met Jimmy once before – I must have been about nine at the time and was with my mother in Arnott Simpson's department store, when she suddenly squeezed my hand and whispered, 'Look, that's Jimmy Logan over there.' Being quite a shy person, it took a lot of pleading on my part to persuade her to approach the Big Star and ask for his autograph. I can still see the look of disdain on his face as he reluctantly signed the scrap of paper she held out. I tend to bin most of the requests I get from professional autograph hounds who have absolutely no interest in me, other than the fact that my signature might fetch a couple of quid on eBay, but as a consequence of that chance encounter with Jimmy Logan I've never refused anyone who has plucked up the courage to ask for my autograph. And here's a piece of advice from me, free, gratis and for nothing – if you achieve a modicum of fame and you find being bothered by the public annoys you, just be aware that the day will come, and sooner than you imagine, when the public won't recognise you or pester you for your autograph any more. In the meantime, you can afford to be a little gracious.

Jimmy had taken the lease on the Empress, an old theatre at St George's Cross that had been closed for years, and had sunk a considerable amount of his own money into reopening it as 'Jimmy Logan's New Metropole'. Unfortunately for Jimmy, the times they were a-changin' and despite the standing the Logan name once carried in Glasgow, by and large the audiences stayed away in their droves. After a couple of years the theatre closed down again and was demolished soon afterwards. But for his first production at the New Metropole, Jimmy had decided to stage a broad comedy called *Love and Kisses*, starring himself as a recently unemployed welder who, aided and abetted by his daft pal (Rikki Fulton), uses his redundancy money to buy a pub. Walter Carr played the cagey inspector from the brewery's head office, while Nellie Norman, a real old stager who had been Jack Radcliffe's comedy partner for over thirty years, was Jimmy's battleaxe of a wife. I saw quite a lot of Nellie over the years, although one Wednesday afternoon when I had come in early for the matinee performance, I saw rather more of her than I would have wished. I was sitting in my dressing room reading a book when I heard a terrible crash followed by loud yells of distress. Rushing along the corridor to see what was wrong, I saw water flooding out from under Nellie's door and threw it open to discover Nellie, with her drawers round her ankles, sprawled on the floor among the shattered remains of the sink.

I have to be honest and say that I didn't really take to Jimmy Logan, finding him something of an arrogant and overbearing bully. One night on stage, he repeatedly ad-libbed a question at me, until I was forced to come back with a lame reply. During the interval I was summoned to his dressing room, where he gave me a stern lecture about professionalism and threatened me with dismissal if I dared to depart from the script again. I later learned that humiliating young performers was something that he liked to do on a regular basis, and although I've no wish to disrespect the man's memory, I can't help but wonder what twisted pleasure he derived from his strange predilection.

The week after the run of *Love And Kisses* ended, an old-time music-hall show opened in the New Metropole. Pete, our stage manager, wangled me a free pass, and I pitched up one evening to see the show. Among the series of tired old turns was a performing-chimp act presented by a husband-and-wife duo. After the show, I went backstage to say hello to Pete and thank him for the free pass. He seemed a far cry from his usual chirpy self. When I asked him what was the matter, he told me in hushed tones about something he had seen earlier that day. On his afternoon rounds he'd been checking that all the dressing-room doors were locked. To his surprise, when he turned the handle of the room that was home to the husband-and-wife chimp act, the door swung open. Inside, sitting on a chair, was the wife who, with one arm around the shoulder of the oldest monkey in her troupe, was in the process of giving it a vigorous hand job. 'Oh dear God!' stammered Pete. 'I-I'm terribly sorry. I didn't mean to . . .'

'It's all right, love,' said the woman matter-of-factly. 'It's not what you think. Close the door and I'll explain.' As Pete sat in the dressing room, trying to avoid the creature's baleful glare, she told him it was necessary to give the chimps regular hand relief to keep them calm, otherwise they became frustrated and started to attack the chorus girls. Pete's experience put a picture in my head that I couldn't get rid of for a very long time afterwards. I wondered, when the woman answered the ad in The Stage saying 'female chimp handler wanted', at what point in the interview did her prospective employer apprise her of that particular duty. In my imagination, I pictured her on What's My Line, performing a little mime to give the panel a clue to her occupation:

LADY ISOBEL BARNET

Hmmm. Tell me, this thing you do – is it a service I could learn to perform?

TRAINER

Oh, yes.

LADY ISOBEL BARNET

Could Gilbert Harding perform it just as well?

TRAINER

Probably not as well as you.

LADY ISOBEL BARNET

Not as well as me? I see . . . Tell me – are you by any
chance a chimp wanker?

EAMONN ANDREWS

How *does* she do it?

After Pete told me that story, I was never able to watch the cheeky
chimps on the Ty-Phoo adverts in quite the same way again.

There seemed to be nothing on the horizon after the job at the
Metropole had finished, so I gladly said yes when Linda, Brian
Pettifer's sister, asked me to be her accompanist around the folk
clubs. Her regular guitarist, Siggy, had died at a tragically early
age but Linda felt it was time she started singing again. There
was a bit of a boom in folk music in the sixties and I had taught
myself fingerpicking guitar to quite a decent standard. Brian and
I were keen folkies, and the pair of us had queued up all night
for tickets to see Bob Dylan at the Glasgow Odeon as well as making
a pilgrimage to London's famous Marquee Club to see Simon
and Garfunkel before they were stars. (If there are any wealthy
autograph collectors reading this, I still have both their signatures
in the back of my 1966 Stage and Television Today diary –
no reasonable offer refused.) On our regular bargain-basement
flights to London, Brian and I often hung out at the Troubadour
coffee house in Earls Court. Everyone who was anyone in the
folk firmament had played its poky little cellar. Owned and run
by a Canadian folk enthusiast named Mike Blume, the Troubadour
was, in the sixties, the Mecca of the British traditional music
scene. Although I couldn't have guessed it then, 'The Troub' was
to play a significant role in my life just a few years down the
line . . .

It was around that time I had my first serious relationship. Irene was a dark-haired beauty who shared my love of folk music and theatre. We went to every play at the Citz and were regulars at the Clyde Valley Folk Song Centre – a big name for a wee place up a close at the back of George Square. We would sit mesmerised, listening to a succession of brilliant artistes like the Incredible String Band, Bert Jansch, Hamish Imlach and Ian McGeachy, a hugely gifted singer/songwriter from the year above me at Shawlands Academy, and who, as John Martyn, was about to make a big splash in the music business.

As so often happens with young love, as we grew older, we began to grow apart. I still had a bit of a roving eye, and when one of her pals spotted me at the Citz with another girl, our days were numbered. So with heart-wrung tears, and warring sighs and groans, we went our separate ways. Realising too late what I had lost, I was bereft, moping around Glasgow with a broken heart and a career that seemed to have ground to a standstill. Then, just when I couldn't see any way forward, Campbell Godley, the indefatigable Laird of Kilbryde, called me from his castle, and my life went off at a sudden and unexpected tangent.

13

Two Virgins

God knows how, but Campbell had managed to get me an interview with Ned Sherrin and John Dexter, who were, respectively, producer and director of a soon-to-be filmed screen adaptation of Leslie Thomas's bestselling novel *The Virgin Soldiers*.[1] John Dexter was a name I was familiar with, after seeing his National Theatre production of *The Royal Hunt of the Sun* when it played in Glasgow. Ned Sherrin I knew as the producer of *That Was The Week That Was*, a hit BBC satire show of which I had been an avid viewer. Still half asleep from catching the midnight flight from Glasgow, I pitched up early next morning at Ned Sherrin's house just off Chelsea's famous Kings Road. A terribly fey young chap ushered me into the drawing room where Dexter and Sherrin were waiting. The walls were covered in production sketches, script notes and headshots of young male actors. I noticed one of the photos was mine. 'Have you ever been a soldier?' Ned Sherrin asked me.

'No,' I answered. John Dexter looked searchingly into my eyes for a long, uncomfortable moment.

'And are you a virgin?' he asked.

'What's the answer that'll get me the job?' I replied.

---

[1] Although I wasn't aware of it at the time, Leslie Thomas's book had been adapted for the screen by a young writer who was making a bit of a name for himself. And although to the best of my knowledge we never met during the filming, John McGrath was to play a pivotal role in my career.

Ned Sherrin smiled and even John Dexter's persistent scowl seemed to soften a little. At the time I used to wear a pair of wire-framed NHS specs like John Lennon's, and I think the combination of the period look and the Glesca attitude might just have prompted their decision to offer me the part of a virgin soldier there and then.

Set in Malaysia during the uprising against British colonial rule, *The Virgin Soldiers* was based on Leslie Thomas's own experiences during his term of National Service. Hywel Bennett, a rising young Welsh star, was set to play Private Brigg, with a strong cast of well-known British character actors like Nigel Davenport, Jack Shepherd and Rachel Kempson in supporting roles. According to the schedule, we would be filming for about three weeks in Singapore, followed by eight weeks on various locations around Saffron Walden that would, with the help of a few lorry loads of plastic palm trees, double as the Malaysian jungle.

I was overjoyed about the prospect of finally working in a big picture, even if the part wasn't the one I was after. I had read the book, and the character I dearly wanted to play was Sandy Jacobs, a Jewish Glaswegian who tries to make himself go deaf as a way of getting out of the army, but Jacobs had already gone to another Scottish actor, Peter Kelly. Instead I would have to be content with being one of the soldiers in Private Brigg's regiment – a bit like those anonymous characters who form up behind the *Dad's Army* regulars at roll call.

I had collected my passport and been given all the inoculations against tropical diseases when I got word that I wouldn't be going to Singapore after all. Due to last-minute budget cuts, only a handful of the principals were getting that little perk. Although I was disappointed, I would still be joining the parade as soon as the company returned to England. Since it would have been impossible to commute from Glasgow, I had to find somewhere to stay in London for the period of the shoot. By a fortunate coincidence, one of the lads from the flat where Pettifer and I often stayed on our London jaunts was moving out. The rest of the flatmates – John,

Brian and Mark, a bunch of fellow Glaswegians – asked if I would be interested in taking his place. Their proposition couldn't have come at a better time and I jumped at the chance.

It was a dark and sleety October morning when I woke my dad and my wee brother to say goodbye. Although I'd told my dad I would just be staying in London during the filming schedule, we both knew that once I was out the door I wouldn't be coming back again. I felt terribly guilty about abandoning my wee brother, who I loved dearly and who looked up to me as his hero, but I knew that if I didn't take this opportunity to break away, all my dreams would die on Glasgow's rainy streets and the rest of my life would be spent in bitter regret.

My second-hand Mini had given up the ghost by then and had been replaced with an old Austin FX3 taxicab, bought for fifty quid from a friend in Edinburgh. As I loaded my few belongings into the boot, I remember thinking it was the modern-day equivalent of wrapping all my worldly goods in a hanky and setting out to seek my fortune. That book of Grimm's fairy tales in the junior section of the Pollokshaws library had a lot to answer for.

The M74 motorway hadn't been constructed yet, and I thought I might actually die of exposure as my heater-less taxi skidded and swerved over the snow-covered Pennines. Finally, just before midnight, I staggered through the door of 61b Talgarth Road, West Kensington, London W14, gratefully accepting the large whisky that was offered to me and drinking a toast to my new home.

The following week at five in the morning, a coach collected my fellow virgin soldiers and me from outside the Hammersmith Odeon and carried us off to start work on the film. As we chatted to each other, we realised none of us had any specific characters, but had been told we would feature in various little cameos. Although we were reluctant to admit it, we were, in essence, a bunch of glorified extras.

Arriving on location at Bury St Edmunds, we were taken two at a time into the make-up room and given authentic 1950s army haircuts. When I finally plucked up the courage to glance at myself in the mirror, I thought I looked like I'd just got out of Barlinnie. Although I was a bit upset, I wasn't nearly as distressed as Davy, the modishly dressed young lad sitting in the next chair to mine. He had clearly spent a lot of time and effort on his carefully coiffured hairstyle, which could easily have taken first prize in a topiary competition. His pleas to the make-up man to spare his crowning glory by gelling it down flat and concealing it under an army beret fell on deaf ears. I could see he was struggling to hold back the tears as his long, flame-coloured locks fell in clumps around his ankles.

Our first week of filming was entirely night shots. A massive locomotive and a string of carriages had been strewn across a field to make it look as if it had been derailed. I had never seen anything on this sort of scale before – this was the Big Picture all right. Each night, dressed in lightweight tropical army outfits, our faces plastered with olive make-up to make us look tanned before being sprayed with glycerine to make us look sweaty, we would fight off a rebel ambush until the dawn brought filming to a welcome halt. Although the scene looks like a sultry night in Malaysia, it was November in Essex and we were absolutely bloody freezing. If you ever manage to catch the film on any of the late-night digital channels, believe me, it isn't pretend fear we're all trembling with.

I had brought my guitar with me, and when Davy discovered we both played, we would bring our guitars to the set and have impromptu sessions during the meal breaks. I soon realised Davy was way beyond my standard, but like most guitar fans, he was more than happy to teach me a few new licks and tricks. One evening he asked if I knew any Jacques Brel songs. I told him I had never even heard of Jacques Brel. When he picked up his guitar and started to sing 'In the Port of Amsterdam', you could have heard a pin drop. The usual noisy chatter in the dining marquee stopped dead as everyone listened in awed silence to Davy's interpretation of Brel's masterpiece. I remember wondering why someone with a talent like that wasn't pursuing a career in the music world rather than taking on small parts and scraping a living running an 'Arts Lab' – whatever that was. After the film ended, we exchanged phone numbers and I promised to come and visit the Arts Lab he ran in Beckenham. But as so often happens in the acting game, we were really only *amis de guerre* – buddies for the duration of the shoot. The next time I heard of Davy was when I was passing the Hammersmith Odeon, the cinema we had once stood outside on freezing winter mornings waiting for the film company coach to pick us up. His name was up in lights on the marquee, but by then – as you've probably figured out for yourself – he had changed it from Davy Jones to David Bowie.

Although I've watched *The Virgin Soldiers* a few times over the years – usually when it fetches up on the digital channels in the wee small hours – I still can't see any sign of Davy. I can spot me, getting my face into shot in quite a few of the scenes. I can spot James Marcus, who played the chief in *London's Burning*, and I can spot Roger Lloyd-Pack, who was Trigger in *Only Fools and Horses*, but Davy Jones? Not a trace – despite the fact that when it pops up on the telly, the film is usually plugged as: *The Virgin Soldiers* – featuring DAVID BOWIE . . .

14

Photo Opportunity

I found myself at a bit of a loose end in the months after the film finally wrapped. I had started singing at the Troubadour with my new girlfriend, Sue, but a share of the ticket sales in its tiny cellar wasn't nearly enough to make ends meet. There was nothing for it – I would have to get a proper job if I didn't want to give up and go back to Glasgow with my tail between my legs.

One of my fellow folkies at the Troubadour told me that Kevin Horgan, a photographer friend of his, was looking for an assistant. I had recently seen *Blow-Up*, Antonioni's film about a trendy fashion photographer, and the thought of being part of London's Swinging Sixties lifestyle interested me more than somewhat. Photography had been a hobby of mine since my mum bought me a second-hand camera from a pawnshop in Pollokshaws, and I had amassed a fair collection of photos, snapped on various productions over the years.

Kevin seemed impressed with my pictures and took me on right away. Panfocal, the company he had just started working for, earned their bread and butter by designing and constructing stands for trade fairs, and when I arrived on the scene, Kevin was in the process of turning a big, disused space into a working studio. It was like being back at the Pavilion as he handed me a pot of emulsion and a brush and invited me to join him in painting the walls a non-reflective black. Not quite *Blow-Up*, but at least it was a start.

The world of commercial photography turned out to be nowhere near as exciting as Antonioni's film. Most of the work Kevin and I did was for things like shopping catalogues. We would spend hours meticulously lighting and photographing sets of engraved crystal wine glasses, or presentation canteens of cutlery, or matching towel sets, or candlewick bedspreads. Everything, it seemed, except the willowy beauties I thought I had signed up for in the first place. The odds of me becoming the next David Bailey lengthened considerably the day we photographed a group of male models for the underwear section of a major home-shopping catalogue. It wasn't until the catalogue had completed its print run – and we're talking tens of thousands of full-colour copies, each the thickness of a phone book – did anyone notice that one of the models had the tip of his dick peeping shyly out below the leg of his shorts. As a result of that little oversight, every copy of the catalogue had to be scrapped, costing the company a small fortune. Needless to say, Panfocal was *not* engaged to do the reshoot.

Somebody had to carry the can for the cock-up (or should that be cock-down?) and I was duly summoned to the Assistant Managing Director's office: a red-faced little despot named Seymour, who handed me my P45 and informed me that my services would no longer be required at Panfocal. I was gutted – I'd never been sacked before, and it was all I could do to hold back a wee sorrowful tear. Kevin didn't react kindly to the loss of his assistant and resigned not long afterwards, taking his clients with him. Due to the sudden loss of income from the highly profitable photographic side of the business, I have to own up to a fair degree of schadenfreude when I heard that Panfocal collapsed soon after, taking Seymour along with it.

My girlfriend Sue and I hosted a regular Tuesday-night folk show in the Troubadour's tiny cellar. One evening, a cool dude in a velvet jacket and slouch hat approached me and asked if he could play a couple of numbers. There were a lot of singers that night, but there was something intriguing about this guy, whose Scots accent didn't quite seem to tie in with his laid-back appearance, so I said

I'd try to squeeze him in somehow. Towards the end of the evening, he sat at the old piano by the side of the stage and sang a handful of his own compositions that blew the usual line-up of guitar-strumming folkies right out the door. That was the start of my long and valued friendship with one of Scotland's real national treasures: Dave Anderson.

Kevin Horgan called me and asked if I wanted to come up and be his assistant in his new studio in Manchester. I didn't really want to leave London, but to make ends meet since losing my regular job, I had been working behind the counter of the Troubadour during the day and washing dishes in the kitchen at night. One evening, up to the elbows in suds, Frank my melancholic fellow *plongeur*, drew me aside. 'Know what I hate most about this job?' he confided. 'Listening to the screams of the drowning cups . . .' That was when I thought it might be a good idea to move on, before I began to hear the screams as well.

15

Back to the Future

Kevin had taken a lease on a once-grand house in west Didsbury, close by the banks of the Manchester Ship Canal. Knowing that the north-west of England was the hub of the catalogue trade, he had opened his own photography studio in Oxford Road and was now completely snowed under with work.

One of the rooms in our big house was rented out to a young couple in the advertising business, Jim and Izz Denley. Not long after I started working at Kevin's studio, one of Jim's old friends came up to Manchester to launch a sister publication to London's successful *Time Out* magazine. One day, Jim asked Kevin if he was free to shoot a photo for the front cover of *Time Out in the North West*, his chum's new magazine. Kevin was too busy, but asked me if I fancied doing it. The main story in that week's issue was about contraception, so I shot a picture of an egg suspended in a net, with the yolk slowly dripping in to the eggcup below. Jim's chum was delighted with the result and asked me to be the magazine's regular photographer. And that's how I came to be a friend and long-time admirer of Jeremy Beadle – publisher, editor, entrepreneur, collector of trivia and human being extraordinaire.

At the time, the workingmen's club scene was booming in the north of England. Like me, Jeremy was a big fan of variety (usually

THERE'S BEEN A LIFE!

the tackier the better), and we would often troop out in my old
Alvis[1] to spend an evening downing real ale and watching the
turns. We saw some big names play these gloriously awful clubs, as
well as some of the most bum-tweakingly awful speciality acts
imaginable. When it came to appreciating naff variety turns, we
were connoisseurs *sans pareil*. Tears of laughter running down our
cheeks, we would speculate as to how and when these poor deluded
sods arrived at their eureka moment – the night the husband leapt
up from the settee, switched off the telly and announced to his wife,
'Sweetheart, I've just come up with an act that'll make us rich. You
bounce around the stage on a spacehopper, wearin' a gold-lamé
bikini, fishnet tights an' a gorilla mask, while I stand in a dustbin
jugglin' empty Vimto bottles and playin' "Land of Hope and Glory"
on the kazoo!'

Although the bottom-of-the-bill spesh acts were always our
favourite part of the show, it was the headline acts that pulled the
punters in. The committees who ran the north of England clubs had
hit on the idea of creating a circuit and pooling their financial
resources to bring over big names from the United States. Most of
the acts, it has to be said, were slightly past their sell-by dates when,
instead of playing to a sophisticated and well-heeled audience at
the Starlight Room, they found themselves performing at the Offal
Trimmers and Tripe Dressers Social Club in the slot between the
bingo and the meat pies.

Jeremy and I went to a club in Oldham one night to see the
legendary fifties singing sensation Johnnie Ray. The club's compère,
an ex-miner with a gammy leg as a result of some dreadful accident
down the pit, but who had since found his metier in the heady
world of show business, limped onstage to introduce the ageing
crooner. 'Right, ladies and gentlemen,' he began, 'here he is. You've
heard 'im on the radio. You've seen 'im on the telly. I like 'im, I 'ope
you will – *Tommy Ray*!' Jeremy had to stuff a serviette in his mouth

---

[1] A clapped-out but classic old convertible I bought for a fiver from Phil, a fellow Scot I met
in a pub, and spent what little spare cash I had on restoring.

to stifle his laughter, as a slightly bemused Johnnie Ray launched into his big hit, 'Walkin' My Baby Back Home'.

Jeremy planned to write a piece for the magazine about the whole northern club phenomenon, so we went back a few weeks later to interview the committee and for me to take the photos we needed to illustrate the article. After sitting through a guy who bashed a tin tray on his head while singing 'Mule Train' and a pair of twin sisters who tap-danced while accompanying themselves on an accordion and trombone, the compère hobbled on to the stage, blew into the microphone a couple of times (why do they always do that?) and called for a bit of hush before introducing The Ink Spots – one of the greatest American doo-wop groups of the forties and fifties. 'Right, ladies and gentlemen,' he announced. 'Here they are. You've heard 'em on the radio. You've seen 'em on the telly. I don't like 'em, you might – *Four Darkies*!'

Jeremy was in hysterics and I laughed so hard a bit of wee came out. Still, despite the hilarity, my heart went out to these four giants of American popular culture. In their day they were headliners. Now, at the fag end of their careers, they were reduced to putting on a smiling, professional front for an audience of disinterested drunks.[2]

Irene, my old girlfriend from Glasgow, had been in my thoughts for some time. I hadn't forgotten her and I was hoping she hadn't forgotten me. On impulse, I wrote to tell her how I was faring. She replied, saying she was at the Glasgow Art School studying jewellery design, and attached a photo of herself looking even more beautiful than I remembered. I wrote back, telling her to look me

---

[2] I got this next story second hand and can't vouch for its authenticity; however, it does have a terrible ring of truth about it. How's this for an intro to end all intros:

A compère is addressing the audience at a workingmen's club somewhere in Yorkshire. 'Right, ladies and gentlemen,' he says, 'before the next turn comes on, I've been asked on behalf of the committee to say a few words about the car park. Now, as you all know, the committee 'as 'ad the club's toilet facilities refurbished to a very high standard at considerable cost. But, despite that, it has been brought to the committee's attention that some patrons are still usin' the car park as a lavatory. In fact, last week, not only did they piss in it, but some dirty bastard shat in it as well.

'Anyway, 'ere she is – LULU!'

up if she ever found herself in Manchester. A week later I met her off the Glasgow train, and before she returned home, she was wearing an engagement ring I bought her from an antique market in Salford.

As Irene was locked into her course at the Art School for the next few years, the logical thing seemed for me to return to Glasgow, even though it went against my philosophy of moving onward and upward. It had been a big wrench when I left my native city to see what the wider world had to offer, and here I was preparing to move back again. I had made a life for myself in Manchester, a life that included some great friends like Trev Hatchett, a brilliant young maths genius whose boundless enthusiasm led to my present fascination with quantum physics; Jim and Izz Denley, a wonderful and clever couple, as much in love now as the day they first met; John Cooper Clarke, punk-poet extraordinaire, who I shared some gigs with in the Manchester folk clubs; Kevin Horgan, my boss, my pal, my guru and my photography teacher; and last but not least, the one and only Jeremy Beadle, who, by the time I left Manchester, had started to compile lists of fascinating facts that he would sell to compilers of radio quiz shows. With a business card that read 'Jeremy Beadle – Curator of Oddities', it was his first foray into a world that would lead him to becoming one of the most famous faces on TV in the eighties.

I had a great time during the years I spent in both London and Manchester, and when I set out to find the path I was meant to follow, I didn't expect for an instant it would lead me back to Glasgow after only four years, but then, as the old saying goes: 'If you want to make God laugh, tell him your plans.'

16

A Splash in the Pool

My fiancée's parents were very liberal-minded people but, understandably, they took a dim view of their daughter moving in to a rented flat with an out-of-work actor, so I accepted their generous offer to stay with them (although *not* in Irene's bedroom) until she had finished college. So, from being something of a free spirit, I found myself having to fit in with other people's rules and regulations – something I've never been too comfortable with and one of the reasons I left Glasgow in the first place.

I knew the idea of a career in photography was behind me now. My photographic heroes were guys like Henri Cartier-Bresson and Robert Capa, and when I first teamed up with Kevin, I had a dream that some day I might work for something like *National Geographic* magazine, travelling to remote landscapes and taking award-winning pictures of extraordinary people and exotic cultures. Maybe if I had found my way into photojournalism instead of teaming up with Kevin, I might have made a different life for myself. As it was, my brief stint in the soulless world of fashion and advertising had all but killed my interest in photography – and besides, I really wanted to get back into acting.

There's still a part of me that regrets the fact I didn't go to drama college. Both Roddy McMillan and Fulton Mackay, two actors I respected enormously (Fulton had played my father in an episode of *Craig*), had both advised me to get out and see a bit of the world before going to drama school. Well, I had followed their advice, and now here I was at twenty-one, back in Glasgow, signing on at the buroo and wondering where the hell my life was heading. If I had gone to the Royal Scottish Academy of Music and Drama I could have got a grant (easy enough back then) which, if not overly generous, would have at least kept the rain off my head for a few years. I've often asked myself why I didn't, and the truth is I was afraid I would fail the audition. Brian Pettifer had been knocked back when he auditioned and I think my logic ran along the lines of 'Well, if I get rejected by the drama college, that's the end of my dream of being an actor.' Absolute nonsense, of course, but in the absence of anyone to tell me otherwise, it seemed a genuine threat to my hopes.[1]

It was the seventies and revolution was in the air – I felt I was a part of the counter-culture that was sweeping away the old values of our parents, replacing alcohol with cannabis and sexual oppression with free love. The problem for me was that none of my new values seemed to square with the life I was living at Irene's parents' house. Most nights, I would wake up around four in the morning in a state of uncontrollable panic – fear and terror running through my mind like rats trapped in my skull. I loved Irene and wanted to spend the rest of my life with her, but what the hell was happening? How had my dreams of independence and liberty come to this – waking up in the attic of a home that wasn't mine and in such a state of alarm that I found it nearly impossible to breathe?

I had lost my way and was spiralling into a state of panic and despair. Finally, out of fear that I might actually be going mad, I saw a psychiatrist. He asked me a few perfunctory questions and told me there was no need to worry – I just had a wee touch of

---

[1] Interestingly, neither Blythe Duff nor John Michie had any kind of formal training either. Out of the *Taggart* team, Colin McCredie was the only – as he would regularly remind us in an exaggeratedly grand manner – 'Classically Trained Actor' so we dubbed him the CTA, but it wasn't long before he became known as the CTC – I'll leave you to work out what the last letter stood for . . .

depression that could be easily treated with a course of pills. No therapy. No information. No discussion about what might have triggered my depression in the first place.

In common with many people who have struggled with the fear of mental illness, I was too ashamed to tell anyone how I felt. I had been brought up to tough things out and 'just get on with it', no matter what life threw at you. I've since discovered that children who fail to grieve properly after suffering a bereavement often fall victim to clinical depression in later life. But all I knew at the time was that I was frightened, vulnerable and desperate, and the antidepressants were the only lifeline I was being thrown.

For the first few weeks after starting my medication I stumbled around like a B-movie zombie. My days passed in a fog of vacuity and when I tried to speak, my tongue seemed to have grown too big for my cotton-wool-stuffed mouth. I tried to act like everything was just dandy, but with the exception of my role in a play called *The Discoverer* for Strathclyde University Players, it must have been the worst performance I'd ever given.

Then one marvellous, brilliant, fantastic morning the sun shone again, and the black clouds that had gathered over my head vanished in the warmth of its welcoming beams. Hallelujah! Praise the Lord and pass the medication. My run-in with what Winston Churchill called his 'Black Dog' was ancient history. I was my old self once again – in fact, much *better* than my old self. I was feeling FANTASTIC. Right – time to hit the boutiques and blow my dole money on some purple loon pants, a paisley-patterned kaftan and a pair of bright-blue, platform-soled clogs. Dear God – why hadn't anyone at the clinic bothered to tell me about the side effects of taking tricyclic antidepressents? Still, at least I hadn't run through the park naked and covered in painted-on rainbows, like quite a few of my fellow sufferers.

Charlie Jamieson and Duncan McCallum, a couple of Irene's colleagues at the Art School, were looking for someone to share their rent and, much to Irene's folks' relief, I moved out of their attic and into a top-floor flat in Gibson Street. It was pretty much what you would expect a student flat to look like in the early seventies – orange walls, mattresses on the floor and the ever-present scent of marijuana drifting seductively down the stairs – but it was a big step towards regaining my lost sense of independence. Campbell, my old agent, had given up the skin trade for running his medieval-banquet caper full time, so the first thing I had to do if I wanted to get back in the game was to find some representation.

There were only two agents in Glasgow at the time, both of them women – Freddie Young and Ruth Tarko. Freddie had been established for quite a time and didn't seem interested in taking on the long-haired, flamboyantly garbed young hippy type who turned up in her office one day. The feeling was kind of mutual – Freddie seemed to me to be part of the old regime, the world of dull weekly rep and safe television drama that I felt needed to be overthrown by rebels and revolutionaries like – well, me, for example.[2]

Ruth Tarko, however, I thought was a bit of a different story. Married to Scots actor Wally Campbell, Ruth had recently started up a theatrical agency from her home in Hillhead. I admired her positive attitude and she seemed keen to have me on her books. We shook hands and I was back in the business again. For the first time in a long while, I felt a sense of optimism returning. I had a new flat, a new agent and a new future. Life was a great big bowl of cherries – right up till the minute the medication wore off.

---

[2] I got to know Freddie well later in life, after I had stopped trying to be Scotland's answer to Che Guevara. She was a wonderful woman, although she could be a little vague at times. Juliet Cadzow, the star of the children's series *Balamory*, was once one of her clients, and told me of the time Freddie rang her up about a possible part in Tennessee Williams' classic drama *The Night of the Iguana*. 'Juliet,' she said, 'I've had an availability check for you from Dundee Rep.'

'Oh yes?' said Juliet. 'What for?'

'Oh it's an American play set in the Deep South. It's by somebody called . . . och, I knew I should have written it down . . . Tennessee Wilson, I think they said.'

'Oh yes,' said Juliet, choking back a guffaw, 'and what's the play called?'

'*The Night of the Wiggy Waggy*,' said Freddie. 'With a name like that, it's bound to be rubbish. Will I tell them you're not interested?'

It was as if I had stepped into a lift and the cable had snapped. I plummeted from the penthouse to the basement in record time. The dark clouds gathered over me again, as the horrors began to chase the terrors round my frantic brain. I held off for as long as I could, hoping it was just a temporary setback, before finally admitting defeat, dragging myself back to the doctor and getting a prescription for another course of antidepressants.

It's interesting to me the way we rationalise negative situations and events in our lives – how quickly we adapt to what once would have been unthinkable, or at the very least unacceptable. Although the rational side of me told me I couldn't go through life being dependent on medication to keep me afloat, my irrational side insisted it was OK to carry on taking the pills. 'I mean,' it cajoled, 'it's not as if you're having electric-shock treatment, or a frontal lobotomy, or having to sit in a padded room wearing one of those natty wee jackets with sleeves that fasten round the back. It's just a course of medication you can discreetly go on every now and again. One tablet a day, that's all, and no one need know your little secret – that deep down, you're really off your fucking rocker.'

When the fog lifted again, I started going up for auditions. As far as Scottish theatre went at that time, my horizons were severely limited. There were the rep companies – Dundee, Perth and Pitlochry, although the last seemed to be strictly for the tourists. There was the Byre Theatre in St Andrews and the Lyceum in Edinburgh. I auditioned for all of them and made a complete arse of myself each time. Although I desperately wanted to be an actor again, I despaired of ever being able to fit into the 'straight' theatre that seemed to be the only option available at the time. While I was in London and Manchester, I had seen fringe shows and arts events that were so much hipper and more exciting than the dreary, dated fare the Scottish reps seemed content to churn out. I had even tried (and failed) to get a production of Dave Anderson's rock musical, *Charlotte Grimm and Foto*, off the ground. I know many people mourn the death of the rep theatres. They were, after all, where most actors, writers and directors learned their craft. But even

97

though I didn't know what it was I was searching for, I knew I wouldn't find it in any of the Scottish rep companies. I had begun to despair. Maybe, I thought, the truth was that I had been a talented teenager, but, like so many other young actors, I had simply failed to make the transition into the adult world.

Despite what she must have started to think was a lost cause, Ruth Tarko sent me for an interview at a new lunchtime theatre venue in Edinburgh. Phil Emmanuel and his business partner John Abulafia had rented a derelict basement below a Chinese restaurant in Hanover Street and named it the Pool Theatre – and for around five bob a ticket, they persuaded local office workers to spend their lunch break watching a play, with a sandwich and a drink thrown in. This sounded much more like the kind of thing I was interested in – a new approach to theatre that owed nothing to the stifling conventions of the past.

Phil offered me the leading role in a new play he was directing – a David Storey piece about a disillusioned young man named Jake, who decides to emulate the Greek philosopher, Crates of Thebes, by taking to his bed and refusing to get up again. I loved it, and played Jake as a thinly disguised version of one of my old chums from Manchester, John Cooper Clarke. It went down extremely well with the audience and the critics and I quickly became one of Phil's regular stable of actors.

Even though the wages at the Pool were below Equity minimum, and I was having to sign on to make ends meet, I felt I had made a real breakthrough as far as finding the way forward was concerned. The work at the Pool was fresh and exciting, thanks largely to Phil's aim of commissioning plays from new young writers who, like me, couldn't find a home in the lacklustre world of the straight theatre. I felt I was a part of an unstoppable wave that was gathering momentum and before long would come crashing through the hallowed halls of the ancien régime and sweep away its crumbling bulwarks. Yes, I know – what a load of pretentious bollocks. But that's what I sincerely believed at the time. It was probably just another side effect of the bloody antidepressants.

My final appearance at the Pool Theatre was in *A Slight Touch of the Sun*, a play by the Scottish poet and radio producer Stewart Conn. I had worked for Stewart in quite a few schools broadcasts and this, his first play for live theatre, was a two-hander with me and an actress named Mary McCusker, and consisted of three ten-minute acts. Act one was set in a travel agent's shop. Act two was on a beach, with act three taking place back at the travel agent's. A few days before we started rehearsals, I came down with a serious dose of flu and spent rehearsals in a bit of a dwam from the combined effects of the flu and the Night Nurse I was downing to keep its effects at bay. On the day of the first performance, Mary and I waited for our entrance cue in the drafty corridor that led to the performing space. As the stage lights went to black, Mary took her place behind her desk in the travel agency. When the lights came up again, I made my first entrance. As I stood looking at Mary, busily tapping away on her typewriter, my opening lines vanished in a puff of smoke. I dried stone dead – not a clue what I was supposed to say to get us going. I prayed Mary would come to my rescue with something – anything – that would jog my memory and kick start the play. No such luck. Mary's typing became more frenetic as she continued to studiously ignore me. I decided to buy myself a little time by leafing idly through some travel brochures in a rotating stand at the side of her desk. Still nothing came to me. I had a sense by now the audience had guessed the lengthy silence was probably not the author's intention. In a cold sweat, the only thing I could recall was that at some point in the first scene one of my lines was the title of the play, *A Slight Touch of the Sun*. Turning to Mary, I said, 'You look as if you could do with a slight touch of the sun.' Her eyes, which were already like saucers, widened to the size of headlights on a small family saloon. Her mouth opened and closed a few times, but other than a few guttural barks, nothing of any help to me came out. In extremis now, the only other thing that came into my useless brain was a stage direction in the script that read: *The young man snorts derisively and gives an insouciant toss of his head.* So I duly gave a derisive snort. Because of my flu, this had the effect of discharging a thick ribbon of mucus from my right nostril. If I hadn't given the insouciant toss of my head immediately after my derisive snort, It would simply have flown out and hit the deck, but as it was, the dangling snotter jerked backwards and clamped onto my downstage ear, leaving it looped across my cheek like a piece of pre-punk jewellery. As the audience were only a few feet away from the stage, I could see them recoil in horror, gagging into their lunch boxes. Realising the ball was now irrecoverably on the slates, I affected a nonchalant manner, peeling off my facial ornament as if it was all part of the play (cue further retching noises from audience) and said something to Mary like, 'See you around, doll,' before strolling casually offstage, where, out of sight of the audience, I fell to my knees in a hopeless morass of snot and despair.

Fortunately, my performance had improved immeasurably by the time Bill Paterson came to see *A Slight Touch of the Sun* . . .

17

Fringe Benefits

I was so skint, I had to do a moonlight flit from the flat in Gibson Street owing a month's rent. My sympathetic flatmates, Charlie and Duncan, told the irate landlord they had no idea where I might be found – in fact, I was back living under Irene's parents' roof once again. When word got out about my disastrous performance at the Pool, my diary was unsurprisingly empty. So quite why I was standing in the Argyll Arcade one day, carrying my guitar case and gazing into the window of the Clyde Model Dockyard, I can't for the life of me remember. What I'll never forget was a voice behind me saying, 'Hello, Alex. How are you?' I looked round and saw a face I didn't immediately recognise. 'Bill Paterson,' said the stranger helpfully, offering me his hand.

Bill told me he had seen me in a few productions at the Pool (including what I had since renamed *A Slight Touch of the Flu*), and admired my work. 'Do you play guitar?' he asked, pointing to my case. When I said I did, he told me he was assistant director of the Citizens Theatre for Youth Company and was looking for someone who could sing and play an instrument, as well as doing a bit of acting and pitching in with the script. Would I be interested in joining them for the schools tour they were about to start working on? I was about to tell him that a schools tour was the last bloody thing I wanted to do, but my instincts told me that this quietly spoken, slightly earnest young chap was not cut from the common cloth.

Bill had been fairly active on the recruiting front, as I discovered when I met the cast of the Citizens Theatre for Youth Company the following week. A young actor named John Bett had caught Bill's attention at the Byre Theatre. Heather Fielding had been one of his fellow pupils on the teaching course at the Drama College; Tim Webb had joined the company at the same time as Bill, and Austen Hyslop, fresh from the Drama Centre in London, had replied to Bill's 'Actor Wanted' ad in the back pages of *The Stage*. As the company was run on strictly democratic lines, I was a bit taken aback to find I was expected to audition for the rest of the cast before they agreed to admit me to their ranks. Still, I needed the work, so I picked up my guitar and ran through a few suitable numbers from my repertoire. After a quick show of hands I found myself on board, and knuckled down to start writing some songs for the upcoming tour.

The show I worked on with Bill, John, Heather, Tim and Austen was aimed at fifteen- and sixteen-year-olds, and dealt with the trials and tribulations they could face when they left school and tried to get a job. It could have been a pretty dry subject, but we all pitched in with the writing, trying to get some serious points across while keeping the ball in the air and peppering the show with comic characters, knockabout sketches and funny songs. We toured around Glasgow in an old Transit van, all of us sharing the twice-daily workload of get-ins and get-outs. The show went down remarkably well with its teenage audience and I found the work challenging, exciting and completely absorbing. It utilised all the skills I possessed – writing, singing, acting and playing guitars, banjos and mandolins. It seemed to me that Bill's little company had taken on the mantle of the old Scottish variety and given it a fresh, new lease of life.

Although I wasn't on a regular contract, I worked with the company as and when they needed my musical skills. On one occasion, I got a panicky call from Bill, asking if I would be willing to take over as assistant stage-manager at short notice – i.e. the next day. Bill explained that the company had devised an interactive theatre piece called *The Pirate Show* for mentally handicapped kids. It involved taking the audience on an imaginary journey to a desert island, where they discovered a chest full of treasure, only to have it snatched away by Black Jake, the scourge of the Spanish Main. The kids had a great time, hauling up the anchor, hoisting the sails and dressing up in pirate hats and waving cardboard cutlasses. Unfortunately, at a performance for around fifty teenage Down's syndrome kids the previous afternoon, the ASM, who doubled as Black Jake, had apparently spent lunchtime in the pub and unwisely decided to beef up his role a little by giving it the full Long John Silver treatment. John, Bill, Austen and Heather looked on in bewilderment as Black Jake triumphantly raised the treasure chest above his head, and launched into an improvised mono-logue of his own devising. 'Arr haarr!' he bellowed. 'Me long-lost treasure chest – at last I have ye safely back in me clutches.' As he stumped dramatically away, his parting 'arrrr!' became a strangled 'arrrgghhh!' as he vanished beneath a howling swarm of solidly built pirates, whose fury at having their treasure stolen from them knew no restraint. Despite the frantic rescue efforts of the cast, the unfortunate Robert Newton impersonator was pummelled to within an inch of his life. Although the ambulance men who took him to the Royal Infirmary managed to revive the spark of life that still remained, there was little likelihood of him joining the show again. When I agreed to take his place, I made no such mistake. With nary an 'arr', let alone an 'arr-Haarrr', my Black Jake grabbed the treasure and was off like a two-bob rocket!

The next major production the Citizens Theatre for Youth company planned to stage was a show based on a recently published book called *A Glasgow Gang Observed*. The author was a young social worker who had been accepted into a local gang and studied at first hand their rules and rituals and their complex hierarchical structure. Though the subject was interesting and insightful, the book itself read like a dull departmental report – but Bill had a few big ideas for gingering it up a little. He planned to turn it into a rock musical called *Real Mental* – a phrase that cropped up regularly in the book. Bill asked me if I would write and play the music, as well as taking on the role of Mark, a straight character who ends up taking a beating from the gang. I knew we needed a great sound, so I called Duncan, my ex-flatmate from Gibson Street. Duncan was an ace guitarist whose band, Joe Cool, consisted of him, a bass player and a drummer. To my joy, all three agreed to join the party.

Instead of taking the show out to school halls, this time we played at the Close – a studio space next door to the Citizens Theatre.[1] The show was a sensation. Our teenage audience had never seen anything like it before – a rock musical that reflected their own lives and didn't patronise or try to preach to them, the reason being that Bill was running a Theatre for Youth company, as opposed to a Theatre in Education company. Same audience – different approach.

Duncan and I had collaborated on the songs and come up with some real belters.[2] More than anything, *Real Mental* had shown me the way forward that I had been searching for. It was everything I thought theatre should be about – fresh, exciting, relevant and, above all, hugely entertaining. *Real Mental* was my eureka moment, and although it would be difficult to top the success of the play, I couldn't wait for Bill to call and tell me what he had in mind for the company's next big show. When he did call, it wasn't exactly the news I had been hoping for.

Peter, the company's producer, was an ex-teacher, who felt that Bill's radical departure from the usual fare of schools theatre didn't quite equate with his own vision of the company's policy. This led to what's euphemistically called 'artistic differences' and Bill tendered his resignation. Such was the loyalty of his little troupe that John, Heather, Tim and Austen resigned in support, leaving Peter to explain to Giles Havergal why such a brilliantly successful theatre company had crashed and burned under his management.

---

[1] We must have been one of the last shows in there, as not long afterwards it was gutted by fire.

[2] I recently sang 'Real Mental', the show's proto-punk title song, to my son Jock, who now has his own rock band. 'Bloody hell, Dad!' he said. 'Did you really write that?' Ah yes, Jocky. Not such an old fart as you thought, eh?

Although Giles asked Bill to take over the running of the company, Bill felt the time had come to move on, and the Citizens Theatre for Youth Company was closed down to be reborn a few years later as TAG – Theatre About Glasgow.

After nearly thirty years of friendship, the only thing Bill and I still disagree about is my firm belief that the history of Scottish theatre from the seventies onward would have been radically different if he had started up his own company and, in the tradition of actor-managers like Wolfit and Olivier, led from the front. Bill was a natural leader – one of those officers in the First World War that you would have run into Hell with. Still, despite his failure to heed my invaluable advice, I have to admit the boy's done not too bad for himself.

In the summer of 1971, Glasgow decided to steal some of the glory from its old rival, Edinburgh, and stage its very own home-grown (or 'haun'-knitted', as some cynics had it) arts festival called Clyde Fair. One of the highlights of the festival was a big theatre production, loosely based on events at Upper Clyde Shipbuilders, where Jimmy Reid, the workforce's shop steward, had recently led an occupation of the yard. Called *The Great Northern Welly Boot Show*, it was co-written by ex-welder and rapidly rising comedy star Billy Connolly, who also starred in the show as a shop steward who leads the employees of a fictitious welly-boot factory in a UCS-style work-in. Although not much known outside of his native Scotland, Billy – or 'the Big Yin' as the Scottish Press had dubbed him (they were still on friendly terms at that stage) – had come a long way since the time we met at Dumbreck riding stables. I had gone to a few of his solo concerts, where I was praying he would just stop talking for a minute or two to give my aching ribs a chance to recover. So I had high hopes of a great night out as I queued up at the King's Theatre for a couple of cheap seats in the upper circle. The show was dire – any of its high points had been undercut by the awful lighting, bad set design and long, unnecessary scene changes. The whole turgid farrago had been directed by Tony Palmer, a fashionable documentary maker who, I thought, as I followed the glum-faced audience back into Bath Street, had clearly never seen a theatre show in his life. Nevertheless, *The Great Northern Welly Boot Show* packed 'em in, and I would have given anything for the opportunity to work with Big Billy. The following year, in circumstances I couldn't have foreseen, or wished for less, I got my chance.

Kenny Ireland, a Scottish actor and an old friend of Bill Paterson, had seen Tony Palmer's production at the King's Theatre and, like me, thought a potentially great show had suffered from a hopeless director, so he had the bright idea of restaging the show the following year at the Edinburgh Festival. With no money to pull off this huge undertaking, Kenny had the brilliant notion of forming a collective, with everyone working for a share of the profits – assuming that at the end of the day there would be any profits to share.

I was on holiday in Paris with Irene, blithely unaware that during my absence, Robin Lefevre, Kenny's choice of director, had been casting for the second coming of *The Great Welly Boot Show* (as it was now called), and three of my mates from the Theatre for Youth Company – Bill Paterson, Johnny Bett and Austen Hyslop – had all been signed up. I was gutted, feeling I had missed out on a once-in-a-lifetime opportunity.

The show was a week into rehearsals when Austen pulled out due to illness. The consultants who diagnosed his testicular cancer told him he had little cause for concern as it had been discovered at an early stage, and although Austen felt confident he would be well enough to rejoin the show at some point during the run, Kenny had to find someone to cover for him until then. That's when I got the call, asking if I was free to start work the following day.

The Great Welly Boot Show opened next door to Waverley Station in a derelict space that had once been a market hall. It was a stroke of genius on Kenny's part to find such a prime location and secure it on the financial basis the rest of us had agreed to: no profits – no rent. Robin, Kenny and Big Billy had made sweeping changes to the original script – the narrative was much simpler and the scene changes that had held up the pace of the Glasgow production had been streamlined into one continuous flow, thanks mainly to John Byrne's eye-popping set design. The production was everything the previous one wasn't and from the moment we opened, we were the hottest ticket of the 1972 Edinburgh Festival.

I had noticed the posters dotted around the festival for a play called *Trees in the Wind*, written by John McGrath and produced by the 7:84 Theatre Company. I recognised McGrath's name from *The Bofors Gun*, a film he had adapted from his own play. Along with political dramas like *The Ballad of Joe Hill* and *Adalen 31*, by left-wing Swedish director Bo Weiderberg, *The Bofors Gun*, starring Nichol Williamson, David Warner and John Thaw, was one of my favourite films.

Some instinct told me I had to see *Trees in the Wind*. Although it was a sell-out and despite having little free time due to the *Welly Boot Show*, somehow I managed to get a ticket for one of their matinee performances. The play was like nothing I had ever seen before. McGrath's visceral script and the riveting performances of Victor Henry and Elizabeth MacLennan had me shaking with emotion. If *Real Mental* was my eureka moment, then *Trees in the Wind* was nothing less than my road to Damascus. I was in a daze as I walked back to the Waverley Market for our evening show, vowing to myself that if I didn't get to be in 7:84's style of political theatre, then I would quit the business and find another way to make a living. This is no exaggeration, nor has time played tricks with my recollection of that day – that was exactly how I felt after seeing that play. As I was to discover, by an extraordinary coincidence (or was it?) John McGrath had managed to get hold of a ticket for that night's performance of the *Welly Boot Show*, and had come away equally inspired by what he had seen. Although neither Bill Paterson, John Bett nor I could ever have guessed it, our individual paths were about to lead us on a journey from a dingy room above an Edinburgh cinema to a place in the history of Scottish theatre.

18

Stage Left

The little team from the Theatre for Youth days were gone with the wind. Austen Hyslop never did return to the *Welly Boot Show*, dying of cancer later that year at the age of twenty-seven. Heather Fielding had married and left the business, and Johnny Bett was busy forging a career as one of Scotland's up-and-coming playwrights. So it was a joy, in the early months of 1973, to find myself reunited with Bill Paterson on a series of schools programmes for STV at their Gateway Studios in Leith Walk.[1]

We had broken for lunch one day when a message was handed to us. It read, 'Please can you call John McGrath.' A jolt of electricity shot up my spine – I felt sure he didn't want to get in touch with

---

[1] I've heard this story repeated so many times now and attributed to so many different sources, that I'd like to set the record straight once and for all, and if you don't believe me, ask Bill Paterson – he was there too! During the period we were working on our schools series, STV also broadcast a daily lunchtime chat show hosted by Bill Tennant. On our recording days, Billy P. and I would take a break so the Bill Tennant show could be transmitted live from the same studio. After it finished, we would return and carry on with recording our own programme. One afternoon, as we came back from lunch, we were tiptoeing round the back of the set just as Bill Tennant was winding up his chat show, which was aimed largely at an audience of housewives. Bill's special guest that day was the eccentric TV cook Fanny Cradock, who had just given a demonstration of how to make perfect doughnuts. As the credits began to roll, Bill turned to the camera and said, 'Well, ladies, I'm afraid that's all we have time for today. Thank you for tuning in, and thanks again to our very special guest. I'll be back tomorrow at the same time, when I hope you'll join me once again. Until then, I hope all your doughnuts turn out like Fanny's.' I'm told you could hear the camera crew's raucous laughter halfway up the Royal Mile.

us to talk about the weather. We rang the phone number on the slip of paper and arranged to meet him in a pub round the corner from the studio. I had never seen McGrath in person, but when a tall, dark-haired, striking-looking man wearing a Mao jacket walked through the door of the pub, it couldn't have been anyone else. After the introductions and the obligatory small talk, he told us he had been so impressed by the talent he had seen at the *Welly Boot Show* that he had decided to start up a Scottish branch of 7:84. He said it was vital to have a cast who shared his political views, as well as his belief in collective theatre, and when he had started asking around for likely recruits, our names kept coming up. The new company's first production, he continued, would be a play about the exploitation of the Highlands, from the clearances through to the current oil boom. Coming straight to the point, he asked if would we be interested in becoming founder members of 7:84 Scotland.

Was it simply coincidence that I saw *Trees in the Wind* the same day McGrath saw the *Welly Boot Show*? Or is it possible to wish so hard for something that you somehow manifest it? Since reading *Bring Out the Magic in Your Mind* all those years ago in Pollokshaws, I shared its author's belief that thoughts, intensely focused, can bring powerful results – I suppose in a religious context it would be called the Power of Prayer. Sound a bit airy-fairy to you? Consider this – quantum physics has demonstrated beyond question that everything in the known universe is interconnected. Ever hear of the butterfly effect? It's the notion that a tiny butterfly flapping its wings in Asia can set in motion a chain of events that eventually leads to a tornado in Kansas. Whatever the explanation, it seemed the cosmic tumblers had clicked into place, finally opening the door to everything I so desperately desired at that point in my life.

It wasn't your average bunch of theatrical luvvies who gathered in a rented room at the top of the Odeon Cinema in Edinburgh's South Clerk Street for 7:84 Scotland's maiden voyage. At Bill's and my suggestion, the third member of our old Theatre for Youth team, John Bett, had joined the company.[2] Also in the cast were McGrath's wife Elizabeth MacLennan, who I had so admired in Trees in the Wind, Dolina MacLennan (no relation), a traditional Gaelic singer with a haunting voice and Alan Ross, a tall, bearded fiddle player. Rehearsals began with McGrath outlining the basic principles of the company, saying there would be no demarcation and that everyone would be expected to contribute to every aspect of the production, from driving the tour vans to researching the material and writing the script. The show, he said, would take the form of a traditional Highland ceilidh, with the cast seated onstage throughout, getting up when it was their turn to perform. He also wanted to celebrate the culture of the Highland communities by having those in the cast who could play an instrument to double as a ceilidh band, playing hooch aye tunes for a traditional Scottish country dance after each show. The set, he said, was to be a giant children's pop-up book that would provide a backdrop for each scene. When he asked if any of us knew anyone who might be capable of realising his concept, I suggested we approach John Byrne, the artist whose brilliant set design I thought had contributed so much to the success of the *Welly Boot Show*. A quick phone call and Byrne was confirmed. So with everything now in place, we launched into rehearsals for a show that consisted of nothing more than a title: *The Cheviot, the Stag and the Black, Black Oil*.

McGrath's directive that everyone should do everything came as no big revelation to Bill, Johnny and me, since that was exactly how the three of us had worked since our old Theatre for Youth days. The dichotomy between theory and practice became apparent, however, when this directive was applied to the dance band – McGrath had decided he would be the drummer, with his brother-in-law Dave handling the bass. Well, big Al Ross was a fine fiddler, Liz played piano and had a fair grasp of the accordion, and I was a

[2] Since there are two Johns at this point in the narrative, to avoid confusion I'll refer to John McGrath simply as 'McGrath' and John Bett as 'Johnny'.

competent guitarist. The fact that neither our drummer nor our bass player had ever picked up an instrument in their lives didn't seem to be a problem.

From the moment we started practising our repertoire of reels, schottisches and waltzes for the tour, it was immediately apparent that, brilliant writer as McGrath might be, as a drummer he was a dead loss. Billy Connolly had once said to me, 'If you've got ten bob to spend on a band, spend nine bob on the drummer.' He was absolutely right – it's the drummer who sets and maintains the tempo, important in a rock band – crucial in a Scottish country dance band. It was clear we would need to bring in an experienced drummer if we wanted to be taken seriously. The ferocity of McGrath's response to this practical suggestion stunned us all. He called an immediate meeting to reaffirm the company's policy that there would be no demarcation and that everyone should and would do everything – and if that wasn't acceptable, then he would have no hesitation in pulling the plug right there and then. His outburst was followed by a stunned silence. We were all more than happy to multi-task, but McGrath seemed to think that Karl Marx's famous dictum 'from each, according to his abilities' actually went on to say 'regardless of whether or not they have any abilities in the first place . . .'

After a few more disastrous band calls, McGrath thankfully saw sense and engaged a professional drummer. Dave was relieved of his bass-playing duties (not half as relieved as we were) and for the first time we actually began to sound like a passable ceilidh combo.

Every morning, we would discuss the issues that McGrath wanted to include in the show, then spend the rest of the day turning them into songs, sketches or direct-to-audience state-ments. One afternoon, Johnny and Bill were working on a scene where the Duke of Sutherland's hatchet man, Patrick Sellar, was evicting an old woman from her burning cottage. For some reason, this slightly overheated piece of melodrama – in particular, Liz's ripe characterisation of the old woman – began to corpse both of them.[3] Johnny's line 'Damn her, the old witch – let her burn!' was cut suddenly short as a heavy book bounced off the side of his head, sending him reeling backwards. His face turned ashen when he realised the book had been thrown by an irate Liz, peeved at his corpsing. 'How dare you,' said Johnny, his voice trembling with anger. 'I will not stay here and be assaulted for eighteen fucking pounds a week.' Picking up his jacket, he walked out the door.

There had been a few disagreements and differences of opinion during rehearsals – an inevitable part of the creative process – but Liz's actions had gone way beyond the pale. Thankfully, over a pint or six in the Abbotsford bar that evening, Bill and I managed to talk Johnny into returning the following day. We had to laugh when he showed us the book that Liz had thrown at him – on the cover, in gold lettering, were the words – and I kid you not – The McPhun Bible.

Over the years, I've been asked about how the 7:84 shows were created, and who wrote what. I've read Liz's version and I've read McGrath's version. Before you read mine, let me start by saying that without John McGrath, there would have been no 7:84 Company, no Cheviot, and, by extension, no Wildcat Company either. It was his insightful political analysis of historical events both in the Highlands and the wider world of international capitalism, coupled with his unquestioned genius as a playwright, that led to the creation of what's now considered one of the most ground-breaking shows in the history of Scottish theatre. What Bill, Johnny and I brought to the party was a ready-made working relationship. We were used to creating something out of nothing and had developed a shorthand style that allowed us the freedom to criticise as well as support each other, with the result that we were usually able to come up with the goods quickly and efficiently. Here's an example – McGrath wanted to include a character who personified the type of fly-by-night speculators whose only interest

---

[3] Corpsing is an old theatrical term for laughing – or, more accurately, trying not to laugh – at an inappropriate moment in the play.

in Highland culture was how to make a fast buck out of it. Bill had a ready-made character he had first conjured up when we were on the schools tours – a wee Glesca fly man who was forever coming up with get-rich-quick schemes, each one more absurd than the last. We would all be helpless with laughter in the back of the van as he regaled us with his latest ventures, such as Govan International Airlines, where, from a disused Scout hut at the back of Elder Park, he operated a fleet of military surplus Lancaster bombers, now tastefully refurbished with the aid of a few tins of Dulux household enamel, a job lot of flock wallpaper and some second-hand three-piece suites from an Oxfam shop in the Gallowgate. When *The Cheviot* needed a dodgy speculator, it was Billy's wee fly man – Andy McChuckemup – who stepped fully formed into the role. While Bill was working on McChuckemup's monologue I happened to tell him about a woeful variety turn I had seen once at the Greenock Empire – a shilpit wee guy in a once-fashionable suit and a terrible toupee who didn't seem to be listed in the programme. 'Picture, if youse will,' he began, 'a tropical paradise – the sun beating down on the golden beaches, the soft, summer breeze gently blowing through the whispering palms, and in the distance, you hear this beautiful melody . . .' I had watched in stunned amazement as he began humming through his nose in a quavering falsetto while deftly manipulating his nostrils in order to mimic the sound of a Hawaiian guitar. Bill howled at the story and, with my blessing, 'picture if youse will' became McChuckemup's memorable catchphrase.

That was typical of how we came up with the material that brought McGrath's vision to life. We would selflessly help each other with ideas and suggestions, some of which were taken up, others ruthlessly discarded if we felt they weren't working. Although there's no question that McGrath was the creative force behind *The Cheviot, the Stag and the Black, Black Oil*, there's also no denying – despite both his and Liz's assertions that we played little or no part in writing the script – that Bill Paterson, Johnny Bett and I had a major hand in its creation.

Shortly before we were due to give a 'work in progress' preview of *The Cheviot* at the What Scotland? conference in Edinburgh, John Byrne appeared with a six-foot-high pop-up book. As we laid it down on the floor of the rehearsal hall and opened it up, we couldn't believe that anything could be so magical. It was a genuine work of art. Its pages, painted in Byrne's distinctive style, opened up to reveal a series of three-dimensional backdrops – among them a crofter's cottage, a Highland glen and a North Sea oil rig. I gazed at it with a sense of wonder I hadn't experienced since the night I saw Curries Waterfalls of Scotland at the old Metropole Theatre.

A symbol of Scotland's reawakening sense of self was the recently founded radical newspaper, the West Highland Free Press. Run from a ramshackle office in Broadford on the Isle of Skye, it sold like hotcakes throughout the Highlands and Islands to a readership eager for the kind of news the traditional Tory-slanted newspapers chose to ignore. Its founder and editor, Brian Wilson (later to become a cabinet minister in Blair's government), had been part of our preview audience and championed the show, publicising the forthcoming tour with a series of interviews and articles in his paper. As a result, when we squeezed ourselves, along with our costumes, instruments, lights and collapsible rostra into two rented Transit vans (one of them with John Byrne's pop-up book lashed to the roof) and set out on the 7:84 Company's first Highland tour, we played to packed houses everywhere we went – in fact, when we mounted the show in Achiltibuie town hall, the audience that night was roughly one and a half times the population of the entire village!

Despite the acclaim and the standing ovations we received on a regular basis, not everyone, it seemed, quite got McGrath's message. After the show one night Johnny Bett happened to overhear a conversation between a pair of well-heeled elderly matrons who had clearly been deeply affected by the issues raised in the play.

'That was absolutely extraordinary,' said one of them. 'I had no idea that Scotland's resources were being exploited like that.'

'Me neither,' said her companion. 'That play certainly opened my eyes, I can tell you.'

'The question is,' said the first lady, 'what on earth can we do about it?'

'Well, it's obvious, isn't it?' her friend replied. 'Put your money into oil . . .'

Although we were aware of the impact *The Cheviot* was having, we were too busy getting on with the tour to bask in our newfound fame. I found my stamina dwindling with each passing week. The schedule was generally along these lines: get up around eight, have breakfast in the B & B, drive to the next gig, unload the vans and do the get-in, set up the equipment, including the heavy wooden rostra we used as a stage, have a technical run, take a break, do the show, strike the set and do the get-out, set up for the dance band, play till midnight (at the earliest), strike the amps and instruments, drive back to the B & B and collapse into bed. Working under the principle that everyone should utilise whatever skills they possessed for the common good failed to address the practicality of the situation. Since I could drive, perform, humph the gear and play for the dances after the show each night, I drove, performed, humphed the gear and played for the dances after the show each night, meaning that my workload was practically double that of those who could neither drive nor play an instrument. Although I loved touring with the show, I would certainly have welcomed a bit more time to enjoy it. I remember Bill Paterson reading aloud a newspaper piece about the Royal Shakespeare Company on tour in America. According to the article, they travelled in a fleet of pantechnicons, with a full crew of stage managers, assistant stage managers, roadies, wardrobe personnel and make-up assistants, not to mention lighting and sound engineers. The final paragraph went something like: 'With the RSC's hectic schedule of three shows per week, it all adds up to a tour that can only be described as gruelling.' If I'd had the energy, I would have laughed even louder.

Since it was the only day of the week when we had a rest, Sundays were always memorable, but one particular Sunday was more memorable than all the others: We had played the show on Saturday night to a wildly enthusiastic audience on one of the beautiful

Hebridean islands, and on the Sunday morning, after a late breakfast, Bill and I decided to go for a wander and see the sights. A mile or so outside the village where we were staying stood a picturesque castle that I immediately recognised from the lid of a hundred shortbread tins. We bought a couple of tickets from a booth by the entrance and in we went. We were gazing out over the ancient battlements at the mist-shrouded hills in the distance when a voice beside me said, 'I really enjoyed the show last night.' I looked round to see a girl who seemed to have stepped out of a Renaissance painting. She introduced herself as Aurora and told us she had been in the audience when we played the village hall the night before. I was so smitten that I could hardly string two words together, happy to let Bill do most of the talking. Aurora and her friend Felicity (Flick) had their own living area in the castle's servants' quarters and we spent a delightful afternoon there having tea and cucumber sandwiches, followed by a conducted tour of the rooms that were generally closed to the public. As she told us the history of the castle, I learned that it had been in her family since they had received it as a reward for their support of King Robert the Bruce, and that she and Felicity were spending their summer break acting as tour guides until the tourist season drew to a close. As Bill and I were leaving, I thought that would be the last I would see of the fairy-tale princess in her enchanted castle, but my heart leapt when she asked if we were free that evening to join the two of them for dinner. When we bowed out of the customary Sunday night piss-up with the rest of the company in the local bar, there were more than a few raised eyebrows as we headed off to spend the evening dining with the lady of the manor and her pal in the castle's great hall.

The late Spalding Gray once said in his journal, 'There are a few rare times in our lives when suddenly, out of nowhere, everything comes together to form a perfect moment.' Of the handful of perfect moments in my life, one of them was standing with Aurora on the castle ramparts that night and seeing the moonlight that danced on the dark waters of the loch reflected in her eyes as she held my gaze for an eternity before I took her in my arms.

From then on, each Saturday night, no matter where we were playing, Bill and I would hijack one of the vans and spend the weekends with our posh new popsies.[4] Bill, though, was much more practical about the whole business than me – I was completely head over heels in love, and, although it was unspoken, I sensed Aurora was too.

Like me, Aurora was engaged, but a few weeks after the tour ended, I learned that she had broken it off. I naively took this as the final confirmation that she and I were destined to spend our lives together. My fiancée Irene had just returned from a month in Tuscany as part of her course at the Art School. When I told her I had met the love of my life, she said that she too had met someone else. With hurt, sorrow and anger on both sides, we parted for the second time. I had staked my future happiness on a gamble that Aurora and I felt the same way about each other, even though deep down I had a feeling that the story of our romance wasn't going to end with the words 'and they lived happily ever after'.

I've always been a hopeless romantic, believing that love conquers all, so it came as a hammer blow while we were playing *The Cheviot* in Brussels as part of a British Council Arts Festival when the Dear John letter arrived. Clearly, older and wiser heads had persuaded Aurora not to throw her life away on someone as socially unacceptable as a common actor. In her letter, she said that she and her ex-fiancé had reconciled and a date had been set for their wedding. I was devastated. In my mind I had seen myself as young Lochinvar, galloping up on a white charger to win my lady's favour – while Aurora's family evidently saw me as a penniless adventurer in a scruffy Transit van. Big Al Ross, our fiddle player, gave me some sage advice concerning affairs of the heart between the upper and the lower classes. 'Aye pal,' he said, slipping a comforting arm round my shoulder, 'ye can get tae shag them, but ye canny get tae marry them.'

---

[4] Billy hadn't wasted much time after dinner that evening either . . .

We had filmed an adaptation of *The Cheviot* for the BBC's Play for Today series. When it went out, the acclaim was overwhelming. My dream of working with the 7:84 Company had gone far beyond anything I could have imagined, but with a broken heart, it all seemed worthless, and I found myself once again battling depression, the unseen but ever-present enemy who threatened to drag me down to the dark place.

As we neared the end of our autumn tour, McGrath called a meeting to discuss the company's next project. Inspired in part by the UCS work-in, he planned to mount a show about the Red Clydeside and the radical labour movement that had grown up in Glasgow in the years leading up to the First World War. He told us he wanted the show to pivot around the life of the great socialist orator John Maclean, and said that he thought the music should be more contemporary than the folksy style of *The Cheviot*. I was well aware of my musical limitations, so I told McGrath about Dave Anderson, my old friend from the Troubadour days in London. I thought Dave could be a major asset for the kind of music McGrath had in mind and I was asked to find out if he would be interested in coming up to meet the company. When I called him at his London flat, his initial reaction wasn't quite as enthusiastic as I had anticipated: he told me he thought that political theatre wouldn't really be his type of thing, but after some gentle persuasion, he pitched up in the wilds of the Highlands one rainy night with his girlfriend Tina in tow. After he had watched the show he grabbed me by the arm and raved on about how he had been totally blown away by *The Cheviot* and had no idea political theatre could be 'so fucking amazing! And so – so – oh fucking hell – where do I sign?'

We had a session back at the digs that night, and Dave played some of his songs to the company. Everyone loved his work and, to his joy, McGrath invited him to join the company and work on the music for *The Game's a Bogey*, as our new production was to be titled.

McGrath had asked me to stay at his spacious family home in Pembroke Square, where Dave would join us each morning to work on the music for the new show, with some of Dave's songs being recycled with freshly written lyrics. The arrangement seemed to be working well, until a few days before Christmas, when Liz ordered me to move out. I was gobsmacked – the only reason I was there at all was to work on the new show. My pleas that I had no money and nowhere to go fell on deaf ears – Liz said it was a long-standing tradition to celebrate Christmas in the house with the family, and I would just have to make other arrangements.

I contacted the nearest social security office to see if they could find me a bed in a hostel. Thankfully it never came to that, as Dave and Tina let me sleep on the floor of their bedsit in South Kensington. Although I was grateful for their hospitality, I felt so aware of putting the mockers on their love life that I spent a lot of my evenings going to the pictures to give them time to catch up.

The 7:84 Company gathered together again early in January 1974 at our old rehearsal room above the Odeon cinema in South Clerk Street. A few new faces had joined us – Billy Riddoch, Terry Cavers and Terry Neason among them. After the success of *The Cheviot's* autumn tour, McGrath had trousered an advance from the Scottish Arts Council to write *The Game's a Bogey*. Picture then – if youse will – the look of surprise on everyone's faces when he announced that he hadn't been able to find time to write the script after all. However he *had* found time to buy a bunch of lined A4 jotters, which he passed out to each of us, saying he had decided it would be best if the new show was written collectively.

As Dr Johnson once observed, 'There is nothing concentrates a man's mind so well as the thought of being hanged in the morning.' Knowing we would be standing in front of an audience at the end of five short weeks, we all worked tirelessly to cobble some kind of a show together in time for the opening night.

Of all the 7:84 shows I worked on, *The Game's a Bogey* is still closest to my heart. The Highlands had been terra incognita to me, but this show was set in my hometown of Glasgow. Bill Paterson shone as John Maclean, the pivotal figure around whom McGrath had woven a tapestry of contemporary characters, including Ina (Terry Cavers), a young lass trapped in an abusive marriage with her violent husband

(Billy Riddoch), and MacWilliam (me), a young tearaway condemned to a series of dead-end jobs before finally being abandoned by a society that cares little for the welfare of its young people. Multiple roles were once again the order of the day as we played teachers, social workers, game-show hosts, whisky-swilling captains of industry and their half-cut wives (Bill Paterson and Johnny Bett as a classic double act that could have come straight from Glasgow's golden age of variety), doctors, narrators, lounge-bar crooners and of course multi-instrumental musicians. Or as Bill neatly put it in the show's intro: 'A cast of thousands for the price of ten!'

One of the highlights of *The Game's a Bogey* was the welcome reappearance of Andy McChuckemup, who outlined his grandiose plans for the regeneration of the city's rundown and redundant docks. Absurdly comical as Bill's self-penned monologue might have seemed at the time, less than a decade later it looked like it had been adopted as a blueprint for the redevelopment of the Clydeside. I can't help thinking that there must have been a few real-life fly men sitting in the audience listening to McChuckemup's philosophy of 'get the contracts, grab the dosh and scram before ye get found oot' and thinking, 'Actually – that's no' a bad idea,' as it seems to have been the primary thinking behind Glasgow's dockside development boom of the eighties and nineties.

After months of dossing on friends' floors and relying on the kindness of strangers, I finally found a home in Edinburgh. Bill was renting a flat in York Place and tipped me off that the bedsit across the landing from him had become available. It made sense to take it on, as 7:84 was based in Edinburgh and I was spending more and more time there.[5] Besides, I needed a change from the depressing

---

[5] From personal experience, I can tell you that there are only three responses from your average Glaswegian when you tell them you've left your native city. They depend on your reply to the question 'So where dae ye live noo?'

America/Australia/Far East – 'Aye, well good luck tae ye, son. If Ah had ma time ower again, Ah'd get oot o' this bloody place an' a'.'

London – 'Is that right? How d'ye like livin' there then? Ah went there wance. Couldny get back quick enough – still, ah suppose ye have tae go where the work is, eh?'

Edinburgh – 'Edinburgh? Whit the fuck wid ye want tae live in Edinburgh fur?'

memories of my old life in Glasgow that still seemed to follow me around like a bad smell. The smart wee bedsit suited me admirably, and I felt my life seemed to be finally getting back into shape. I had enough money to live on (just), a measure of recognition, a great social life and, unlike most of the places I stayed back in Glasgow, I enjoyed the novelty of looking out of the window each morning and taking pleasure in the fact that the buildings opposite hadn't been demolished during the night.

The only thing lacking in my Edinburgh life was someone special to share it with. Johnny B. had found a partner with a beautiful young actress named Desi, and Bill always seemed to have a succession of splendid girls trooping through the door of his flat. Although I'd had a few 'pictures and a poke' relationships, there was no one special in my life, most likely due to the fact that I've always been very particular about the kind of girls I fancied. They say most men marry their mothers – I think my template for female beauty stemmed from my regular boyhood trips to the Kelvingrove Art Galleries, where I was surrounded by depictions of women by some of the world's greatest artists. Although I envied those of my chums who were a lot less fussy than me and consequently spent a lot more of their evenings having fun, I kept telling myself I wouldn't drop my standards in order to get someone to drop their drawers.

When a special someone did appear in my life, it was a case of Cupid's arrow straight through the heart. I was at a wee gathering in Bill's flat one Saturday night when I caught sight of a girl who took my breath away. A century before, she would have been a model for the pre-Raphaelites. Graceful and willowy, with long dark curls that tumbled over her shoulders, I couldn't take my eyes off her. Towards the end of the evening, there was a bit of a singsong, and when I sang an old Scots ballad, she joined in, harmonising effortlessly in one of the purest voices I had ever heard – it was as if we had been singing together all our lives. I knew then I had no option but to do whatever it would take to win her heart. I made some discreet inquiries about her and discovered her name was Alison, that she came from Tillicoultry, that she was a daughter of the manse and that she was a recent graduate of Stirling University. I also discovered that she already had a boyfriend – OK, an inconvenient but not insurmountable obstacle in the path of true love. Then I learned her boyfriend was no other than my flatmate and dearest friend, Bill.

'In love, as in war, go all out and let the chips fall where they may' was a piece of advice that stayed with me since I first heard it from a poet in the Troubadour. I was in a terrible predicament. I knew without a shadow of a doubt that this girl was the one for me, but I've always prided myself on my loyalty to friends. I couldn't betray Bill like that, no matter how strong my feelings for Alison were. Next morning, as Bill and I met over cornflakes in our shared kitchen and groggily eased ourselves into Sunday, I casually asked him how long he had known Alison, and if they were making any big plans for the future. With a sigh, he said the relationship wasn't going anywhere, and they had decided to break up. It was the greatest news I could have heard. A few days later, I called her up and asked if I might see her again. To my joy, she said if I hadn't called her, she would have called me.

She invited me over that evening and we talked late into the night. I said that I didn't want to risk ruining our fledgling romance by moving too quickly, and that we should take things slowly and get to know each other – plus, out of respect, we should allow a decent interval before springing the news on Bill. Alison was of the same opinion and we agreed we should see each other only at the weekends and not rush into things until we were absolutely sure of our feelings for each other. Two days later all our good intentions went to hell in a handcart when, to her parents' disapproval and Bill's surprise, she moved in with me.

All things considered, Alison and I couldn't really continue living across the landing from Bill, so we found a garret flat to rent in a terrace named, by one of life's odd coincidences, East Norton Place, and struck out as fellow travellers on life's journey. At last, I was finally living the life I wanted – La Vie Bohème – although when I think back to my time with Alison, perhaps The Wild Years might be a little more descriptive.

19

Brush Up Your Erse

For most of the Edinburgh-based Scottish acting fraternity, social life at the time centred around either the Traverse Theatre in the Grassmarket or the Abbotsford bar on Rose Street. There were other less salubrious haunts too, where serious drinkers like Martin Black, Jimmy Kennedy, Ronnie Letham, Harry Stamper and Roy Hanlon would gather (all fine actors, all great company, all now dead). One of these drinking dens was a bar in Thistle Street that, apart from catering to thirsty thesps, also provided a haven for a horde of fanatical Scottish Nationalists. Aside from their hatred of the English, the only other thing these big, hairy, bearded buggers had in common was their deep-rooted misogyny – no women were served in the bar. Even though it had recently been made unlawful for bars to discriminate on grounds of sex, this place had craftily got round the rules by having only one lavatory, so that if any women strode in and tried to order a drink they would be refused on the grounds that since there were no separate toilet facilities for women, it was illegal to serve them. One evening, apparently, a lone female wandered into the crowded bar and headed straight for the cludgie. On opening the cubicle door, she screamed at the sight of a huge red-bearded Highlander, kilt howked up round his waist and peeing like a fire hose. 'Dinnae worry, lassie,' he growled with barely a backward glance, 'I have the beastie by the throat!'

Speaking of pubs, I made a series of TV ads at the time for the *Sunday Mail*. In them, I played a reporter phoning my editor with Sunday's forthcoming scoop. The final tag line of each week's ad was the editor's gravelly voice saying: 'The *Sunday Mail* – if it's going on, it's going in!' One Friday night as I visited the loo in the Abbotsford bar, I noticed on the recently installed contraceptive dispenser, some wag had written: 'Durex – if it's going on, it's going in!' Ah yes, recognition indeed![1]

The Game's a Bogey tour had been another big success for 7:84. We had toured central Scotland and Ireland with the show, playing to packed houses in civic theatres and community halls, staying true to McGrath's philosophy of bringing theatre to the people. For the final two weeks of the tour, we were booked into the Glasgow Citizens, where its artistic director, Giles Havergal, even though his style of theatre was radically different to our own, recognised the quality and integrity of our productions and welcomed us with genuine enthusiasm. When Johnny and Bill and I asked him how our old schools company was faring, he told us how he had recently engaged a new director who, to his horror, turned out to be a covert member of the Workers' Revolutionary Party.

The WRP were a bunch of Trotskyites spearheaded by Vanessa Redgrave – a radical proselytiser who saw no irony in waging the class war while at the same time sending her kids to public school. Throughout the seventies, scores of actors seemed to have been creepily replaced with almost identical alien counterparts. What used to happen was that a fellow actor who you hadn't seen for a while would ring you up saying he was back in town and did you fancy meeting up for a drink? When you turned up at the pub, he would be sitting there with another out-of-work actor by his side. After introducing his chum, the evening would start off pleasantly

---

[1] A day or so after the original Durex machine was replaced with one that dispensed novelty contraceptives of assorted colours, beneath the list of available hues such as 'Passionate Purple' and 'Romantic Red' was added – in a suspiciously familiar hand – 'In ye go Indigo'.

enough with the usual theatrical chit-chat and gossip, then, a few pints later, the pair of them would suddenly morph into automatons, fixing you with a calm, flat-eyed stare and inviting you to 'join them' – it was like finding yourself in a remake of *Invasion of the Body Snatchers*. This 'hi mate – long time no see – let's meet up for a drink' act was the WRP's standard procedure for recruiting actors whose careers hadn't quite gone as hoped, and convincing them that their lack of success was due to the pernicious effects of the global banking system and/or the rise of the multi-national corporations which deprived actors like them of the right to control their own destiny. One of the WRP's aims was to take over Equity and run it according to strict party principles – although how they thought Equity would survive after the majority of its members stopped paying their dues to a bunch of incompetent prats who couldn't run a ménage, never mind a union, didn't seem to bother them. Another step on their road to world domination was to infiltrate, and then take over, existing theatre companies. This, sadly, was the situation at the Citizens Theatre as we prepared to stage *The Game's a Bogey* there. The new Theatre About Glasgow ('TAG) director turned out to be a covert WRP member whose first artistic decision had been to sack the regular company and replace them with a cast of fellow travellers. This idiot then had the gall to demand that Giles and the board of directors offer his actors lifetime contracts. If I had ever harboured the slightest notion that the WRP might have had something worth saying, it was dispelled when I heard that. I mean, what kind of an actor, if they have even a grain of ambition, would want to tour round schools for the rest of their lives? I discovered *exactly* what kind of an actor when, out of curiosity, I went see the TAG company perform at a nearby school. I was staggered: if 7:84 represented the best of seventies political theatre, this lot had to be the worst of the worst. Not only had they mounted a rip-off version of *The Game's a Bogey*, but the cast – all of them Londoners – hadn't even attempted anything approaching a Scottish accent. Thanks to the WRP putting on that tripe in their school hall, there must be a generation of kids who grew up

125

believing that once upon a time, working-class Glaswegians spoke like the cast of *EastEnders*, while their leader, John Maclean, sounded remarkably like Dick Van Dyke in *Mary Poppins*.

On the day of *The Game's a Bogey*'s opening, the TAG/WRP Company decreed a meeting with us, to insist we join them in occupying the theatre until Giles agreed to meet their demands. It all ended rather abruptly when McGrath grabbed their director by the scruff of the neck and booted him out the stage door. *The Game's a Bogey* spent its final two weeks playing to packed houses and glowing reviews, and, I'm glad to say, after a bit of legal wrangling, Giles was finally able to rid himself of his nest of vipers.

Kenny Ireland, the friend of Bill's who had been largely responsible for the success of the *Welly Boot Show*, invited Johnny, Bill and me to a meeting, saying he had a project he wanted to talk to us about. Best known for his brilliant comic portrayal of inveterate Scottish shagger Donald in ITV's *Benidorm*, in the early seventies Kenny was running the Young Lyceum Company, and had secured serious funding for a big production that was to be the showpiece of the 1974 Official Edinburgh Festival. Penned by the Young Lyceum's writer in residence, Irish playwright Sean McCarthy, *The Fantastical Feats of Finn McCool* was to be an all-singing, all-dancing, pan-Celtic musical extravaganza based on the tales of Fionn MacCuill and the Fianna – a warrior band who roamed around ancient Eire doing daring deeds and righting wrongs in a mythical Golden Age. Kenny told us that he would be directing the show and that John Byrne had agreed to be the set designer. He didn't have to twist our arms too hard when he asked if we would be interested in joining the cast. It sounded like a belter and we shipped aboard there and then. As we all repaired to the pub to raise a glass to the venture, Kenny mentioned that he still hadn't come up with anyone suitable to handle the music. At the time, I was daft about an Irish band called Planxty, who were the Beatles of Irish traditional music. I put them forward as a possibility, not really believing for a moment that they would give up their well-paid concert dates to be a pit band at the

Edinburgh Festival. When I played one of their albums to Kenny and Sean, they were bowled over and swiftly arranged a meeting with the band in Dublin. To my joy, Planxty, whose line-up at the time consisted of Christy Moore, Andy Irvine, Liam O'Flynn, Johnny Moynihan and Paul Brady, immediately agreed to arrange and perform all the music for the show.

By bringing together Sean McCarthy's idiosyncratic script, John Byrne's visionary designs, Planxty's thrilling music and a bunch of actors who were well established on the alternative theatre scene (a term I've never understood – I mean, what exactly is the alternative to theatre?) Kenny hoped to capitalise on the growing success of fringe productions by staging a Big-Budget, Mega-Fringe show. Tony Haygarth had agreed to play Finn, the eponymous hero of the piece. Bill Paterson and Patrick Malahide were Cam and Mac, the show's double-act narrators. Johnny Bett played, among various other characters, Aengus, God of the Birds. Hamish Imlach was cast as Surly the Giant, while I was Diarmuid O'Dyna, whose opening line was, 'I am Diarmuid, the handsomest of the Fianna' – a line I might have been able to say without raising a snigger if I'd looked like Robert Redford. At rehearsals I begged Kenny and Sean to drop it or change it, but to no avail. On our opening night, however, my toe-curling intro line proved to be the least of my worries.

On paper, the show had everything going for it – great set, great music, great cast – but somehow, the sum of its parts didn't quite add up to the whole. Rehearsals got off to a good start, with Kenny encouraging us to play around with the script. Whatever ideas anyone came up with, no matter how outlandish or just plain daft, were given equal consideration and added to the brew. This created a great freewheeling atmosphere for a while, but as our opening night grew closer, the mood darkened as we all realised the show was lacking any real shape or focus. It was a classic case of – as Hamish Imlach succinctly put it – 'too many bloody Chiefs an' no' enough fuckin' Indians.' Sensing disaster, Kenny transformed overnight from avuncular team coach to grim-visaged dictator as he belatedly tried to turn a nebulous mass into the big success the Festival Committee were counting on.

On opening night, things started well enough. Awed by John Byrne's dazzling set and thrilled by Planxty's spirited overture, the audience's excitement lifted all our spirits – it seemed possible that we might be on to a winner after all. When I made my first entrance, clad from head to foot in tight black leather, my opening line didn't elicit the sniggers I had been expecting. I felt my confidence grow as the audience warmed to my performance, which went swimmingly – up until my big fight scene with a pair of characters wearing leg-extenders, American football helmets and wielding a couple of baseball bats (don't ask!) called the Two Sons of Morna. Hans Mater, the fight director, and I had worked out a carefully choreographed routine that climaxed with me running between them and skidding to a halt before deftly finishing them off with my sword. Unbeknown to me, the long incline we staged the fight on had just been given a fresh coat of shiny varnish, and instead of skidding to a halt, I slid onward for what seemed like at least another yard before unexpectedly finding myself horizontal and in mid-air. As I fell, I instinctively put my right arm out and landed on it with a bone-jarring crack. Feeling no pain, I leapt to my feet and carried on the fight sequence where I left off. It was when I went to swing my sword to dispatch the Two Sons of Morna that I realised all was not as it should be. Try as I might, I couldn't raise the weapon higher than my waist, which made for an interesting spot of improvisation. My adrenaline-fuelled brain was frantically working on two levels – dealing with the moment-to-moment playing of the scene while trying to figure out what was wrong with my right arm, which refused to bend at the elbow. 'You've only numbed it,' I told myself. 'It'll wear off in a few minutes – just keep going.' The Two Sons of Morna must have been as bewildered as the audience when, in a brilliant flash of inspiration, I ran round behind them, booted them both up the arse and shouted, 'Die, ya bastards!'

My next scene followed on directly. It was a Monty Pythonish notion of Diarmuid, the Great Lover, sitting at home with his feet up reading the *Irish Times*, grunting the occasional 'Yes dear – no dear' from behind his newspaper while his wife (Jeni Giffen) prattled on about domestic trivia. As the scene started, I realised I couldn't lift the paper up to my face – and not only that, but my arm was starting to hurt like hell. In the middle of Jeni's monologue, I stood up and looked out at the audience. 'Ladies and Gentlemen,' I said, 'I'm afraid I can't carry on because I . . . I think I've broken my arm.'[2] This brought a huge laugh from the audience, who obviously thought it was all part of the play. 'No, really,' I said, 'I'm no' kidding.' This got an even bigger laugh. Dazed and on the verge of collapse, I uttered the immortal words: 'Is there a doctor in the house?'

Luckily there was, and the doctor who responded to my distress call diagnosed a dislocated elbow and had me carted off to the Royal Infirmary to have my arm re-set. Afterwards, as I was leaving the hospital in a post-operative fog, I was dimly aware of Tony Haygarth – Finn McCool himself – being pushed past me in a wheelchair, still in costume. 'All right, our kid?' he asked as he was trundled into the emergency department. It turned out that early on in the show, Tony had felt something go in his back and, like me, tried to carry on as normal. Taking advantage of the show being cancelled, he had called the hospital and been taken in for a spinal examination.

Both Tony and I were back in the show the following night, he with a surgical corset under his costume and me with my arm in plaster. We might have been the first victims of what quickly became known as 'The Curse of Finn McCool' but we certainly weren't the last – the dressing room started to take on the appearance of a makeshift field hospital as the casualty list grew with each performance.

Kenny's vision for the show had been largely inspired by a European theatre company who had taken the festival by storm the previous year. *Orlando Furioso* was a big, freewheeling theatrical

---

[2] Jeni told me afterwards that she thought I was about to say 'because I can't work with this bloody awful actress any longer.'

extravaganza full of stilt-walking, juggling, fire-breathing, tumbling and acrobatics, which presumably all the cast members had spent endless hours perfecting. Unfortunately, circus skills simply weren't part of the average Scottish fringe actor's repertoire, with the result that Kenny's grandiose vision of hi-octane physical theatre had little chance of success. Let me give you an instance of the gulf between ambition and realisation. Kenny had asked John Byrne to design a narrow walkway, high above the audience's heads, that would run all the way round the auditorium before sloping down at a steep angle to meet the thrust stage. Early on in rehearsals, I watched as he told Johnny Bett his idea for Johnny's entrance as Aengus, God of the Birds. Pointing to a big set of feathered wings and a pair of roller skates, Kenny told him that he wanted Aengus to skate along the walkway, race down the slope and shoot up over a ramp, then land in the middle of the stage, extend the wings with a flourish and say, 'I am Aengus – god of the birds'. John looked at Kenny, looked at the ramp, looked at the wings, the skates, and looked back at Kenny again. 'Fuck that!' said the god of the birds tersely. Interestingly, Johnny was one of the few actors to survive the run without requiring any medical attention. In fact, the show seemed so jinxed that we turned an old theatrical superstition on its head – anyone saying the words 'Finn McCool' in the dressing room had to go outside, turn around three times, spit and say 'Macbeth' before being allowed back in!

There was one night I'll never forget. As part of the plot, Diarmuid falls in love with Finn's wife and steals her away. There follows a big, dramatic confrontation as Finn tracks them down and angrily demands Diarmuid's death. Half the Fianna take Finn's side, while the other half plead with him to let Diarmuid live. Finn has to make a choice – kill Diarmuid and destroy the unity of the Fianna, or allow him to live and lose his beloved wife forever. The scene was staged with me facing downstage, while the rest of the Fianna, with Finn at their head, stood with their backs to the audience. There was a tense, dramatic silence as Finn made his decision. 'Very well,' he growled to his men, 'I will let him live.' Then, turning back to me, he roared, 'But get you out of my *sight!*' I think it might have been the extra stress on the word 'sight' that evening that caused Tony's top set of dentures to shoot out of his mouth. That on its own would have been enough to reduce me to hysterics, but what really finished me off was when, without missing a beat, he grabbed his gnashers in mid-air and stuffed them back in. Other than Tony, I was the only one who saw it happen. How I managed to bark out the last few lines before my exit I'll never know, but the audience must have been a bit bewildered by Diarmuid O'Dyna's rapid transformation from dashing hero and seducer of men's wives to a giggling idiot with a stream of wee running down his leg.

There was a legendary review for a West End play that went: 'The set was wonderful – unfortunately, the actors kept standing in front of it.' Sadly, that wasn't a million miles away from the sort of notices *Finn McCool* garnered, but for all the lousy press, we constantly played to full houses, and judging by the response of our audiences, they seemed to have had a great night out. I made a lot of new friends, some of whom are now old friends, and whenever we meet, we always end up talking about how much we enjoyed the show and what a great experience it all was. Kenny Ireland, who sadly passed away during the writing of this book, was a genuine visionary who never took the easy way out, and if *The Fantastical Feats of Finn McCool* was a failure, it was a glorious failure – Terry Gilliam would have loved it. So well done, Kenny old pal, and a belated *go raibh maith agat* from the handsomest of the Fianna.

A few weeks after *Finn McCool* closed, the 7:84 Company gathered together to start rehearsing our next show. The stunned silence that followed McGrath's announcement that yet again he hadn't found time to put pen to paper was broken by Bill and Johnny, who expressed their exasperation in no uncertain terms before heading out the door. Although I felt like following them, I stayed because I couldn't bear the thought of the company going down the tubes.

Johnny and Bill's exit left a terrible vacuum, particularly when it came to writing the show, which was called *Boom!*[3] After the impact of *The Cheviot*, our Highland audiences were eager to see the company's next offering. I could sense their disappointment as they found themselves sitting through what amounted to a lecture tour with a few sketches and songs thrown in to keep them from nodding off during the long, dreary sections where the cast stood in line reading out extracts from the thrillingly titled *Life in a Chinese Village During the Cultural Revolution* – a book that Liz was passionate about. It was full of lies and half-truths that would have made Josef Goebbels blush, with passages such as:

> When the villagers heard that the revolution had been
> successful, they marched up to the Landlord's house and
> told him that he would have to leave, so he packed up
> his belongings and went away from the village with his
> wife and children and we never heard from him again.

Every time I read this propagandist tosh out to our audience, I knew a more likely scenario was that the villagers butchered the Landlord's family in front of him before sticking a bamboo pole up his jacksie and parading him round the village – you know, the things oppressed peasants tend to do when they discover the rules have been abolished. As the tour went on, out of boredom and devilment, Dave, Doli and I began to replace the villagers' names with the names of Edinburgh Chinese restaurants, or made-up names like Hoo He, Hi Ho and Sum Yung Guy – until the night Liz threw an almighty wobbler and threatened to bring McGrath up to give us all a salutary lecture in political discipline. All in all, I thought *Boom!* was a lot like the puppet show I'd seen at the Salvation Army hall in Pollokshaws. The thinking behind both of them seemed to be that it didn't matter how bad the show was, as

---

[3] Although *Phut!* might have been a more apt title for the dreary mishmash that was finally patched together.

long as it delivered the message. In fact, *Boom!* would probably have gone down a whole lot better if we'd thought to throw out sweeties after the final song.

We were playing the final two weeks of the show at the Citizens Theatre, when Donny MacLeod came back to see me after the show. Donny, his sister Margaret and fellow musician Noel Eadie were in a brilliant Gaelic band called Na h-Òganaich (Young Blood), whose exquisite harmonies and contemporary arrangements had earned them a reputation as one of the best traditional groups around. As we chatted, I sensed that this was more than just a social visit, and I was right – Donny told me that Na h-Òganaich had been asked to take part in a tour of America the following month, and since Noel wasn't able to take that amount of time off from his post as a lecturer, would I be interested in taking his place?

I had dreamed about travelling to America ever since my uncle Hughie had emigrated to New York when I was five, and now, twenty years later, I was being offered an amazing opportunity to see a country I only knew at second hand from books, comics and cowboy movies. When I burst through the door and told Alison I was off to America for three and a half months, I was surprised to find she didn't seem to share my elation. In my excitement, I hadn't considered the possibility that my news might not be quite so thrilling to the person who was going to be left behind to mind the shop. But work has always been my first priority, and despite the occasional hint from Ali that she might not be waiting for me with open arms when I got back, nothing would have prevented me from embracing an amazing opportunity like this.

20

The Magical Misery Tour

The tour Na h-Òganaich would be part of was called *Scotland on Parade* – a live version of a then popular TV series called *Songs of Scotland*. The man behind both shows was legendary BBC Scotland producer Iain MacFadyen, whose main claim to fame, apart from churning out the kind of tartan kitsch that should have died out with Harry Lauder, seemed to be the ability to be constantly sucking a mint imperial, despite the fact that no one ever saw him put one in his mouth. My old friend, TV director Hal Duncan, who had started his television career as Iain's assistant, once described him to me as a 'chain-sooker'.[1]

Na h-Òganaich were scheduled to perform three numbers in the show, so I spent a few weeks practising my guitar, mandolin, whistle and bodhran parts while learning the Gaelic lyrics of the songs using phonetics – the same way I'd learned the Gaelic songs in *The Cheviot*. I was delighted when I heard that an old pal of mine, Tony Roper, would be in the show, giving of his Rabbie Burns. I was even more delighted when I learned that Isla St Clair would be adding a touch of glamour to the proceedings. I had met Isla once or twice before, most memorably when Bill Paterson and I, as

---

[1] When Iain passed away, one of his friends told me there had been a major turnout of Scottish celebrities at his funeral service. 'Ah've never known showbusiness folk be that quiet,' he said. 'When Iain's coffin was carried into the church, you could've heard a Pan Drop . . .'

Andy McChuckmeup and his latest protégé, glitter rock star Boaby Dazzler, inadvertently sabotaged her third (and unasked for) encore at a charity event with a raucous but – judging by the audience's relief – welcome interruption. At the photo shoot for the *Scotland On Parade* programme I was wowed by Isla's natural beauty. She seemed genuinely pleased to see me again, and I caught myself murmuring, 'Get thee behind me, Satan – but not too far . . .'

The tour kicked off in Newfoundland. Although the stark beauty of its rocky terrain looked as familiar as Scotland's Western Isles, it was the furthest I'd ever been from home. Despite trying to come across as the well-travelled, seasoned trouper, in truth I was beside myself with excitement. Headed by *Songs of Scotland* star Alastair MacDonald, the *Scotland On Parade* company, with its complement of pipers, dancers, singers and musicians piled into a chartered Greyhound bus and began a journey that would take us through most of America's fifty states as well as the occasional foray into neighbouring Canada.

Morally and ethically questionable as it might be, there's an old theatrical adage: 'Adultery doesn't count on tour'. Realising I would be without what the French call *une copine* for the next three and a half months, I thought it wouldn't be a bad idea to make a bid for Isla before some other silver-tongued lothario got in there first. By the time the tour reached Cape Cod, Donny found himself short of a roommate – I had moved in with Isla.

I knew I was the envy of all the guys on the tour (apart from several of the male dancers of course), but behind my cocksure facade I felt like a cheap gigolo. The affair seemed to have happened so suddenly that I hadn't paused to consider the emotional impact of opening one door before closing the other. Still, what was done was done, and it *was* going to be a long tour . . .

The more time I spent with Isla, the more I realised I wasn't the only one putting up a front, and sensed that, like me, the ready smile and jaunty self-assurance masked a sensitive soul with a wounded heart.

I'm still not quite sure why our affair went so wrong so quickly – in the blink of an eye, it seemed I had gone from dreaming about the pair of us teaming up and going on the road together to telling her angrily that she was perfectly capable of carrying her own bloody suitcase up to our motel room. In normal life, if a relationship hits a bump in the road, you can usually retire to lick your wounds in private. In the hothouse atmosphere of a concert tour, however, privacy isn't an option. Feigning indifference to the odd sly smirk behind our backs, Isla and I shifted seats to either end of the bus and poor Donny – who hadn't been slow off the mark in nabbing a cute wee dancer for himself – found his style severely cramped when his crestfallen room-mate moved back in.

America, the country I had so longed to see, whizzed past the coach window in a disjointed flurry of images: an Indian reservation that looked like a run-down Glasgow housing scheme, with banged-up gas-guzzlers parked haphazardly in the rubbish strewn streets;[2] the awesome grandeur of the Canadian Rockies, where our tour bus was stranded overnight in a blizzard of epic proportions; western sunsets that made me think of a favourite childhood song, 'Ghost Riders in the Sky'; a home that was an old aeroplane fuselage mounted on struts and sticking out from the side of a hill; endless shopping malls with JC Penney stores, multiplex cinemas and identikit fast-food franchises that prompted one of the wee dancers to point excitedly out of the coach window and say, 'Look – they've got Kentucky Fried Chicken here as well!'

The show played mainly in small towns scattered throughout America and Canada as part of a circuit run by the mighty CBS Company, who provided the towns' civic auditoriums with regular quotas of shows and events from around the globe. *Scotland on*

---

[2] Things have changed radically since then. The US government in the nineteenth century solved the 'Indian Problem' by dumping the defeated tribes on areas of land that were deemed worthless. Because they aren't subject to state or federal anti-gambling laws, the new generation of Native American Indians have built mega casinos on their reservations that bring in billions of dollars in tax-free revenue, much of which is used to provide schools, hospitals and welfare for their own people.

Parade was just another part of CBS's cultural sausage machine for regional theatres that subscribed to their tour list. We would often meet our audiences afterwards at a reception in the theatre foyer, where they would invariably come out with stuff like, 'You know, I'm Scotch too – my great-great-grandfather was a Macdonald.'

'Aye,' I would whisper to Donny, 'Ronald fuckin' McDonald!' What I couldn't understand was why these Elmer Y. MacTavish the Thirds and their Crimplene-clad wives couldn't be content with just being Americans. These endless meet 'n' greet sessions left me with a deep admiration for skilled professionals like Prince Charles, who manages to appear genuinely interested in assemblies of beaming sycophants while restraining himself from butting them resolutely with his forehead.

The endless tedium of small-town America was broken by the occasional stopover in genuinely interesting places like Leadville, a Colorado mining town where a velvet-suited Oscar Wilde, lily in hand, had once lectured the local miners on the finer aspects of the aesthetic movement and while there reportedly saw a sign in the local saloon saying, 'Please don't shoot the pianist, he's doing his best.' Leadville stands eleven and a half thousand feet above sea level, and the air was so thin that when we played the show that night there was a nurse standing by in the wings with a mask and a tank of oxygen. I don't know if the audience noticed that during some of the livelier jigs and reels, a dancer or two would occasionally totter offstage for a quick blast of life-saving oxygen before tripping gaily back on to rejoin the troupe. We also played a show in Dallas, where our driver took us along Dealey Plaza, scene of JFK's assassination and where, in a seedy nightclub after one Jack Daniel's too many, I borrowed a guitar from the resident band and gave an impromptu rendition of Hank Williams' 'Lonesome Blues' that went down like a lead balloon. As I took the long, lonely walk back to my grinning companions, one of them patted me on the shoulder and said, 'Never mind, at least you can always say you've got somethin' in common wi' President Kennedy – ye baith died in Dallas.'

As lonely days turned to weeks and lonely weeks to months,

there were more than a few times when I genuinely thought I was going to crack up under the strain. My affair with Isla had been a terrible mistake, and my attempts to make up and at least be friends fell on deaf ears. I was almost physically ill with homesickness and, hypocritical as it may seem, I missed Alison terribly. In fact, if I hadn't felt such a strong sense of loyalty and commitment to Donny and Margaret, I would have jumped ship in San Francisco, gone AWOL and to hell with the consequences.

I thought maybe if I tried to write something that would amuse me, it might keep my mind occupied and help to beat the blues. As a boy, I was a huge fan of Lobey Dosser, the cartoon strip in the *Glasgow Evening Citizen*. Lobey's creator, Bud Neill, had the brilliant notion of setting Glasgow in the Wild West, where, despite their ten-gallon hats, six-shooters and feathered war bonnets, the inhabitants of Calton Creek were as Glesca as mince an' totties. As we travelled across Arizona, the desert scenery brought Neill's timeless creation to mind once again, and I began to think about the comic possibilities of Glasgow relocated to some other unlikely part of the world. A memory came back to me of travelling on the Glasgow underground a couple of years before. The carriage was packed, and as the doors were about to close, the tall, turbaned guard called out in a rich Indian accent, 'Mind your heids.' Everyone burst out laughing, which, judging by the guard's broad grin, seemed to be the intended result. His hybrid Glasgow/Indian accent struck me as being a contemporary version of the Glasgow/ Italian 'Hey! Get-a-oot o' ma café, or ah'll-a-call-a-da polis!' accent that had so tickled my parents' generation. The comic potential of an East–West culture combination struck me as having great comic potential, as to the tune of Harry Lauder's 'I Love a Lassie', the words 'I've got a granny, and she's a Hindustani' suddenly sprang into my head.

I waited until I had completed the chorus before I sang it to the rest of the bus. It went down a storm and became the theme tune of the tour – even Isla joined in the hilarity. Once I had the basic template for the song, I added to it whenever a word or phrase would pop into my mind. It was just the remedy I needed – my mind was constantly busy trying to come up with Indian words that had found their way into our language from the time of British Raj and couple them with Glaswegian words that rhymed. Finally, after some tortuous thinking, I had a complete song:

Chorus: Ah've got a granny and she's a Hindustani
She's ma Hindustani granny fae Bombay
And when she makes me chapattis
Wi' curried mince an' tatties
Ah'm vindaloo a'day.

Now ah'll tell ye a story, an' ah hope it disnae bore ye
Of ma grandad's derring-do in Hindustan
He wiz oot there huntin' badgers
Wi' some dukes an' maharajahs
He was a very sporting sort of man.
Well wan day while in the jungle
Wi' his auntie an' his uncle
A maiden called him over with a wave
She said, 'Sir, I beg yer pardon
But is this the Perfumed Garden?'
He said, 'Naw, it's jist ma Auld Spice aftershave.'
Chorus

Well they vowed they would marry, so she bought a
    tartan sari
Then Grandad spent a very sleepless night
For one unanswered question gave him nervous
    indigestion
Did she kick wi' the left fit or the right?
Now he didnae want a rammy, so he went tae see a
    swami
Who whipped oot his crystal ball and had a keek

Then pronounced – in Hindustani – 'She's no Billy, or no
    Danny
In fact, religion makes the lassie Sikh.'[3]
Chorus

Now Grandad wiz nervous, when they held the weddin'
    service
In a wee Masonic hall in Kathmandu
While the band played 'Colonel Bogey', they were
    married by a Yogi
Who had jist got back fae knifin' Mad Carew[4]
Then they stood an' posed for photies, in their dungarees
    an' dhoties
While the home-made Eldorado flowed like wine
Then hauf the guests got scurvy aff the Cooperative
    purvey
While the other hauf quite suddenly went blind.
Chorus

Well that's the end of the raga, and Granny's little saga
Ye'll be pleased tae hear that she's still goin' strong.
Now she drives a double-decker, every Friday doon tae
    Mecca
Where the faithful play at bingo a' night long
And with his bowler hat on, Grandad marches with his
    baton
For the flute baun' at the Delhi Orange halls
You should see their banners sway, on the road to
    Mandalay
As they sing, 'We'll guard old Delhi's walls.'
Double chorus to finish.

---

[3] As in: 'Ah'm feelin' a bit seek.' (Glaswegian for *sick*.)
[4] A reference to the brilliant old music hall monologue, 'The green eye of the little yellow god' by J. Milton Hayes, which Johnny Bett and I used to perform as a party piece – you should check out the original.

As the daft Indo-Scots rhymes came flooding in to my head, I realised I was really writing it for my old friend and folk hero, Hamish Imlach. Although as Glaswegian as they come, Hamish was actually born and raised in Calcutta at the tail end of British colonial rule. There are dozens of scurrilous tales told among folkies about Hamish. My favourite is about the time he had spent most of the day drinking in the Scotia, a well-known folkie pub in Glasgow's Saltmarket. Suddenly remembering he was booked to appear in Edinburgh that evening, he downed a final pint of Guinness, grabbed his guitar case and started legging it up the Saltmarket to catch the next train. Now, whether it was the effect of the Guinness being shaken up as he ran, or whether one of the Scotch pies and pickled eggs he had consumed that afternoon was slightly dodgy, we will never know. All we can say for certain is that, somewhere en route to Queen Street station, Hamish shat himself. In a blind panic and with an inundation of malodorous cack coursing down his legs, he spied a clothes boutique called 'Jean Genie'. Running in and grabbing the largest pair of jeans he could find, he threw them down on the counter along with a wad of cash. Apologising profusely to the lady he had barged in front of, he explained he was in a tearing hurry as his train was about to leave. Without waiting for his change, he grabbed the bag from the counter and ran to the platform where the Edinburgh express was just about to depart. With a superhuman effort, Hamish squelched frantically up the platform, yanked open a door and hurled his guitar, the poly bag and finally himself into the already moving carriage. When he finally got his breath back, he headed straight to the toilet, where he peeled off his underpants and trousers, rolled them up in a bundle and pushed them out through the top of the lavatory window. After wiping himself clean, he opened the bag from the jean shop to find that instead of the pair of XXL Wranglers he expected, he found instead a ladies cardigan in a rather fetching shade of lavender. Weighing up his options and concluding he had none, he turned the cardigan upside down and carefully slid his legs into its sleeves. Hauling it up, he managed, with some difficulty, to fasten its dinky little pearl buttons around his ample waist. Unfortunately, by the very nature of the garment's design, it left a big gaping triangle that formed a picturesque frame around his wedding tackle. Ever resourceful, Hamish utilised his wide-brimmed panama hat as a sort of codpiece, sauntering nonchalantly past the gaping throng at Waverley station, and into legend.

After the rapturous reception 'Hindustani Granny' received on the coach, Alastair MacDonald asked me if I had written anything that might be suitable for a new album he was planning to record. I sang a few of my compositions to him, but it was 'The Music of the Highlands', a song I had co-written with John McGrath for *Boom!*, that really seemed to hit the mark. Alastair loved it and asked me if he could use it as the title song of his new album. I said I would be delighted, but that as John McGrath was co-author, he would have to seek his permission as well. Alastair said he would do that on his return to Scotland.

As the tour neared its end, I'm glad to say that Isla and I patched up our differences and became friends once more, and for the first time in a long while, I started to feel positive again. I had a long-held ambition to be a singer/songwriter, and now I had a comic song of my own that I hoped would start the ball rolling. Not only that but 'The Music of the Highlands' looked as if it would have a fresh lease of life instead of being buried along with the dud show it had been written for. Oh yes, the future was already looking much brighter . . .

As I walked out of passport control at Prestwick Airport, Alison was waiting for me. I couldn't have been happier to see her, although as she started to tell me about the surprising and unexpected change in our living arrangements, a wee inner voice was telling me there might be some serious bridge building to be done.

Understandably concerned about their only daughter's vagabond lifestyle,[5] Alison's parents had given her enough money to buy a home for herself. While I was in America, she had quit the buzz of

---

[5] Understandable, that is, now I'm a respectable, middle-class parent myself . . .

the city centre for a two-bedroom flat up a close in Portobello, a once popular holiday resort on the Firth of Forth whose main, if not only, claim to fame was the fact that in 1870, Harry Lauder had been born there in a little cottage in Bridge Street.

As fully paid-up members of seventies counter-culture, Alison and I set about turning our new home into party central – it wasn't uncommon, after a riotous booze and pot-fuelled party at our flat, for guests to wake up the following morning in a tangle of limbs, only some of which were their own. Back then, it seemed that we were living the perfect modern relationship. Not for us the dull and repressive mores of the older generation – we were pioneers of a sexual revolution that would sweep away the hypocrisy of the stereotypical male–female relationship forever. We were young, we were hip, and we were having too much fun to notice that we were, in the words of the old Hank Snow song, 'doin' ninety miles an hour down a dead-end street'. By the time we saw the brick wall, it was way too late to hit the brakes.

Do I regret the free and easy life I led in the seventies? Do I blush when I look back? In answer, here's a quote that's dear to my heart: 'On my deathbed, I think I shall probably regret the things I didn't do, rather than the things I did.'

Out of the blue, I got a call from Robin Hall. Since he and his singing partner Jimmie Macgregor had called it a day, he had become the presenter of a popular weekly folk series for Radio Scotland. When he asked if I would be interested in doing a spot on the show, I thought it might be the perfect opportunity to give 'Hindustani Granny' its first public airing.

I was more than a wee bit nervous when Robin introduced me to the studio audience. This was my first attempt at a solo performance and I felt that a lot hung on the success or failure of this gig. After a couple of Scots ballads I finished my set with 'Hindustani Granny'. The studio audience laughed all the way through it, and the cheers and whistles that greeted its final chorus were more than I could have hoped for. Clearly the studio audience had enjoyed it, but what about its impact in the bigger world? I didn't have to wait too long for an answer – the producer called me about a week after the broadcast to say the switchboard had been buzzing off the hook and they had received an unprecedented amount of letters, all of them asking the same question – where could they buy the record?

I have a personal theory. I've held it for a long time and now I'd like to share it with you. I call it the 'Big Bucket of Shite' theory, and it is simply this: the moment you start trying to achieve a measure of personal success in Scotland, the Fates allocate you a wee guy whose sole purpose is to follow you around with a big bucket of steaming ordure. If, by some miracle, you do manage to attain a modicum of success, the moment you step into the spotlight to take a bow – SPLAT! – the wee guy chucks the Big Bucket of Shite all over you – and hell mend you for thinking you were something special in the first place.

A few weeks after my song was aired, I received a formal letter from the publishing giant who owned the copyright of all Sir Harry Lauder's works. They were far from pleased that a parody of 'I Love a Lassie' had been used on the BBC without their permission. Oops! It hadn't actually occurred to me that I would need permission to use Lauder's tune. After all, for a song wee Leo McGuire wrote for Billy Connolly, he used 'The Road to the Isles' as its melody – and on one of their albums Robin and Jimmie had used 'I Love a Lassie' for the old Glasgow street song, 'I love a cookie, a Cooperative cookie'. So I dashed off a polite letter to EMI, apologising for my oversight and asking permission to use Sir Harry's melody. When the reply dropped through my letterbox and I tore the envelope open I failed to spot the wee guy with the Big Bucket of Shite stepping purposefully out from the shadows. SPLAT! My request had been turned down flat. Despite promising to donate the royalties to charity, I was told I would never be allowed to record what the *Sunday Post* had dubbed 'The funniest Scottish song since Duncan Macrae's "Wee Cock Sparra".'

Over the years I've met a lot of folk who grew up singing the song and are taken by surprise when I tell them I wrote it. Although I was saddened that I'd never get to record 'My Hindustani Granny', I was made even sadder when my old 7:84 buddy Terry Neason dropped it from her repertoire after being told by some self-appointed spokesperson for Glasgow's Asian community that they considered the song racist. For obvious reasons, I think it best if I keep my thoughts about that absurd allegation to myself.

The final nail in the coffin of my failed attempt to become a successful singer/songwriter was when Alastair MacDonald called me to say that 'The Music of the Highlands' was the opening track of his new album – but when he approached John McGrath to seek his permission as I had asked him to do, McGrath claimed the song was entirely his own work and that I had nothing to do with writing it. I was completely stunned. I couldn't understand how my one-time hero could stoop so low as to cheat me out of my share of the song's royalties. I decided against seeking legal redress because, as Bill Paterson said once when I was sounding off about McGrath's duplicity, 'Whatever the man's faults may be, he gave us so much more than he ever took.' I knew he was right, so in the end I let it go. I have no idea how much or how little 'The Music of the Highlands' made over the years, but even though I never made a penny from it and I may not legally hold the copyright, it's still my bloody song!

The long years of silence between McGrath and me ended when he was terminally ill and called me to say how good he thought I was in *Taggart*. We had a long chat about the old times, and when I finally put the phone down I found myself convulsed with grief. At his funeral not long afterwards, Bill, Johnny and I bid a sincere and emotional farewell to the man who had been such a crucial part of our lives.

The weeds had been steadily growing between Alison and I, and we had both started to think that it might be time to call it quits, when I received an offer to present a schools television series for BBC Scotland at their Queen Margaret Drive studios. It wasn't exactly the direction I had been hoping my career would go in, but in the absence of anything else, I grudgingly accepted it. There was a cast of three, one of whom was a strikingly attractive young actress named Sally Kinghorn. After rehearsals one day, I hesitantly asked her out for a drink and got an unequivocal knockback in return, but as the weeks went went on, I thought I saw an occasional glimmer of interest in the depths of her dark-brown eyes, but when the series ended we politely said our goodbyes and went our respective ways. Like the majority of friendships that blossom over the course of a run, it seemed we were just another couple of ships that passed in the night. The trouble was, I couldn't quite seem to get her out of my mind. Whenever I thought about her I felt a real pang of regret that she hadn't got to know me a bit better – I had a notion we might have made a good team.

21

Borderline Success

I've always found losing myself in a project the best way to beat the blues, and when, after a longish stretch of being out of work, the offer of a great part in a new play came my way it sounded like just what the doctor ordered.

Although now much altered, in 1975 Irvine was still the sleepy wee town on the Clyde coast where, as a boy, I had spent happy times among its sand dunes and souvenir shops on day trips with my uncle Willie. Now I was back there working for a recently formed outfit called the Borderline Theatre Company. Thanks largely to the drive and commitment of local entrepreneur and arts activist Eddie Jackson, Borderline had secured enough of a grant to maintain a theatre company whose principal remit would be touring around Ayrshire schools and communities with small-scale productions. They had recently hired a new artistic director, Stuart Mungall, who came up with the brilliant notion of asking Billy Connolly to write a piece for the company. The result was *An' Me Wi' a Bad Leg Tae* – still one of the fondest memories of anything I've worked on before or since.

Set in Partick, Connolly's childhood home, the plot, such as it was, hinged around youngest son (Sandy Morton) returning from a tour of duty in Belfast to the welcoming arms of Father and Mother (Bill Paterson and Betty Gillan) with a litre of duty-free whisky in his kit bag. With the arrival of uncle Peter and his brassy wife (Jimmy Kennedy and Sarah Ballantine) they settle in for an evening's drinking and reminiscing. The boy's tales of soldiering for Queen and Country cause a flare-up between him and his communist older brother (me). The rich cast of characters was completed by the nebby wee upstairs neighbour (Carey Wilson), on the mooch for a free bevvy.

Given his hectic touring schedule, Big Billy turned up at rehearsals as often as he could, chipping in the odd rewrite (not that the piece needed tinkering with) and seeming happy enough to take on board any suggestions that had arisen during the rehearsal process. Although theatrical superstition forbids any presumption of success, I think we all secretly believed that come opening night, we might just have something a little special to put before the patrons of the Harbour Arts Centre.

One day, shortly before we were due to open, Billy turned up in the morning and stayed till after lunch. As always when he put in an appearance, rehearsals would grind to a halt as he distracted us with his endless fund of stories. Over lunch, he told us he was heading off to London to be a guest on Parkinson the following night. At that time the *Michael Parkinson Show* was the biggest thing on TV. 'I've got this great joke I want to tell on the show,' he said. 'Frank, my manager, doesn't want me to tell it, but I think I will anyway.' The following evening the entire cast of *Bad Leg* gathered round a wee portable telly to watch Billy rattle off a string of hilarious Glasgow stories, tell the joke about the guy parking his bike in his dead wife's bum, and transform overnight from a local hero to a National Institution.

Our instincts about *An' Me Wi' a Bad Leg Tae* were spot on. From Irvine to the Edinburgh Festival, via community centres in Ayrshire and Kilmarnock and finally rounding off with a triumphant run at London's Royal Court Theatre, *Bad Leg* played to full houses and glowing notices everywhere we went. Of course it wasn't all plain sailing – to ease the tedium of long winter nights playing the show round bleak Ayrshire towns and villages, we would occasionally (oh, all right, frequently) replace the cold tea in the big bottle of Johnnie Walker with the real McCoy. One night, at a thankless gig in a primary school hall in Stuarton, I'm ashamed to say we completely overdid it and found ourselves in theatrical hell as a result. There's a pivotal moment towards the end of the play where Sandy Morton's character is slumped in the chair in a drunken sleep while Jimmy Kennedy and I talk about the army in less than complimentary terms. Then I say something about how 'it's the capitalists who start the wars, but it's the mugs who fight them', at which point Sandy wakes up and says, 'Who are you callin' a mug?' This leads to a violent physical confrontation that triggers the show's moving and dramatic climax. At least that's what was supposed to happen. Here's what actually *did* happen that night:

> *Sandy sits slumped in his chair in a drunken sleep as Alex's character, John, speaks his mind about the role of the army in society.*

> ALEX
>
> Aye, it's the capitalists that start the bloody wars, but it's the mugs that end up fightin' them . . .

> *Silence*

> ALEX
>
> Aye, it's mugs like us that fight the capitalists' wars for them . . .

> *Still nothing. The cast begin to shift uneasily.*

> ALEX
>
> I'm tellin' you, it's the bloody capitalists that start the . . .

> *He is interrupted by a comically loud snore.*

Alex glances nervously at the rest of the company. All he sees is the look of panic in their fixed expressions. Finally, after what feels like a very long time, Jimmy Kennedy, as Uncle Peter, makes a valiant but misguided attempt to get the train back on the track – he leans over to Alex and murmurs

JIMMY

Ah think he's fell asleep, John!

Breaking into a cold sweat, Alex has to think fast. He grips Sandy's shoulder and gives him a vigorous shake.

ALEX

Hey, young yin – wake up will ye! Ah was just sayin' it's the capitalists that—

There is a loud grunt as Sandy's eyes blink blearily open, then, realising he has actually fallen asleep onstage during a live performance and woken up with the audience staring at him in expectation, his entire body convulses as if his chair has been electrified, and he pitches forward, gabbling in an unknown tongue while simultaneously producing a resounding fart. This has the effect of reducing the rest of the cast to a state of hysterics, which they struggle valiantly to control while sputtering out the remainder of their dialogue.

Mercifully, the play ends shortly after with Bob, Bill Paterson's character, having a heart attack. At that point, Sandy, Jimmy and I were supposed to rush over, pick Bill up and carry him out the door. Unfortunately, the supposedly lifeless Bob was shaking with laughter so much that Jimmy Kennedy lost his grip and Bill's head bounced off the stage with a resounding thwack.

That was the final nail in the coffin. Realising the ball was well and truly burst we just cut the rest of the lines and dragged the convulsing corpse offstage before collapsing in the wings in a hysterical heap of laughter and shame.

As Bill and I were loading the set into the touring van after the show that night, an elderly lady came over to us. 'Well done, boys,' she said, 'that was just great – professionals couldn't have done it better . . .'

Alcohol seemed to play a central role on those Borderline tours. Soon after we finished touring the *Bad Leg* show, I was invited back to take part in *The Wallace*, a specially commissioned play written by historian John Prebble, whose 1963 book *The Highland Clearances* was one of John McGrath's main inspirations for *The Cheviot, the Stag and the Black, Black Oil*. Now, a brilliant historian Mr Prebble may have been, but a brilliant playwright he certainly was not. Nevertheless, during the brief rehearsal period, Sandy Morton, Paul Humpoletz, Carey Wilson, Jimmy Kennedy and I did our best to breathe some semblance of life into the leaden dialogue and thunderously dull scenes.

Our first performance, at a school hall in Dreghorn, set the tone for the rest of the tour. The teachers used our visit as an excuse to have a fly fag break in the staffroom, leaving the overcrowded hall totally unsupervised. Gathering in the wings before the start of the show, we exchanged a few concerned glances, as the usual murmurings from the auditorium sounded more like feeding time at the zoo.

Our worst fears were confirmed as soon as the play got underway. After a minute or so of relative quiet while the teenage mob sized up the presentation before them, the noise level began to creep up and up, to the point where the cast could barely hear themselves speak. Sandy Morton's Wallace declaiming his intention to send Proud Edward's army homeward to think again was lost beneath a wall of sound that Phil Spector would have envied. No one intervened. No outraged head teacher silenced the hall with a threat of swift and terrible retribution. All we could do was carry on regardless, although I realised our prospects were unlikely to improve when I peered through the gap between the curtain and

151

the wings to see, huddled amid a fug of cigarette smoke, five or six of the wee sods running a card school in the fourth row.

With an 'Art of Coarse Acting' type medieval costume of tabard and leggings, I played a minstrel, whose narrative ballads linked the scenes together. As I stood in the wings waiting to make my first entrance, I tried to boost my flagging spirits with the thought that the kids might quieten down when I came on. I mean, at least I was something different – a musical turn who might just appeal to them and catch their interest. As my cue came and I strode to the front of the stage, the audience quietened down. Thankful that my instincts had proved correct, I was just about to start my song when a voice said, 'Heh, look! Ye can see that cunt's ba's through his tights!' For the rest of the show I played the minstrel as a hunchback, with my lute doubling as a makeshift codpiece.

Eddie Jackson had been having a difficult time persuading Ayrshire County Council to continue their financial support, so the success of *The Wallace* was crucial to Borderline's future funding. The final show, timed to coincide with the anniversary of Wallace's death, was to be a special open-air performance among the ruins of Arclowdun Castle, reputedly the home of Wallace's mother. It was to be a gala presentation in the presence of Irvine's Lord and Lady Provost, the council's funding committee and our author John Prebble, who had flown from his home in Canada especially for the occasion. Jimmy Kennedy, who had played Uncle Peter in the *Bad Leg* show, had been cast as the Lord High Archbishop of Scotland, a part calling for a deal of gravitas and authority. A dear man and a wonderful actor, Jimmy was known to have a fondness for the odd refreshment before, during and after a performance, and at Eddie's pre-show meet 'n' greet, held amid the picturesque ruins that served as our backdrop, it's just possible that he may have had one too many glasses of the free Asti Spumante that was being passed around. The play seemed to be going down well with the local bigwigs, up until the moment when King Edward, wanting to know the strength of Wallace's army, called for his loyal archbishop. After a short delay, Jimmy tottered from the wings, his bishop's

Moffat Street in the 1950s, with Auld Nick's lum lowering over the far end . . .

On my beloved three-wheeler.
Back court, Moffat Street, 1954.

My mother and me at Saltcoats, 1954.

My first school photo. Oatlands Primary, 1955. I'm the dapper little chap second from the left in the back row. My pal Rab is on the far right of the back row, and poor wee David is the lad with the frilly shirt in the middle of the second row.

My parents, John and Sarah, circa 1956.

At the RSAMD's junior course, 1965.

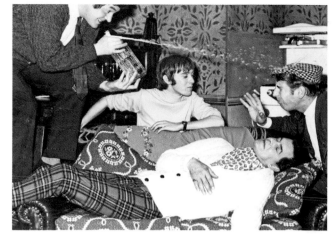

Left to right: Jimmy Logan, me, Rikki Fulton and Walter Carr on the sofa in *Love and Kisses.* New Metropole Theatre, 1966.

On location for *The Virgin Soldiers*, 1969 – no sign of young Davy Jones unfortunately . . .

The Great Northern Welly Boot Show, Edinburgh, 1972. Bill Paterson and Billy Connolly are second and third from the right. Me and Johnny Bett are fifth and sixth from the right.

Hamish Imlach and me in *The Fantastical Feats of Finn McCool*. Edinburgh Festival, 1974.

Isla St Clair, *Scotland on Parade*, 1975. Isla's expression tells you all you need to know about our relationship at that point in the proceedings . . .

Mr Merlin's Marvellous Magic Show (AKA Peter and Penny's Panto) 1976.

My favourite photo of myself – I loved being a gallus Glasgow Dame. Citizen's Theatre, 1976.

Bill Paterson and me (I'm in drag!) in John Byrne's *Writer's Cramp*. Edinburgh Festival, 1977.

Three cheeky chappies. Left to right: Bill Paterson, John Byrne and me in 1977 shortly before starting rehearsals on *Writer's Cramp*.

Paying tribute
to Stan Laurel.
Hollywood, 1979.

The lovely Aimi
MacDonald.
*Do You Come Here
Often?* 1979.

Captain Cranstoun.
A Question Of Guilt, 1980.

My dad and me in 1985 – pals again.

Dorset, 1985. One of my fourteen different characters in Bill Douglas's *Comrades*.

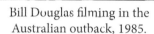

Me and Clint Eastwood. *White Hunter, Black Heart,* 1990.

Bill Douglas filming in the Australian outback, 1985.

Left to right: Jim Carter, me and Dudley Moore camping it up on set. *Blame It On The Bellboy,* 1991.

Cheer up for God's sake! *This Is Your Life,* 2003. Behind me, left to right: Ronnie Christie, Colin McCredie, Kevin Horgan, Jake Auerbach, Jeremy Beadle and Clare Grogan.

At the helm of *The Edinburgh Trader, Pirates Of The Caribbean,* 2006.

John Michie, me, Blythe Duff and Colin McCredie from *Taggart.* Cannes TV Festival, 2008

My family. Left to right: Jock, Sally, me, Jamie and Rory, September 2014.

mitre at a rakish angle and a pair of stained Hush Puppies peeping out from under his cassock. Weaving his way to the centre of the stage, he stood swaying unsteadily, using his jewel-encrusted crosier as a buttress. Sensing disaster, an ashen-faced King Edward pressed   gamely on with the scene. 'I have ten thousand yeoman,' he boomed imperiously. 'Five thousand archers and above two thousand knights. These peasants – these rabble who dare defy me – what is their number?'

'Ach,' said the Lord High Archbishop of Scotland, fixing his sovereign with an unsteady gaze. 'There's fuckin' millions o' them!'

My final engagement with the Borderline Theatre Company was on a totally different footing. My old chum Campbell Morrison had taken over as their artistic director and asked me if I would be interested in writing something for them. I had got to know Campbell when, in the wake of the Workers Revolutionary Party fiasco at the Citizens for Youth company, he was appointed director of the newly created Theatre About Glasgow (TAG) company. For his first production, he had come up with the notion of a wee show about the history of Scottish variety that would tour round pensioners' clubs and old folks' homes. Knowing my enthusiasm for the variety era, Campbell asked if I would be interested in being part of it. It didn't exactly sound like a step up the career ladder to an ambitious young actor like myself, but in the absence of any other offers, I reluctantly accepted. To my dying day I'll be so grateful that I did. Apart from a first fateful meeting with a brilliant young Glaswegian musical director and actor named Patrick Doyle, who is now one of the world's leading composers of film scores, I can honestly say that nothing I've ever done, either before or since, has given me as much artistic and personal satisfaction as that little tour. Pat and I quickly realised we shared a love of Scottish variety in all its awfulness as well as its glory and worked in tandem to create a damned fine little production. Making a virtue of the fact we had a minuscule budget, we came up with the notion of using the old theatrical term 'living out of a trunk' as our central image. We raided the Citz prop store for an old wicker basket and plastered it with travel stickers of the Scottish seaside resorts a travelling troupe of variety turns might have played in days gone by. We would set the basket centre stage, pulling the costumes out and changing in front of the audience as we introduced the next item. With Pat on keyboards and me on guitar and ukulele banjo, our little company sang old numbers, recited monologues, staged some patter routines and soft-shoe shuffled their way through the show. The response from our elderly spectators was fantastic. Most of them knew all the old songs and joined in with gusto. Every gig was like a party. It was on this tour I truly realised why we have performers in the first place. Our wee concert brought such joy to some fellow human beings who had been written off and ignored by society, most of them spending endless hours sitting in a shabby day room, bored, isolated and waiting for the inevitable. 'Yer show's like a breath o' fresh air, son' was the general response. When the tour ended, I vowed one day I would somehow get the financing to establish a company to tour old folks' homes on a regular basis. Sadly, like many a well-intentioned notion I've had over the years, it came to naught. Still, you never know – maybe one day, before I find myself sitting in the old stagers' home watching *Taggart* repeats on the Yesteryear Channel, I'll dig out our old script and call in a few favours.

'Listen,' Campbell said, 'I'm looking for a Christmas show and I was just wondering if you might be interested in writing one for us.' Why ask me, you might wonder. Well, the previous Christmas I had played an Ugly Sister for Giles Havergal in *Cinderella* at the Citizens Theatre, a part that had originally been offered to Bill Paterson. Giles had asked me to play Buttons, but a traditional Glesca Dame was something I longed to play, and when Bill turned down the part my instincts told me to go for it. Giles seemed a bit taken aback when I asked him if he would consider letting me take the role, but to my joy he agreed, casting a handsome young actor named Hilton Macrae as Buttons instead. Our Cinders was a beautiful and talented young dancer named Annette. As soon as I saw her I knew something was going to happen between us, and despite fearsome competition from other cast members in general, and Hilton in particular, she and I fell into each other's arms one night between shows.[1] Romance apart, my instincts about playing the Dame proved right. Exhausting as the work was – three shows a day sometimes – I loved every minute of it and the response from the audience was brilliant. Giles must have enjoyed my performance too, as he invited me back to play the Dame for four years on the trot. There are a lot of arty farties who look down on pantomime as a low form of theatre, and I'll grant you there's a lot of old tat out there around Christmas time, but having written, directed and performed in panto, my love of it has never diminished.

Pantomime is a noble tradition with roots going back to Italian *commedia dell'arte* troupes of the sixteenth century and, it can be argued, even before that. Some theatre historians believe panto's origins can be traced all the way back to the 'Pantomimus' of classical Greek theatre, and on through the Roman Saturnalia celebrations, when men would dress as women, women as men, masters as servants and vice versa. It provided a welcome safety valve for the pressures of everyday life – the world turned upside down for a brief, anarchic period. The *commedia* companies that toured Britain in the seventeenth century, with their silent (speaking onstage was forbidden by Oliver Cromwell's Puritan parliament) and slyly subversive comedies were known as 'Mimis' – hence the 'mime' in pantomime. It was these itinerant players who kept the torch of this ancient tradition alight and sowed the seeds of a convention that over the centuries evolved into a unique form of theatre that exists nowhere else in the world but Britain – and to me, that's something that any genuine lover of the performing arts should hold in high esteem.

---

[1] I suppose it must have looked pretty bizarre, Cinderella and her ugly sister winchin' the face aff each other, but hey – that's panto for you!

As I began to mull over ideas for Borderline's Christmas show, I knew there was no point in writing something involving a big cast or elaborate scene changes. I thought back to a husband-and-wife team who used to put on a wee magic show in our local swing park in Pollokshaws during the summer holidays. They had a canvas booth, similar to the sort of thing used for Punch and Judy shows – only instead of puppets, they stuck their heads through gaps in a backcloth and operated a pair of doll's bodies attached beneath. The images of the wee magic show and its living puppets came back into my mind so vividly, I knew it would make the ideal starting point for my first attempt at writing a show on my own.

I handed the finished script to Campbell a few months later. Almost the entire contents from my mental stockpile of old variety gags and business found its way into the piece – one-liners, cross talk, double acts, stage magic and comical capers along with a handful of songs I had written specially for the show. I used my imagination to turn the little husband-and-wife magic show I had seen in the swing park all those years ago into something called *Peter and Penny and the Marvellous Magic Show*.

The size of the cast had been dictated by Borderline's limited budget and the number of members in their regular company. Sandy Morton would be Mister Merlin. Terry Neason was the Govan Fairy, while the villain – The Great Bahooky – I had written specifically for my pal Carey Wilson, who, apart from being a wonderful character actor, was also gifted with a superb singing voice.[2] For his comic sidekick, I knew that no one else could play it as well as an actor I had recently worked with on a schools telly programme. As I started to write the character of Bumble, in my mind's eye he had the look, the presence and the impeccable comic timing of the wonderful Gregor Fisher.

I was in rehearsals for the Citz panto when Eddie Jackson called me with some bad news – Campbell Morrison had been sacked.

---

[2] As well he might, for someone whose father was the legendary Scottish tenor Robert Wilson.

His replacement, Morag Fullerton, was someone I knew only as an actress, but Eddie seemed to place great faith in her abilities as a director, so I left the show in her hands and got on with rehearsals at the Citz.

Towards the end of our first week, Freddie Boardley, a member of the Citz company who hailed from Ayrshire and had a friend in Borderline's stage crew, casually mentioned he had heard that the *Peter and Penny* cast had walked out. I flew downstairs to the stage door and rang Borderline. Eddie filled me in on the situation. Sandy Morton, who seemed to be under the illusion that Borderline was a people's theatre collective, had objected to Gregor earning slightly more than the rest of the cast. The show's musical director and the two youngsters playing Peter and Penny had joined him in flinging down the gauntlet, none of them having grasped the fact that Gregor was worth a hundred times more than the basic wage Borderline was paying him. The result of Sandy's misguided idealism was that three professional performers unexpectedly found themselves on the dole that Christmas, while Morag frantically phoned around trying to find last-minute replacements.

Through Freddie Boardley, my regular conduit for info about the situation at Borderline, I learned that the musical director had been replaced with some guy who was a drummer round the local pubs. Then, to cap it all, I learned that Jimmy Kennedy had been cast as Mister Merlin. Oh Jesus! Did Morag really think a man who had trouble synchronising his right arm with his left leg when walking down the street could actually sing, dance and perform magic tricks at the same time? My paranoia escalated to a whole new dimension and I called Eddie, insisting I see a run-through of the show – no easy matter to arrange since I was so tied up at the Citz. After settling on a date, I turned up in Irvine to find the doors of the theatre locked and nobody home. I hung around for an hour or so then drove back to Glasgow with dark thoughts wheeling round my mind like Van Gogh's crows in a cornfield. How badly wrong had things gone if they were afraid of letting me see a preview of my own show? Through sheer desperation, I threatened to take out an injunction stopping the production if I didn't get to see a run-through before opening night. My presence was met with an undisguised wall of hostility as I took a seat in the stalls of the Ayr Civic Theatre for what I feared was going to be something of an ordeal.

Even before the show went up, things got off to a bad start with the overture – instead of the jolly medley of all the show's songs as my script stipulated, the MD played a selection of Christmas carols on his Casio organ that sounded like an homage to Les Dawson. To my surprise, Billy Connolly's one-time partner, Tam Harvey, had been engaged to complete the musical line-up. Fine folk guitarist as Tam was, the fact that he seemed to be improvising riffs from an entirely different production didn't do much to undo the knot in my stomach. Finally, the tabs opened to reveal quite a nice little set. I had plenty of time to admire it during the uncomfortably long pause before Jimmy Kennedy as Mister Merlin lurched on to the stage, dressed in what looked suspiciously like an ankle-length frock with some glittery stars and crescent moons sewn on to it. He wore a long ash-blonde wig of the kind you buy in party shops for hen nights, topped off by a pointy wizard's hat made of cardboard that had been stapled together to form a rudimentary cone. The snappy lyrics of Mister Merlin's opening number may as well have been sung in Sanskrit for all the sense I could make of them, while the magic trick that accompanied each verse either failed to come off (I can still see Jimmy struggling to pull a bunch of silk flowers from his sleeve the wrong way round) or was simply non-existent. Still, the show's opening number was considerably enlivened when, during his dance routine, Jimmy suddenly and unexpectedly took a header into the orchestra pit. Clambering back onto the stage, he stood there in a daze, his pointy hat crumpled beyond repair and his off-centre wig covering one eye and making him look like a failed Veronica Lake impersonator.

It wasn't *all* bad. Given the awfulness of the prevailing circumstances, Simon Tate and Elaine Collins made a sweet and engaging Peter and Penny, Terry was on top form as the fairy, while

Carey and Greg lit up the stage with their flair and professionalism. Looking back, I understand how difficult it must have been for Morag to recast a show halfway through rehearsals, but at that point I was not in the mood to be charitable. I had lavished so much care and attention on this, my first solo effort, and to see it turn to shit before my eyes was more than I could bear. When the first act finally staggered to a halt, I stood up and told Morag that I thought her production wasn't fit to put before a paying audience. Realising there was nothing I could do to fix things before they opened, I wished them all good fortune and drove back to the Citz, where I danced, joked and sang my way through the afternoon matinee, hoping the audience wouldn't guess how close Dorah the Dame was to having a fit of the screaming abdabs before their eyes.

As a postscript, I'm pleased to report that my firstborn survived its troubled delivery, going on to become a real wee perennial and garnering some great reviews along the way. Oh, and despite our falling-out, I'm happy to say Morag and I eventually fell back in, working together again thirty years later in *Taggart*, where she directed some of our very best episodes.

22

Gone in a Flash

Sally Kinghorn, the actress I had desperately fancied on the BBC schools series we worked together on, had come to see me in the *Bad Leg* when we played the Edinburgh Festival. She was very complimentary about my performance and I had the feeling her previously stand-offish attitude towards me had mellowed somewhat, so a few months later when I discovered she was playing the Fairy at the Pavilion panto, I decided to return the courtesy and pay her a visit. Memories of operating the lighting board came flooding back as I took my seat in the crowded auditorium and waited with some anticipation for Sally's first appearance. Following a rousing medley of tunes from deservedly forgotten musicals, the keyboard, bass and drums combo that constituted the Pavilion Theatre Orchestra struck up a magical tinkling intro as the house lights dimmed and a single spotlight picked out a graceful little fairy ballerina making her entrance from the wings. I thought she was excellent, and after the curtain came down, I went to see her in her dressing room. She was surprised and delighted and gave me a warm welcome. I couldn't stay long, as she had to get ready for the second house, but as we said our goodbyes I asked how she found working at the Pavilion. She paused for a moment before telling me about her opening night.

As a graduate of the Arts Educational theatre school in leafy Hertfordshire, Sally had never been exposed to the kind of rowdy, 'oot for a rerr terr' audiences that were the mainstay of the Glasgow Pavilion. She said that as she stood in the wings, listening to the cacophony from the high-spirited crowd, she began shaking with nerves. When her cue finally came, she stepped into the blinding glare of the follow spot, skipped gracefully on to the stage and started her opening monologue – 'Fairy tales are told, old and new. And here is one especially for you.'

As she carried on with the rhyming couplets, she said she became aware of something that sounded to her ears like a giant crisp packet being scrunched up. As the crackling sound increased in volume, it was accompanied by gales of laughter from the audience. Glancing down she finally saw the source of the hilarity – the riser, a type of microphone that, as its name implies, comes up through a small trapdoor at the front of the stage, had caught the front of her ballet skirt, pushing it flat against her bodice and giving the audience an unexpected display of her very unfairylike Marks & Spencer knickers. Rattling through the rest of her lines, she beat a hasty retreat accompanied by chorus of cheers, catcalls and wolf-whistles. The Alexander Brothers were more than a little put out when instead of the round of applause that usually greeted their appearance, they bounded on to a raucous chant of 'Bring back the Fairy! Bring back the Fairy!'

As I left her dressing room, I had a definite feeling that there was something between us – but I wasn't quite ready to take the plunge into another relationship just yet, so once more we parted as just good friends.

23

That's Entertainment?

Mervyn Williams, a senior producer at BBC Wales, got in touch with me to say he was a fan of *The Cheviot* and had the notion of putting together something in a similar vein about the early days of the Chartist movement. I was keen to gain more experience of writing for TV, so I travelled to Cardiff to start researching and scripting the story of Dic Penderyn, a Welsh hero who was hanged in 1831 for taking part in a political uprising. One of Mervyn's cast was Stan Stennett – someone I had known since I used to read about his adventures in a comic called *TV FUN*. Along with fellow luminaries like Arthur Askey and Jimmy Edwards, Stan had his very own cartoon strip: *Stan Stennett, The Cardiff Cowboy*. With a ten-gallon hat and a guitar strung round his neck, he was pictured as a globetrotting entertainer, travelling the world on his bandy little legs and getting into comical scrapes that usually ended up with him saving the day and tucking into a huge plate of bangers 'n' mash as a reward. I have to say that meeting someone you've only known as a cartoon character is a little daunting – a bit like finding Biffo the Bear or Desperate Dan standing next to you in the pub one night.

After rehearsals each day, Stan would drive out to the nearby seaside resort of Porthcawl where, every summer for the past twenty-odd years, he had produced, directed and starred in his own variety show at the Grand Pavilion Theatre. Over lunch in the canteen, he asked me if I fancied driving out with him on the Saturday to catch the final show of the season. Since my offer of a fun-filled weekend in the Gower Peninsula had been cruelly rejected by Mervyn's PA, a green-eyed, raven-haired Celtic warrior princess,[1] I was at a loose end and grateful for Stan's invite. As things turned out, I ended up with more indelible memories than I would have got from a few nights in a cheap hotel with Merv's secretary.

As I looked at the publicity photos in the theatre foyer, I noticed that every turn had appeared on *New Faces* – a talent show that gave unknown acts a chance to perform before a panel of judges who would offer praise or criticism and award them marks out of ten. I have to confess I never missed an episode, and judging by the acts on the bill that night, I guessed Stan must have been a regular viewer too – getting in touch with the also-rans after they had been given the bird and offering them a summer season in Porthcawl for two bob and a balloon.

For a connoisseur of tat variety, the evening was sheer delight. The first act on the bill was a ventriloquist, whose claim to fame – as Stan rather insensitively pointed out in his introduction – was the fact that the judges on *New Faces* awarded him zero points, saying he was the worst vent act they had ever seen. Sadly, instead of being smart enough to turn it to his advantage by becoming the funniest bad vent act in the business, his big mistake was in thinking the judges were wrong. Breezing on with a suitcase on a stand, he started his act by opening the lid, thrusting his arm in and pretending to be grabbed by whatever was inside. All was revealed when he pulled his arm back out again – dangling from it was a long, furry creature of indeterminate shape that looked like it had escaped from a vivisection lab, only to misjudge its timing while crossing a busy road. Beaming at the audience, the vent started his patter.

'Well,' he said to the furry thing, 'I hear you've been a bit of a naughty boy today. Is that true?'

---

[1] At least, that's the role I was hoping she would adopt over the proposed weekend.

'Ggghhhhrrr!' it answered.

'It's not true? Well I heard you were a *very* naughty fellow indeed. Why don't you tell the ladies and gentleman what happened to you on the way to the theatre tonight?'

'Ggghhhhrrr-hhgggrr arrhgg hggghhrrr!' came the reply.

It took a minute or so of listening to the act before it dawned on me that the reason I couldn't understand what the creature was saying was not, as I first thought, because it was speaking Welsh, but rather the ventriloquist's inability to master the basic art of speaking intelligibly without moving his lips. Finally, and much to the audience's relief, he crammed the thing back into the suitcase – but the act wasn't over yet. After yet another mock struggle, he hauled out a second creature that, apart from the colour of its fur, was virtually identical to the one he had just put away.

'Well,' he said, 'I hear *you've* been a very naughty boy too. Is that right?'

'Gghhrrr-hhrrgghhhrrrr!' it replied . . .

One of the highlights of Stan's show was the Scena. Pronounced *shayna*, it's the old Yiddish word for 'beautiful'. In a variety show it's the big production number that winds up the first half. Usually set in some glamorous foreign location, it involves the entire company parading around in colourful costumes while singing a medley of popular songs. In Stan's Scena, the setting was 'Gay Paree' and the cast, dressed as debonair boulevardiers, pencil-skirted *grisettes* and beret-wearing onion Johnnies, strolled along a chic Parisian street to the accompaniment of an accordion-playing waiter. So far, so ooh la-la – except if you looked a bit closer at the big, grey building on the backcloth, which although intended to depict the elegant exterior of a Parisian café, seemed to have a distinctly Cambrian look about it. A clue to its origin was to be found above its neo-Gothic entrance, where the legend 'Cardiff Town Hall' could still be seen through the thin coat of grey emulsion that hadn't quite managed to blank the lettering out. However, the illusion of Gay Paree at the height of the Belle Époque was completed by a hastily daubed silhouette Eiffel Tower soaring majestically above the distant but unmistakable silhouette of Cardiff Docks.

To open the second half with a bang, a local dance school hoofed their way through a number described in the programme as 'A lively Expresso Dance Routine'. Next, out came Stan in his Cardiff Cowboy gear, cracking some old chestnuts and singing a couple of country and western numbers before introducing Bill the Yodelling Cobbler. I thought I must have misheard, but no. On marched a moustachioed burgomaster in full Tyrolean dress – lederhosen, knee-length socks and a trilby with a shaving brush sticking up from the brim. He started his act by setting down a gaily painted shoemaker's workbench, complete with hammer and nails and festooned with multi-coloured leather strips. Then he started yodelling while skipping round the stage, pausing only to pick up a couple of leather strips and tack them together in time to the jolly oompah music on the backing tape. The thrilling climax of Bill the Yodelling Cobbler's homage to the art of the Swiss shoemaker was when he proudly held aloft the finished pair of shoes he had just made. Whatever you thought of Bill the Yodelling Cobbler's act, you certainly couldn't accuse him of misrepresentation.

A half-cut Red Indian fire-eater who inadvertently set his war bonnet alight; an aging soubrette with a vibrato you could have stuck your head between; a husband-and-wife act who teetered around on stilts, the wife playing the washboard, the husband singing a George Formby medley while playing the ukulele[2] – these were just a few of the gems from what must have been one of variety's last gasps. So thanks to Stan Stennett, my one-time comic-strip hero. Thanks to your thoughtfulness and generosity I spent an evening I've never forgotten – though God knows, I've tried.

---

[2] Microphone stands are generally designed for performers of average height. In the singing stiltwalker's case, the microphone reached only as high as his crotch, so you couldn't actually hear a word of his songs. If he had only learned how to sing through his todger, chances are the act would be headlining in Vegas by now.

24

'An Extraordinary Trio'

In the spring of 1977, Bill Paterson starred in a half-hour radio play. Produced by Marilyn Imrie, and with Walter Carr as the narrator, *Writer's Cramp* took the form of a series of letters written by one Francis Seneca McDade, the creation of the artist John Byrne. Not content with being a brilliant painter and set designer, John had now turned his hand to writing. It was J. M. Barrie who said, 'There are few more impressive sights in the world than a Scotsman on the make.' Byrne's shrewd take on Barrie's observation was to replace the word 'impressive' with 'hilarious'. Through his copious correspondence, McDade brags, girns and scrounges his way through a less than glittering career as a hack writer who re-invents himself as a naive artist – clearly a parody of Byrne's own success story as viewed in the distorting glass of a fairground mirror.

Since the radio play, Byrne had expanded the script with a view to mounting it as a fringe production at that year's Edinburgh Festival. Bill agreed immediately to his suggestion that he recreate McDade for the stage, but pointed out that since the script was written for a large cast – some fifteen or so characters – the practicality of getting that number of actors to work on a profit-share basis was pretty unlikely. 'What if we put it on with a cast of three?' he asked Byrne. 'With me as McDade, and Alex Norton and Johnny Bett playing all the other characters – that might be a more practical proposition for a no-budget fringe show.' Byrne gave his consent and Bill asked Johnny and I if we would be willing to work for nothing to make the stage version of *Writer's Cramp* a possibility.

If an actor is exceptionally lucky, there are maybe one or two times in his career when a script comes his way that he would happily give his right arm to be a part of. *Writer's Cramp* was one of those scripts. After reading it through, we all knew it was absolutely outstanding. The problem was, with no money for props, costumes or sets, let alone the hire of a hall (assuming we managed to find one at such a late date), how the hell were we going to pull it off?

The answer was to beg, borrow and steal everything we needed. Favours were requested and old pledges redeemed with interest. Dave MacLennan and Dave Anderson, late of 7:84 and now striking out on their own with the Wildcat Company, loaned us some of their lights and stands. Nadia Arthur, 7:84's wardrobe mistress, generously agreed to scrounge all the costumes we needed. Byrne's wife Alice volunteered her services as wardrobe assistant, dresser and general gopher, while Johnny Bett managed to sweet-talk a blonde bombshell he had met in the Traverse bar into being our stage manager.[1] All we needed now was a venue. Steve Clarke-Hall, Johnny's brother-in-law, came up trumps by giving us free use of an empty space in Calton Studios, a film production facility he owned near the bottom of the Royal Mile. At least we didn't have to worry about finding a director, since Byrne's intention was to direct it himself.

As we gathered together in Calton Studios for the first morning of rehearsals, I must have been too distracted to notice the wee guy with the Big Bucket of Shite waiting patiently in the shadows. The first inkling that all was not as it should be was when Byrne announced that as he was busy finishing off a commission for the trustees of the Kelvingrove Art Galleries, he wouldn't be free to direct the play after all. In the absence of a sealed envelope marked

---

[1] Like Ulla the blonde secretary in Mel Brooks' *The Producers*, the fact that Johnny's stunning protégée had absolutely no experience of stage management didn't seem to concern him overmuch.

'Plan B – to be opened only in the event of the director leaving you all up shit creek', we concluded that there were only three options open to us:

1. Abandon the whole affair and go home
2. Direct it ourselves
3. Try to find another director at a day's notice.

We had spent a great deal of our own and other people's time in getting things to this stage, so option one seemed like a premature admission of defeat. We might just pull off option two, but we all agreed it would be better if we had an objective eye out front. Option three seemed like our best bet, but where were we going to find a director who was clever, sympathetic, willing to work for nothing and free to start the next day? As we discussed the possibilities, one director's name came up so often that we agreed unanimously to grant him first refusal.

Robin Lefevre had directed the 1971 revival of *The Great Welly Boot Show* and we thought his combination of artistic sensibility and down-to-earth practicality would be a major advantage for the production. Robin's only request, when we called him at his London flat, was to see a copy of the script. We sent it overnight delivery, and the following afternoon he walked through the door of Calton Studios.

'This is a goldmine,' he said after our first read-through. 'Our job is to sift through the dross, dig out the nuggets and polish them up.' We all agreed – as it stood, John's script had far too many characters with far too much to say, most of which detracted from the seriously funny stuff. Since our author was *in absentia*, we spent most of our first week working on the script – or 'digging out the nuggets' as Robin put it. I remember feeling a bit uneasy about making any alterations without Byrne's consent: after my recent experience at Borderline, I knew how it felt to be shut out of the proceedings. I suggested it might be a good idea to consult John first before making any serious changes. So when he arrived the following afternoon, I expected a few sparks to fly – but I was completely unprepared for the phone call that woke me shortly after midnight:

RING-RING.
'Hmmm?'
RING-RING.
'Hello?'
'It's John here.'
'John?'
'Byrne.'
'Oh, John. Er – what can I do for you, John?'
'Just to let you know – this is *my* play.'
'Umm, yes, yes of course it is, John. What's—?'
'It's not some 7:84 production. I own the copyright. It's my play – is that clear?'
'Yes of course. Is there some—?'
'*My* play, *my* copyright. Understand?'
'Sorry, John – understand what exac—?'
CLICK. Brrrrr . . .

Over the course of the rehearsal period, these midnight calls became a regular occurrence, but the show we were all working so tirelessly on was due to open in a fortnight, so despite the Kafkaesque atmosphere, we carried on regardless.

The morning after *Writer's Cramp* opened, I went out early to get the papers and see what the verdict was. The notices were unbelievable, with critics exhorting festival goers to kill for a ticket. The BBC's daily radio review of the festival proclaimed it 'not just the funniest show we've seen at the Festival, but the funniest show we've ever seen at *any* Festival'. A few days later, we were the proud recipients of *The Scotsman*'s Fringe First award, but still Byrne was far from happy and continued to make his dislike of us known in no uncertain terms. As Robin said about the pall of gloom that hung over the show, 'It's like being on holiday wi' your teacher!'

The final kick in the teeth was when a producer at Granada TV approached Byrne with a view to filming our production of *Writer's Cramp*. He agreed on condition that none of the original cast would be in it – with the result that the astonished producer pulled the plug on the project.

John Byrne was, and is, an extraordinarily gifted man who had written a brilliant comedy, and Bill, Johnny and I had been extremely fortunate in having been given the opportunity to perform it. But in my view Byrne had been equally fortunate in having three actors who were up to the task of 'digging out the nuggets' and turning his script into the smash hit it became. Why he took against us so vehemently is still a mystery to me, although as a well-known Hollywood director once said, when telling one of my friends about a famous movie star who hadn't been the easiest person to work with, 'In my experience, great talent seldom arrives unaccompanied . . .'

25

Off to See the Izzard

Despite all the traumas, *Writer's Cramp* was a real watershed in my career. After our run at the festival we took it to London's Bush Theatre, where Duncan Heath, an agent who had just started up his own business, came to see me in it and took me on. We were the toast of the town – everyone who was anyone squeezed into the tiny pub theatre and lingered in the bar afterwards to offer their congratulations. One of our admirers was Bryan Izzard, a flamboyant, larger than life character who had become Head of Light Entertainment at STV. In his chequered career, Bryan had produced more turkeys than Bernard Matthews, as well as popular shows like *On the Buses* – a comedy series I could never watch without imagining how depressed I would feel if I was one of its regulars. Izzard took Bill, Johnny and me out for lunch at a posh Soho restaurant and told us, as he puffed at his big cigar, that he was going to make us all stars. I have to confess, this was the sort of thing I wanted to hear, but not necessarily from the man who had been responsible for sending Rikki Fulton's career into free-fall when he was STV's Head of Light Entertainment once before in the late sixties. Bryan and Rikki's first (and only) venture was a series of six comedies, with Rikki playing a different character in each one. Were they any good? Sadly, we'll never know, because the night after the first episode was aired to scathing reviews, STV's Hope Street studios were mysteriously burgled. I say 'mysteriously' because the only items stolen were the tapes of the five remaining episodes of Rikki's series. Was it a put-up job? Did Rikki (as the gossip of the day had it) hire a professional burglar to save his reputation? Well, as a former STV employee who was there at the time once said to me: 'If Supercop was on the case, he wouldny have to look too far to find the guilty party . . .'

The first of Izzard's Faustian temptations was to invite the three of us to appear in STV's New Year show. To that end, he had hired a professional gag writer to come up with a handful of sketches for us. We told Izzard we felt they weren't for us (we thought they were shit) and would prefer to write our own material. During the show's live transmission, I have to say that our stuff had the studio audience laughing, cheering, whistling and clapping – a far bigger response than that received by the show's host, cockney comic Mike Reid.

Although we had gone down a storm on the Hogmanay show, both Bill and Johnny decided that there was no role for them in Izzard's grandiose plans for our future as TV's latest comedy team, and bowed out. Even though I was aware of his reputation as a schlockmeister, I thought I would stick around for a bit longer and see if I could find a way to play the game to my advantage. I wanted to write for TV and reasoned that there would be more chance of it happening if I was on the inside looking out, rather than the other way round.

One of Bryan's other 'discoveries' was a talented and vivacious young singer named Diane Langton, a West End musical performer whose star seemed to be on the rise. He decided to build a show around her that would show off her talent. Imaginatively titled *The Diane Langton Show*, it was due to be broadcast on Valentine's Day. The concept was that Diane would be the only woman in an all-male cast (John Cairney, Chic Murray and me), with an all-male audience. The problem was that very few people responded to the newspaper ads inviting them to apply for tickets, so, come the evening of the recording, only about a third of the seats had been taken up. There was a part of the show where Diane was supposed to walk among the audience and pretend to flirt with them while singing 'My Funny Valentine', so wee Bobby the wardrobe master was ordered to go out and return with around fifty men. Picking up strange men was, allegedly, something to which Bobby was not entirely unaccustomed, but rarely fifty at a time. Now, if the show had been recorded, say, at London's Talk of the Town Theatre, you just might have been able to round up fifty good-looking, sophisticated and smartly dressed males at short notice. Unfortunately, since our show was being recorded in Cowcaddens, the best wee Bobby could rustle up (and then only after the promise of free drink) was the throng of half-cut regulars from the nearest boozer. My heart went out to poor Diane as she glided seductively among the audience, ruffling someone's hair or perching on someone else's knee, while trying not to react to the forest of hands that were grabbing her backside and causing the odd quaver in her voice as she gamely carried on like the trouper she was.

My swansong under Bryan's tenure at STV was *Do You Come Here Often?*, a series conceived by Peter Barber Fleming, the dynamic young producer who had taken Bryan to see me in *Writer's Cramp* at the Bush. I thought it was a great idea – a wee Glasgow dance hall during the war, a perfect vehicle for comic situations with Yanks, Poles, spivs, GI brides, lovelorn lassies looking for a lumber and everything else that was going on in that colourful period in Glasgow's history. A nostalgic half-hour sitcom with singing, dancing and Glasgow patter – how could it go wrong? Well, here's how. 'Have you heard of Cliff Hanley?' Bryan asked me. 'He's agreed to write the scripts for us. Terribly clever little chap – he actually played in a dance band during the war you know.' My heart sank like a stone. I had read, and loved, Cliff's autobiography, *Dancing in the Streets*, a comic and warm-hearted memoir of Glasgow life in the thirties and forties. Unfortunately, by the late seventies Cliff's wit was mainly confined to the bar of the BBC club, where he was the resident jester.[1] Cliff was a clever and

---

[1] Until the arrival of Billy Connolly, who one wag described as 'Cliff Hanley on stilts wi' a banjo!'

inventive man who could create songs, sketches and topical gags at the drop of a hat, but had absolutely no form when it came to anything as demanding as writing a comedy series that Izzard assured me would knock *Dad's Army* off its number one spot in the ratings.

While *Dad's Army* had the brilliant Arthur Lowe in the leading role, we had Ronnie Fraser, a character actor who, thanks to a lifetime of serious boozing with mates like Richard Harris and Richard Burton, had just been handed the yellow card by his doctor, with the result that he was so shaky from withdrawal symptoms he could barely remember a line of his dialogue. Our John Le Mesurier was an actor named Stephen Hancock, who for years had played Emily Bishop's mild-mannered husband Ernie in *Coronation Street*. When he had the audacity to ask for a pay rise, the producers told him they would consider his request and get back to him. So, picture his surprise at the next read-through, when he discovered the following stage directions in his script: *As Ernie and the robber struggle, the gun goes off and Ernie falls to the floor – dead.* This dramatic reversal of fortune had occurred only a few months before he joined our merry band, and poor Stephen still seemed in such a state of shock that I wondered if maybe he secretly believed he really had been shot and was now in a section of Hell specially reserved for soap actors who tragically misjudge their status. Una McLean was the wisecracking manageress (at least she would have been if Cliff's scripts had provided her with any decent wisecracks), and Nellie Norman, seemingly none the worse for her sink-breaking turn at the New Metropole, was the old dragon in the box office.

The eye candy came in the shape of Aimi MacDonald – 'the lovely Aimi MacDonald', as she was always introduced when she played the hostess of *At Last the 1948 Show*, John Cleese and Graham Chapman's precursor to *Monty Python's Flying Circus*. Aimi was a tall, leggy blonde who had been a Las Vegas showgirl and had a fund of tales about the place that made Martin Scorsese's *Casino* seem like the 'Little Stories from the Police Courts' in the *Weekly News*. She and I hit it off right away – I've always had a thing for tall, leggy blondes and she liked younger men who had a thing for – well – tall, leggy blondes, so we enjoyed a delightful wee arrangement that buoyed us both up through the long dreary weeks that stretched ahead. Una summed up the likelihood of us getting a second series one morning at the read-through. 'Great script,' she whispered to me. 'D'ye think Cliff'll send us the jokes later?'

I knew we were on a hiding to nothing with *Do You Come Here Often?*, but I still saw my future in TV comedy so, after a lot of thought, I finally hit on an idea that I thought might just take a trick. My notion was to option the rights for Sir Compton Mackenzie's two books, *Whisky Galore* and *Rockets Galore*, and commission Ewen Bain, the sharp wit behind Angus Og, the *Daily Record*'s satirical cartoon strip, to take Mackenzie's classic tales, update them and put the characters in a series I provisionally titled *Oil Galore*. The basic premise was the discovery of a major oil field just off the coast of Mackenzie's fictional isle of Todday, which spurs the wily inhabitants to try to keep the prospective bonanza to themselves by declaring independence from the mainland. Naturally, the British government and the big oil companies would have other ideas, which would set the scene for a rich stew of comic characters, confrontations and complications.

Once I had drafted a synopsis, I took it to my friend and mentor in STV, Peter Barber Fleming. Peter thought it was a winner and said he would very much like to produce it. A meeting was arranged with Bryan Izzard, who said he thought it had some potential and asked me to leave the synopsis with him while he thought it over. Later that day Peter called to tell me that as soon as I had left the meeting, Izzard had jumped up and down with excitement, saying that it was the best idea for a comedy series he had ever heard in his life. I was totally over the moon – this could be the turning point of my career. 'Have you registered your synopsis with your agent yet?' asked Peter.

'No, not yet,' I answered. 'Why?'

'Please don't say you got this from me,' he said, 'but Bryan said he was going to register your idea with his own company and claim it for himself.' I felt the blood drain from my face. The man who told me he would make me a star was about to steal my work and elbow me out of the proceedings without a second thought? I realised Izzard was lacking in the taste department, but I hadn't realised he was completely devoid of decency too.

Whether Izzard ever did register my idea as his own or not I'll never know. All I do know is that nothing ever came of *Oil Galore*, and soon afterwards, he departed from STV with a fat bonus, never to return. In his autobiography, Rikki Fulton scathingly dubbed Bryan 'the Fat Boy', but I think my personal term for him, 'the Izzard of Dross', might have been more on the money.

26

Make or Break

Since my prospects of a career as a writer at STV appeared to have hit the skids and the seventies renaissance of popular Scottish theatre seemed to be on the wane, I decided to try my luck in London again. Over the years, Alison and I had our share of tearful separations and emotional reunions, but as I stowed my suitcase in the boot of my car and bid a tearful farewell to the girl I once thought of as the love of my life, we knew that it was, in the words of Fletcher of Saltoun, 'The end o' an auld sang . . .' With a parting kiss, Ali wished me luck as I set off once more on the road less travelled, hoping beyond hope that it wouldn't lead over a cliff.

Starting life over again is never an easy thing. I had exchanged the familiarity of my circle of friends and my home in Edinburgh for a rented flat in Maida Vale, an affluent but dull part of London I once heard described as 'the undiscovered country from whose bourn no traveller returns'. Soon after moving in, I glimpsed the dark crows as they began circling the cornfield again. I tried my damnedest to be positive and believe things would improve as I adjusted to my new life, but scarcely a day went by that I didn't want to call Alison and beg her to take me back. I had no friends to speak of in London, and having little to offer them in return for their favours, the few old flames that had bothered to keep in touch with me gradually faded out of the picture. I had never felt so lonely in my life.

I was offered the part of a sex-mad Egyptian lothario in a play at the Bush Theatre – *The Tax Exile* by Johnny Gems. It was a darkly funny character part that I thought I could shine in. Between the read-through and the opening night, however, something must have gone very, very wrong. When the reviews came out, most of them liked the play well enough and praised several of the cast by name, but not a single reviewer mentioned me. It was a humiliating blow. Still, at least one of my fellow performers thought I was good – the bluff Lancashire actor whose gloriously ripe performance as the eponymous tax inspector had stolen the notices. He offered me a piece of advice concerning critics. 'Fuck 'em!' he said. 'The fuckers aren't even worth fuckin' ignorin'.' Relatively unknown then, it was as Reg Holdsworth, the outrageously on-the-make manager of *Coronation Street*'s Bettabuys supermarket, that Ken Morley was to become one of the best-known faces in the pantheon of British TV's comedy characters.

My agent had put me up for a major new BBC drama called *A Question of Guilt*, a six-part series based on the true story of Mary Blandy, a seventeenth-century spinster who was hanged for murdering her father. The part I was up for was Mary's lover, an impoverished Scottish aristocrat who woos her with an eye to getting his hands on her not inconsiderable dowry, and when her father opposes the marriage, he tricks the girl into poisoning him. A leading role in a big-budget production was a long way from anything I had any experience of so, even though the interview had gone well, I simply put it out of my head. When my agent rang the following morning to congratulate me on landing the role, I knew I had just been given the opportunity that an actor can wait a lifetime for. My gamble had paid off: this was the break I had turned my back on everything back home for, the reason I was living on my own in London. So why, half an hour later, was I curled up on the floor in the throes of a full-blown panic attack with a single thought racing round my mind on an endless loop: 'Why now? Why did my break have to come now?'

It's when we're forced into confronting our true selves – the person behind the persona – that we discover who we really are. The flimsy carapace that hid my growing sense of failure had been shattered by the news. I felt I was facing a challenge for which I was totally unprepared. Having made something of a name for myself in fringe theatre productions with tiny budgets and audiences of a few hundred at most, I was now being offered a leading role in a major TV drama that must be costing a fortune and would be watched by an audience numbered in millions. I felt I had no aptitude for the job whatsoever. Oh Jesus, why hadn't I gone to drama college and learned to be a proper actor when I had the chance? I knew it would be madness to say no to this one-time-only gift, but as the starting date drew ever nearer and I began the pre-production sessions of costume and wig fittings, it felt like the half of me that believed I could pull it off was fighting a pitched battle with the half that was hell-bent on destroying what little self-confidence I had left. Trying to resolve the civil war that was raging in my mind didn't leave me with too many reserves to concentrate on the job in hand.

There's an old saying in the business when you feel you can't go on: 'You need to visit Doctor Footlights.' It means that the act of walking onto the stage and getting the first few lines out will somehow dissipate all the demons that have been plaguing you beforehand. From personal experience, I've found there's a deal of truth in it – there were times during the Citz pantos when I was so exhausted or flu-ridden I could barely crawl from my dressing room to the stage, yet I would spend the next two hours singing, dancing and running around like a dervish, only to crawl back to my dressing room after the curtain had fallen. Unfortunately, Doctor Footlights must have been on a sabbatical when I started work on *A Question of Guilt*. Throughout the entire two months of the schedule, I lived in daily expectation that I would be taken aside and told I was being replaced with a proper actor. I had to struggle to suppress an overwhelming sense of dread every time I went before the camera – the camera whose dispassionate eye, I believed, would see through the mask and reveal the shy wee boy from Pollokshaws who had got away with pretending to be a grown-up for such a long time.

Throughout the shoot, one of the things that helped buoy me up was a notion I clung to like a shipwrecked sailor to a broken spar: I would use the money I was earning from the series to finance a trip to Los Angeles. Jean Gilpin, an actress I had become friends with when we worked together at the Citz pantos, had recently moved there and I took it into my head that after I'd wrapped I would go and stay with her and see if I could make a fresh start in LA. Of course! It was a brilliant notion – the perfect antidote to all my worries. Not for a single second did the phrase 'running away from failure' ever enter my mind.

27

California Dreamin'

Hollywood played a major part in shaping my childhood, portraying America as an enchanted realm where, if you believed strongly enough in yourself, anything was possible. To me, it was the land of dreams, with nowhere more dreamlike than California. I had fallen in love with America's west coast when I was on tour there and vowed that one day I would find my way back again. Well, I had earned enough for the airfare, so if not now, when? Although I had managed to get through the personal hell of *A Question of Guilt* without fainting or weeping tears of blood during the close-ups, I knew in my heart I had been tried and found wanting. It seemed to me that wherever my road less travelled was leading, it wasn't towards a glittering career in British television drama. What the hell, I had nothing to lose. If my fortune wasn't to be found in London's friendless streets, why not see what Hollywood's star-spangled boulevards had to offer.

Jean sounded a bit taken aback when I called to tell her I was flying out. In my grandiose scheme of things, I hadn't considered the possibility that there might be any problem in lodging with my old panto chum – after all, she did say that I was welcome to pay her a visit once she'd settled in LA. Or was it the other way round? Well, anyway, what matter? I had booked a plane ticket and there was no way I was going to allow a petty little detail like whether

Jean actually minded me suddenly turning up on her doorstep to dampen my enthusiasm for the Next Big Adventure.

Within a few days of bedding down on Jean's sofa, I realised that landing on her out of the blue might not have been one of my more rational decisions. She had barely settled in the city herself and was busily engaged trying to establish her own life there. Not that she wasn't hospitable, far from it – Jean has the biggest heart of anyone I know – but not having a car meant that whenever I wanted to go anywhere I had to rely on Jean driving me there and back in her little Karmann Ghia. That our friendship continues to this day speaks volumes for her kindness and generosity of spirit.

Jean had a job as a 'meeter and greeter' each evening in one of Hollywood's more fashionable eateries.[1] Concerned about me spending most nights sitting at home, she would ask some of her friends to call in on me now and again and take me out for a drink or a meal. One evening, she phoned from the restaurant to ask if I would like to go on a blind date with one of her pals. Never having been on a blind date in my life, I said yes. About half an hour later, I answered a knock at the door. Now I don't know if you've ever seen any of those Tex Avery cartoons from the forties, where, whenever the zoot-suited wolf spies a glamorous dame, his eyes spring out on stalks, his tongue rolls out like a red carpet, jets of steam blow out of his ears and his heart threatens to burst out of his chest to the accompaniment of bells, whistles, ships hooters and fire alarms. Well, hold that image in your mind's eye when you picture me opening the door that night to Jean's friend Mimi. I was so knocked out by the sun-kissed, green-eyed, golden-haired vision before me that as I stepped back to usher her in I tripped over a footstool and went arse over tit – not the most auspicious impression

---

[1] Unless you're a movie star, every actor in LA has a second job. In fact, one of the first 'in' jokes I heard there was about two guys meeting for the first time. One says to the other, 'What do you do for a living?'

'I'm an actor,' the other guy answers.

'No kidding – me too!' says the first guy.

'Really?' says the second guy. 'Which restaurant?'

to give a beautiful girl on a first meeting. Anyway, after an unforgettable evening at a swanky Japanese restaurant high up in the Hollywood hills with the fairyland lights of the city twinkling below us, when I hesitantly asked if I could see her again, she gave me a sweet little kiss and agreed to a second date.

I wanted to stay in California forever. I loved the weather, the scenery, and the beautiful beaches where you could sit on the deck of a tavern with a glass of Californian champagne and watch the sun setting in the Pacific Ocean. Why the hell would I want to go back to the dismal, lonely life I was leading in London? I needed to find out how the system worked in Hollywood and pestered Jean to let me go along with her when she went to casting sessions. The reality of trying to make it as an actor in LA was brought vividly home as I stood with her in the long lines of hopefuls, with their glossy 10x8 photos that made them look far more attractive than they really were – but it was their resumés that were the most telling. I was amazed by the fact that would-be actors with nothing much going for them would hope to impress casting directors by including parts they didn't actually get! For example:

STAR WARS – FEATURE FILM. DIRECTOR GEORGE LUCAS – THIRD X-WING PILOT – TWO RECALLS.

COLOMBO – TV SERIES. DIRECTOR ALAN SMITHEE – HISPANIC DRUG DEALER – THREE RECALLS AND SCREEN TEST.

I thought it was all a bit like India, where, if you don't pass your final degree, you can still earn a decent living by putting up a sign saying 'UNIVERSITY OF CALCUTTA. BSc – FAILED' and charging a lower fee than your more successful fellow students.

Many of these wannabes operated a mutual support system – bringing a fellow actor along to act as a confidence booster and tell them how terrific and awesome and incredible they were as the casting queue inched slowly forward. The thing that really made my bum tweak, though, was the fact that people would actually dress up for these auditions – you could always tell where a casting session was taking place by the line of pirates or aliens or 1930s gangsters stretching around the block, every one of them prepared to do whatever it took to get a foot on the ladder of movie stardom. As I soon discovered, *everyone* is an actor in LA: the stunning waitress who serves you breakfast, the Latino guy who's filling your car with gas, your chiropractor, your dentist, the pair of cops sitting in their patrol car nibbling hi-bran muffins – they all have agents and carry membership cards for the Screen Actors Guild. In Britain, being an actor is still regarded as having some social caché – not so in LA, where, if you're not a movie star, you're a complete nobody. It's a city filled with ordinary folk from ordinary Midwestern towns who woke up one morning and felt called to risk everything – their homes, their families, even their sanity – to follow a vision, not of the Devils Tower in Wyoming but of the big HOLLYWOOD sign in Griffith Park. Surely my aspirations were more realistic than theirs. I had been in successful theatre productions and had actually been cast in a few films – not just got a couple of recalls. But the knowledge that I had blown what should have been my big break continued to haunt me, and deep down I knew the truth was that I was chasing the same dream as all the cowboys, pirates and spacemen in the cattle calls, with just as little chance of it ever becoming a reality. It seemed such a short time ago that I had a real bubble going for me, with critics, casting directors and audiences praising my work and hinting at a great future. It all meant nothing now, as a long litany of failures ran through my mind. I had recently broken up with Alison, my long-term partner; John Byrne, a man I admired and was proud to call a friend, had turned on me for no discernible reason; after disagreeing over a proposed tour of *Writer's Cramp*, the days of the 'Extraordinary Trio' were over, probably forever; I was alone and friendless in an anonymous flat; I had failed in *The Tax Exile* and blown what should have been my big break in *A Question of Guilt*; and here I was, hoping, like Chaplin's little tramp after falling on his backside, that

I could just pick myself up, brush myself down and, with an insouciant shrug of the shoulders, stride jauntily towards a new horizon.

The breakdown, when it came, hit me like a runaway freight train. I had spent the day with Mimi at the beach and had gone back to her apartment, where, after a candlelit dinner, she put on some romantic music and snuggled down next to me on the sofa. As I took her in my arms for the big clinch, I felt myself starting to tense up as somewhere inside my head a cheap radio with tinny speakers began to blare out random snatches of songs, loud bursts of electrical static and strange voices that jeered and mocked me. 'I'm sorry,' I blurted, as I broke free from her embrace. 'I can't do this – I just can't. I don't know what the hell's happening to me.'

When Jean came back that night from work, she found me curled up in a foetal ball on her sofa, crying and shaking with terror as my heart threatened to burst out of my chest, and the babble in my mind became more and more strident.

I was saved from going completely off the rails when, the following day, Freddie Boardley, my old chum from the Citz pantos, rang Jean to say hi, leaving him speechless when he realised it was me on the other end of the line. It turned out that he and a few of his pals were having a lads-only holiday at a beachside motel in Santa Monica. I had never been 'one of the lads' in my life, but Freddie and his pals welcomed me into their fold and, thanks to their earthy Scottish humour and freewheeling attitude to life, I laughed so much during the rest of my stay that I got myself back on something like an even keel. So thanks, Freddie, my dear old friend, you threw me a lifeline when I felt I was going down for the third time, and I hope that some day, some way, I'll be able to repay the huge debt of thanks I owe you.

28

Magic Moments

'Bill Forsyth,' said Lindy, my new agent at Duncan Heath Associates. 'Do you know him?' I had to confess the name didn't ring a bell. 'Well he's a young Scottish film director and wants to know if you'd be interested in taking a part in something he's about to start shooting.' I was back in my dreary little London flat and desperate for a project that would stop me spiralling down to the dark place again, and this sounded like it might just be it. 'Anyway,' she continued, 'it's set in a school, and the part he wants you for is one of the teachers. He says he was a big fan of the 7:84 Company – in fact, he wants John Bett and Bill Paterson for it too.[1] I think it's a really great little piece and I think you'd be very good in it. I'll have the script biked over to you now.'

After I finished reading Bill's screenplay, I punched the air with joy. *Gregory's Girl* was exactly what I needed at this point in my life.

One of the many delights of working on Bill's film was being reunited with one of my all-time comic heroes, Chic Murray, and although the great wee scene we had together didn't make the final cut, it was, as always, a pleasure and a privilege to spend time in his company. So permit me, at this point, to share a few reminiscences about one of the most unforgettable men I've ever met.

---

[1] As it turned out, Bill Paterson wasn't available and the part of the PT teacher was taken instead by Jake D'Arcy.

Chic and I were on location together in Fingal's Cave for a weird and wonderful film called *Scotch Myths*. After we finished, we were dropped off at a small hotel on the island of Mull where we would be billeted for the next few days. As we stepped through the door, we suddenly found ourselves in a scene familiar to any fan of old cowboy movies – the noisy bar became silent as soon as the locals caught sight of us. Domino games halted in mid-chap. Glasses of whisky hovered midway to open mouths. There was a long, uneasy pause as Chic and I stood watching them watching us. Finally, a grizzled fisherman rose slowly and purposefully to his feet, swaying slightly as he fixed his one good eye on Chic. 'I was walking down the road,' he said in a mock-Kelvinside accent. 'Well, I knew I was walking *down* the road because I could see the bottom of the road coming towards me . . .' When he had finished speaking, a red-haired lad of about sixteen stood up and, with a similar drawl, said, 'I bumped into the wife the other day. I said "Hello dear" – I call her "dear" because she's got two antlers sticking out of her head.' Then, like the famous 'I'm Spartacus' scene, one after another, every customer in the bar rose to their feet and gave their impression of Chic's unique delivery. 'We chatted about this and that. He said, "What d'you think of this?" and I said, "Oh, I don't think much of that . . ."'

On and on it went. Chic, standing quietly throughout, acknowledged their tribute with an occasional smile, a raised eyebrow or a nod of approval. I remember thinking, as I looked on in astonishment, that however bizarre life might be at times, nothing would ever be more bizarre than standing next to Chic Murray in a Hebridean bar full of Chic Murray impersonators.

Chic was one of the most extraordinary men I've ever met – a surrealist in the same category as Salvador Dali or René Magritte. For Chic all the world was a stage and all the men and women merely players, to be disported as the fancy took him. I remember his daughter Annabelle telling me about the occasion when the two of them were walking along London's Oxford Street and Chic hailed a smartly dressed businessman striding along the pavement.

'Excuse me,' said Chic, 'could you tell me where the nearest sandwich bar is?'

'A what?' he said.

'A sandwich bar,' Chic repeated patiently. 'I'm feeling a little peckish and I'm looking for a sandwich bar – can you tell me if there's one nearby?'

'A sandwich bar?' said the gent, quizzically. 'You're looking for a sandwich bar?'

Chic had had enough. 'Never mind,' he said, pointing across the street, 'there's a camera shop – I'll eat a camera.'

Another indelible memory of working with Chic on *Scotch Myths* was when we were standing on Oban pier waiting for the film crew to finish capturing a few shots of the sunset before turning the camera on to us. A passing group of elderly American tourists had stopped to watch the proceedings. Chic clocked them and began shaking his head gravely and sighing deeply. After a moment, one of them made the fatal mistake of asking him if he had any idea what the camera crew were filming. He gave me a sly glance as his countenance grew even more solemn. 'Terrible tragedy,' he said. 'Absolutely heart-breaking.' As his audience listened raptly, he told them how a pair of young lovers – 'a local Romeo and Juliet' as he put it – had plunged hand in hand off the pier because of their family's disapproval over the match. Some of the ladies were dabbing hankies to their eyes as the group started to move quietly and respectfully away, but Chic wasn't ready to let them off the hook just yet. 'But all may not be lost,' he continued. Pressing a hand to his heart, he went on to tell them how the sharp-eyed skipper of a trawler had spotted the pair of young lovers being sucked into the gaping maw of a passing whale shark, and that even now, a flotilla of fishing boats was trying to locate the leviathan in hopes that the couple would be rescued, Jonah-like, from its belly and returned safely to their now remorseful and understanding parents. I realised that day that I had been granted a unique insight into Chic's *raison d'être*. Why bore people with dull facts they'll instantly forget, when you can offer them a thrilling fiction they'll always remember?

Here's my final reminiscence on Chic. In 1985 I was in Glasgow for a TV job and, on one of my days off, I had gone into the booking hall of Queen Street station to buy a day return ticket to Edinburgh. I had been standing in the lengthy queue for a few minutes when I became aware of some kind of commotion at the information counter on the other side of the hall. One of the voices sounded terribly familiar. I looked over to see none other than the Great Man himself, having a noisy debate with a flustered and hapless-looking booking clerk. 'So you mean to tell me that there's no observation car on the three-fifteen to Lesmahagow?' Chic was saying in a belligerent tone of voice. 'N-n-no, there isn't,' stuttered the little scarlet-faced assistant, looking like a startled rabbit caught in the headlights of an oncoming truck.

'Well, if I get the two-twenty-seven to Leuchars and change at Hamilton, will there be an observation carriage on that train? I had a splendid view of the Rockies from an observation car last time I travelled across Canada, and I wouldn't want to miss seeing the Campsies in a similar fashion.'

'I'm awful sorry, sir,' said the wee clerk, clearly fighting the urge to duck under the counter until Chic had gone, 'but we don't have observation cars on *any* of Scotrail's services.'

By now I had left the queue and made my way over to Chic's side. It had been a few years since we last met and I was a bit shy about approaching him in case he might not remember me, but I couldn't let the opportunity to renew our acquaintance pass by. I got as far as 'Hi Chic, I—' when he suddenly spun round, eyes ablaze with indignation.

'How dare you importune me in this manner,' he roared. 'Are you aware of who I am and my standing in this city?' I felt the blood drain from my face as every head in the booking hall swivelled to see what the uproar was about. I tried to speak, but no sound came out as Chic continued at the top of his voice: 'Now you listen to me, young man. Once and for all. I have absolutely no desire to accompany you to the gents' toilets for purposes I couldn't begin to guess at – now be off with you and ply your foul trade elsewhere before I call the police!'

The faces of the shocked onlookers had begun to swim in and out of focus as Chic slipped a friendly arm round my shoulder and whispered in my ear. 'Great to see you again, son – fancy a wee cup o' tea?'

Of course it was all a set-up. Chic had clocked me the moment I walked into the station and had engineered the performance at the information desk as a sting to lure me into the role of the hapless gump in his improvised scenario. I mean, why just say hello when, with a little sleight of hand, you can transform a chance meeting into a brilliant piece of absurdist theatre worthy of Ionesco?

After leaving Queen Street station under the glare of a hundred pairs of eyes and a chorus of tut-tuts, we sat in a wee teashop catching up on each other's recent pasts. Chic did most of the talking, telling me about the offers of work that were constantly coming his way – films, TV series, cabaret bookings on glamorous cruise ships. The main problem, he said, was deciding which to choose and which to turn down. He told me about various skits and sketches he was busy writing, which I, if I fancied it, could play a part in. I knew, as did he, that all of these offers were notional rather than tangible. Chic just wanted me to believe that he was still in demand – still at the very top of his game. As we took our leave of each other, shaking hands and agreeing to keep in touch more often, our waiter hovered expectantly. 'Was everything to your satisfaction, sir?' he asked.

'First class,' said Chic. 'Tell me – are you allowed to accept tips?'

'Oh yes, sir,' said the waiter eagerly.

'Here's a good one,' said Chic. 'Never tie your shoelaces in a revolving door.'

Less than a month later I learned that Chic had passed away.

'National Treasure' is a title that's in danger of losing its rarity value these days, but if there was ever a worthy candidate for the designation, it surely must be the irreplaceable Chic Murray. To work with him was a privilege I'll always remember. To be publicly ridiculed by him was a privilege I'll never forget.

29

Wide of the Mark

Lindy called to say she'd got me an audition with the Royal Shakespeare Company. Wow! This was serious stuff – a chance to improve my craft by working with the crème de la crème. What did I have to offer the RSC, though? My knowledge of Shakespeare was pretty limited, so I thought maybe the versatility that seemed to have served me well enough in the 7:84 Company might do the trick. At my audition, after reading a couple of prepared scenes, I gave them a taste of my musical prowess by playing a couple of lute pieces I'd transposed for the guitar and demonstrated my expertise on the bodhrán. To my surprise, I was offered a place in the company for the new season at Stratford upon Avon. I knew this was a break most actors would kill for, but after mulling it over for a day or so, I said no. Memories of the miserable years I spent at Shawlands Academy still haunted me and I felt I was never cut out to be a little cog in a big machine. Of course I'll never know if the decision I took was the right one – all I knew was that my instincts were telling me that it wasn't the path I needed to follow at that time. 'You'll have such a wonderful time there,' Lindy pleaded, trying to get me to see reason. 'Every actor who works at the RSC gets Stratford-itis and never wants to leave.' The thought of getting 'Stratford-itis' simply reinforced my decision to turn the RSC's generous offer down – I had left Scotland to make a fresh start in London, and I didn't feel I had been there long enough to leave

London for another fresh start in Stratford. Besides, my goal was to work in television and film, and with the experiences of *Writer's Cramp* and *The Tax Exile* still fresh in my mind, I had taken something of a scunner to the stage. Rightly or wrongly (probably wrongly) I just couldn't see myself fitting in at 'the Big School', as Bill Paterson dubbed the National Theatre when he starred there in Richard Eyre's production of *The Good Soldier Svejk*.

When Lindy left Duncan Heath's a few years later to start her own agency, she was astute enough to spot the potential in another young Scots actor, Ewan McGregor, who became her star client and brought her all the kudos I signally failed to do. Due to her departure, I had been assigned a dynamic and fearless young agent named Michael Foster, who had an awesome reputation in the business as someone who didn't readily take the word 'no' for an answer,[1] and it was largely thanks to Michael's dynamism that I appeared in so many films throughout the eighties. The way it worked was this: Duncan's agency was something of a one-stop shop for movie production. As well as actors, Duncan had some of the top names from every aspect of the film world on his books – writers, directors, producers, editors, cinematographers – and could put together a complete package for a film company. Naturally, when it came to casting, his agency's clients were first through the door and, thanks to Michael's sterling efforts on my behalf, my career began, at last, to head along the path I really wanted to follow. Allow me to skip ahead a few years, to give you an example of one of the films Michael put me into as part of a production package.

Remember Kevin Costner's *Robin Hood*? Of course you do – who could forget Alan Rickman as the Sheriff of Nottingham, stealing Costner's big Hollywood movie from right under his nose. Remember

---

[1] I was told by another of his clients about the time he was having a meeting with Michael in his office when his phone rang. 'Do excuse me,' he said as he picked it up. 'It's from LA – very important, been waiting all day for this.' The very important call went something along the lines of 'Hi, Michael here . . . I'm sorry, *how* much? . . . Oh fuck off!' before the phone was slammed back down again.

Patrick Bergin's *Robin Hood*? The low-budget British-made film that was released around the same time as Costner's, with Uma Thurman as Maid Marian, Jurgen Prochnow as Robin's nemesis and me as Harry, the one-time leader of Robin's outlaw band? No? Well, if you do, you can number yourself among a select few. God knows how these things come about, but while Mr Costner was filming his multi-million-dollar epic less than twenty miles away from our location, we were struggling with a low-budget production that was under constant threat of having the plug pulled on it. Apart from its unfortunate timing, the film's main problem was its leading man, Patrick Bergin, a handsome young Irish actor who had just arrived hotfoot from Hollywood after starring opposite Julia Roberts in a film called *Sleeping with the Enemy.* Now, as you can imagine, playing Robin Hood in a fast-paced action adventure film requires a fair amount of, well – action. Unfortunately Patrick was apparently suffering from an unknown malady that left him as weak as a kitten, with the result that he flatly refused to ride a horse or take an active part in any of the film's action scenes – something of a drawback in a role that requires quite a lot of riding and fighting. However, he did impress me mightily the day we filmed the famous scene where Robin shoots at the target and splits his rival's arrow along the length of its shaft. In our version, the scene went like this: Little John sticks his quarterstaff upright at one end of a clearing in the forest while Robin and I attempt to hit it with one arrow each. I get first go, and although my arrow doesn't split the staff, it strikes it and glances off again – all in all, a pretty impressive feat. Everyone thinks the contest is in the bag, until Robin takes aim and splits the staff in two. Now, even though in reality my arrow missed the target by a mile (the close-up, where my arrow glances off the staff, was filmed later using a skilled archer), I had to act like I thought I was the victor. The camera was still running as Patrick stepped up to the mark, drew back his bow, loosed his arrow and sent it through the centre of the staff, splitting it clean in two. The scene, which would have been fantastic, was completely unusable due to all of the merry men yelling 'Fuck me!' in near perfect unison.

Despite a two-week recess while Patrick checked in to a private clinic to recuperate from his mystery ailment, the movie was finally completed, with a stunt double wearing a rubber mask of the top half of Patrick's face and taking over all his action scenes. If you ever manage to catch the film (it pops up occasionally on one of the digital channels) watch the action scenes carefully – even in mid close-up you'd be hard pressed to spot the switch.

Apart from the uncertainty about whether it would ever be completed, *Robin Hood* was a joy to work on. Having watched it a few times over the years, I still think it stands up – although if you picture Costner's big-budget blockbuster as a supertanker, then we were the unfortunate pedalo caught in its wake.

30

The Horse Whimperer

I was asked if I would be interested in being in a pilot that Rowan Atkinson was about to do for the BBC. Since I played a cameo role (actor-speak for a small part) in his short film *Dead on Time*, Rowan had gone from strength to strength, most notably as a member of the hugely popular comedy series *Not the Nine O'Clock News*, and was now an established TV star. The pilot was set in what the wardrobe designer called the 'Tudorbethan' period, and was called *The Black Adder*. Rehearsals were held at the BBC's rehearsal halls in North Acton (known with some irony as 'the Acton Hilton') and my character was a belligerent Scots general named McAngus, whose presence at court threatens to queer Blackadder's pitch. After coming up with a cunning plan that culminates in an abortive attempt to hang me, Blackadder and I have an elaborate swordfight that ends with me deftly flipping the sword out of his hand and threatening to run him through. During the take, as Rowan's sword flew out of his hand, I felt a little sting on my face. It was only when the scene was over that I noticed the trickle of blood running down my cheek – the tip of his blade had nicked me just under my right eye – half an inch higher and there would have been no point in me ever watching any more 3D movies. A month or so later, I got a call to say that the series was going ahead, and would I be willing to re-shoot my particular episode.

Shortly after, I found myself sitting astride a huge shire horse on location at Northumberland's historic Alnwick Castle, wearing a big over-the-top helmet with deer antlers sticking up from it, chainmail leggings and a sheepskin jerkin festooned with swords, daggers, clubs, bows, arrows and a spiky mace. For the first series, the era had been changed and Blackadder was now a medieval princeling with Brian Blessed and Elspet Gray as his parents. For my first shot, I had to ride down a steep path at the back of the castle. It had snowed heavily overnight, and the going was pretty dodgy. 'Just take it real easy,' said the horse master, 'the path's very slippery and the horse is a bit skittish.' Oh shit – that was all I needed to hear. 'Just go at walking pace and you'll probably be fine,' he said. I think it was the word 'probably' that sent my already shaky confidence plummeting to my boots. The director called 'Action' and I urged the horse forward, its hooves sliding and skittering as it walked warily down the slippery slope. Thinking how boring this snail's pace was going to look on camera, I decided I needed a bit more speed. Forgetting I was wearing spurs, I dug my heels in; the horse let out a terrifying whinny and started to gallop down the hill at full tilt. Both my feet were jerked out of the stirrups and my ill-fitting helmet slipped down over my eyes, rendering me completely blind. Yanking the reins back and yelling obscenities had absolutely no effect as the horse thundered on regardless. The noise in my ears was deafening as all my armour and weapons crashed up and down in time to the hoofbeats – it was like being in a Tokyo hardware store during an earthquake. The thought that came into my head as I clattered along was that if I fell off, not only would I break my bloody neck, but as I hit the ground, the likelihood was that I would be skewered by the assortment of swords, daggers and weaponry strapped about me. With no way of getting my feet back in the stirrups I had one option open to me: gripping the horse's flanks with my thighs as tightly as I could, which, thank God, kept me in the saddle until the big bastard finally ran out of steam and I managed to dismount. It wasn't till the following morning that I realised just how tightly I had been gripping the horse, as for the next few weeks I had to soak myself two or three times a day in baths of scalding-hot water to help ease the agony of my screaming thigh muscles.

After location filming was completed, we started rehearsals back at the Acton Hilton for the studio scenes. I was surprised to find Rowan was playing his character differently – in the pilot, Blackadder was the cynical, smooth-talking opportunist he was in the following three series. However, for the first series he had decided to play him as an unctuous little weasel with a squeaky voice.[1] I played the same character as before, but since the series was now set in the medieval period, I based my look on a bas-relief carving I had seen in a museum, depicting a Roman soldier about to dispatch a fallen Celtic warrior. It was the warrior's long, braided hair and heavy moustache that inspired me. Whether Celtic warriors still looked like that during the Dark Ages was anyone's guess, but it certainly made Lord Dougal McAngus look a bit bloody fearsome.

We were rehearsing McAngus's first appearance in the castle. As written, he rides his horse into the great dining hall, clambers over the table and parks himself next to the Queen. Helping himself to a hunk of meat, he leans over to the Queen and says, 'You must be the King's bit of way-hay-hay, eh?' I thought way-hay-hay was a bit 'Carry On up the Castle' so I suggested an alternative – a story I got from my old chum John Bett, which had me choking with laughter. John, something of a flamboyant dresser at the best of times, was having a drink in a Glasgow pub one evening when a wee guy in a shabby raincoat and bunnet approached him. 'Excuse me,' he said, 'but would ah be right in thinking you're an artist of some kind?'

'Yes, I am actually,' replied John.

'Ah thought so,' he said. 'Are ye a painter?'

'No,' John replied. 'I'm an actor.'

---

[1] Even the most die-hard fans seem to agree that the first series may not have been Blackadder's finest hour.

'An actor?' said the wee guy. 'An actor, eh? Ah could tell by your unusual demeanour that ye were somethin' to do with the arts. Tell me – do you go down?'

'I beg your pardon?' said John in astonishment.

'You know,' he replied. 'Rumpy pumpy!'

I told our director, Martin Shardlow, this story. 'Oh, no,' he said dismissively, 'the audience won't understand "rumpy pumpy", so let's just stick with "way-hay-hay" if you don't mind.' Rowan, who had been quietly listening, walked over.

'Actually, Martin,' he said, 'I think Alex is right. I think the meaning is pretty clear in the context of the action – and besides, rumpy pumpy *sounds* funny.' Rowan's decision was final – way-hay-hay was out and rumpy pumpy was in. When Brian Blessed heard me say it in my opening scene, he exploded with laughter and promptly worked it into one of his own scenes. Almost immediately after the episode went out, any newspaper photo of a public figure who had been caught with his pants down was invariably accompanied by the words RUMPY PUMPY in huge type. So I think I can genuinely put my hand on my heart and say that rumpy pumpy became the ubiquitous catchphrase it is today because of my appearance in *The Black Adder* – compilers of *The Oxford Dictionary of Slang*, please take note.

31

Back from the Brink

'What are you doin' in *that*?' said Billy Connolly when we met at a party in Peter McDougall's house. '*That*' was *Playaway*, a long-running BBC kids' show in which I was a regular member of the cast. Billy's question took me aback, and I wondered if the rest of my friends were wondering the same thing. What *was* I doing in *Playaway*? The answer? – having the time of my life!

It all started because the BBC had decided to shoot two episodes of *Playaway* in Scotland. The series producer, Anne Wreay, had been asking if there were any Scots actors who could sing and play an instrument as well as write some daft songs and comic sketches, and my name had been put forward as a likely candidate. Anne called my agent and arranged for me to meet the female casting director who was in Scotland to audition likely candidates for the show. On a rainy Glasgow evening, guitar in hand, I pitched up at her hotel. She invited me up to her suite and I ran through a selection of songs while she ran through the contents of the mini-bar. She seemed to like my stuff and asked me to stay for a glass of wine. Three bottles later, I was astonished to find myself in the old casting-couch scenario. I was familiar with tales of lecherous producers seducing gullible young starlets with empty promises of fame and fortune, but not for a second did I consider the possibility that I would find myself on the receiving end of it. However, my hostess's plans for a night of unbridled lust were not to be – as she went to slip into something more comfortable, I quietly slipped out the door. 'The fuckin' castin' couch? Furra fuckin' kids' show?' I muttered to myself as I staggered to the nearest taxi rank. 'Fuck that! Who the fuck wants to work in fuckin' kids' fuckin' telly anyway?'

Since I failed to come up with the goods the night before, you can imagine my surprise when my agent rang to say I'd been offered the job. I started to write some songs and sketches, and a couple of weeks later, in a Dumfries hall packed to the rafters with Cubs and Brownies, I sang, played my guitar and performed with one of *Playaway*'s stalwarts, Anita Dobson. I enjoyed it enormously, and if it led to nothing more, at least I could say I had given it my best shot.

My best shot must have gone down well enough with the heads of the BBC's children's entertainment department. Not long afterwards, Anne Wreay called to say that one of their regulars was leaving at the end of the current series and would I be interested in taking his place? I told her I would, and she said she would send me some tapes so I could see the standard I'd have to follow. When I watched them, I was quite impressed by the chap's singing voice, and thought he played the guitar rather well. In case you're wondering, my predecessor was a young actor named Jeremy Irons.

Thanks to *Playaway*, the legacy of variety was very much alive and kicking. The series' leading light was the wonderful Brian Cant, who, along with regulars like Nerys Hughes, Floella Benjamin and the show's musical director, Jonathan Cohen, soon made me feel a valued part of the team. I was finally living out my dream of being a variety turn – writing and singing comic songs, as well as acting in sketches and patter sequences. The thought that in some small way I was helping keep variety alive by playing it to a new, young audience gave me a real sense of satisfaction.

I found Brian Cant to be a man of great warmth, integrity and talent, and over the time we worked together we became very good friends. For many years, first as the voice of classic children's puppet series like *Camberwick Green*, *Trumpton* and *Chigley* (for which, he once told me, he had never received a penny in royalties), then as the presenter of *Playaway*, Brian had given years of sterling service to the children's department, so when I heard a rumour that the BBC were thinking about letting him go, I was deeply shocked. As we neared the end of the current series, I was asked, strictly off the record, how I would feel about having my own show – a prospect, I have to admit, I found very tempting. I felt very fortunate to be earning a good living doing something I really enjoyed and had a real flair for – so why did I hear an alarm bell clanging in the distance? Believe me when I tell you that the answer came in a vision. One morning, I had what I can only describe as an epiphany. I saw myself walking down one of the long corridors in TV Centre. A sign saying CHILDREN'S ENTERTAINERS THIS WAY pointed towards a closed door. I pushed it open and stepped through, realising too late that it opened on to a sheer cliff face. As I plummeted downwards, I saw far below me a big deep pit, littered with the mouldering remains of former kids' show hosts. I decided there and then that, joyful as my time in the BBC Children's department had been, it was time to move on. When I was asked to sign up for another series of *Playaway*, I had a good excuse to say no – I was in Hollywood, following the Yellow Brick Road yet again.

32

Somewhere Under the Rainbow

Thanks to the regular income from *Playaway*, for the first time in years my life had become agreeably pleasant: I was living in a lovely flat in Belsize Park, one of the prettiest parts of London; my flatmate Steph and I had become great friends; and although Sally Kinghorn and I had both wondered whether we were doing the right thing when I moved to London while she stayed in Edinburgh as a regular member of Leslie Lawton's rep company at the Lyceum Theatre, the fact of the matter was that we were both ambitious, single-minded professionals who had chosen to put our careers before our personal lives. So when she called to say she had finished at the Lyceum, moved back to London and was living in nearby Primrose Hill, I hesitated before agreeing to meet for a drink and a catch-up, wondering whether our past relationship, joyful as it had been, had run its course. As we caught up on each other's lives, I realised I still felt a deep affection for her, and since both of us were still single and fancy free, we began to see each other again on a fairly casual basis. As time went on, I began to think that maybe settling down together would be a good plan, but there were still a couple of things in my life that I needed to sort out once and for all before I considered making any serious commitments . . .

When I worked with Ronnie Fraser on *Do You Come Here Often?*, he said something to me that I had taken very much to heart: 'Don't splash about in the puddles, old son – dive into the sea.' Ronnie had clearly practised what he preached – a Bonnybridge boy who had carved out a nice career for himself as a character actor in some big Hollywood movies. Well, if Ronnie could do it, why couldn't I? I hadn't lost my thirst for a crack at the movies, and with the few quid that I had managed to save from *Playaway*, I bid an emotional farewell to Sally and headed back to LA, gratefully accepting my friend Jean Gilpin's offer to stay in the spare bedroom of the smart little house she was renting in north Hollywood. I had come a bit more prepared this time, with a work permit, a new set of photos, a resumé and a professionally made showreel of my TV and film work – all of which I hoped would help lead to a career in the movie industry, where my long-held ambition lay.

Jean had arranged a small gathering in the charitable hope that I would make a few new friends and start having a social life. Among her guests was Mimi, the girl I had blown my chances with last time around by having a wobbler. She was even more alluring than I remembered, and as we chatted, I sensed a distance between her and her current partner, a pleasant enough man who clearly worshipped the ground she trod on. I had a sensation that we might have some unfinished business to resolve, and if my instincts were right, I thought this time around things might be very different. If I'd had an inkling of just *how* different, I would have run out and jumped on the first plane back to London.

Mimi too must have thought there was something that needed sorting out, as she called me a few weeks later to ask if I fancied spending the weekend with her on the coast at Big Sur. It was unforgettable, and the start of a torrid affair that carried on behind her boyfriend's back until, much to his ire, she finally gave him the heave-ho.

I can't say I wasn't aware that Mimi might have a few complex issues regarding relationships: the first inkling that there might be choppy waters ahead came when she introduced me to her parents. Her Swiss-born father had written and directed several successful European theatre productions before being pushed by his fiercely ambitious wife towards what she hoped would be a glittering career in Hollywood. Sadly, things started to go awry when she took it upon herself to start negotiating with the major studios on her husband's behalf: 'My husband requires a personal assistant. My husband requires a larger trailer. My husband requires . . .' Hollywood is a small community, and eventually word went round not to employ Mimi's father at any cost. The final nail in the coffin of his career was when his wife discovered he was having a torrid affair with a young starlet and went completely off the rails. The affair ended immediately, but when the Valium her shrink had prescribed kicked in, Mimi's mother took the rather unusual step of inviting the ex-mistress into the family circle, where she became a friend and confidante, even to the extent of passing on her cast-off clothing to Mimi. I never really appreciated the true meaning of the phrase 'a spoiled child' until I saw Mimi wriggling coquettishly on her father's lap, dressed in his ex-mistress's cast-offs and speaking to him in a little-girly voice, while through a haze of Valium, her mother looked on and smiled approvingly.

Ignoring yet again the wise old saying, 'Never sleep with anyone who has more problems than yourself,' I moved into the little Spanish-style bungalow Mimi rented in West Hollywood (which, as she told me matter-of-factly, she had managed to get for a song by sleeping with the landlord), and for a time, everything seemed to be going pretty well, until the morning I stood in stunned silence listening to her ex-boyfriend leave a message on her answering machine, saying how much he had enjoyed the wonderful lovemaking session they had when she had dropped round to see him on her way to work.

It seemed my rocket to the moon had turned into Apollo 13, so I packed my bags and drove back to Jean's house, where I sat in her backyard, pouring my heart out to her. Her partner, Phil, suggested that I might benefit from a few sessions of Rebirthing, the New Age therapy movement that he had helped co-found. When Jean had first told me about the Rebirthing movement and said she was training to be a practitioner, I have to say I wondered whether my dear friend had been sucked into one of the bizarre cults that seem to spring up so often in that part of the world. Rebirthing certainly sounded weird enough, involving a breathing technique that supposedly led to a breakthrough in terms of self-awareness. Thinking I didn't have anything to lose and maybe something to gain, I lay on the sofa and let Jean guide me through the process.

There's an old saying about philosophy that goes, 'A philosopher can look at an apple, observe its colour, contemplate its shape and its weight, but it's only when he tastes it that he truly understands what an apple is.' Since I was a teenager I'd had an insatiable curiosity about Life, the Universe and Everything, reading the *Tibetan Book of the Dead*, the Hindu Upanishads, the writings of Krishnamurti, books on Japanese Zen and Chinese Taoism – even signing up for a course of lectures in metaphysics when I first moved to London. Through the writings of Alan Watts, I had learned about nirvana – the state of bliss that Buddhist monks were supposed to attain after years of meditating at the feet of an enlightened master – but nothing in any of the books I read, the lectures I attended, or even the hallucinogens I had tentatively experimented with back in the day prepared me for what happened next. As I lay there breathing deeply with Jean's voice guiding me, I felt my legs being drawn up and my arms contracting until finally I found myself in a foetal position. I kept nodding off, but Jean would prompt me to stay awake and carry on with the breathing technique. After enduring this self-inflicted torture for about half an hour, the words 'what in the name of God am I doing?' came into my mind. It was the last rational thought I had, before the cosmic express whisked me off to Nirvana Central at the speed of light.

There's probably only one thing more boring than someone telling you about their dreams, and that's someone telling you about their spiritual experiences, so I'll cut to the chase and say that after years of reading, deliberating, musing and pondering, I finally tasted the apple.

For a moment that could have been an eternity, I was at one with everything. The material world ceased to be, and the too, too solid flesh that constituted my physical being simply evaporated as I became a wave in a sea of pure bliss. Trust the Yanks – too restless and impatient to spend half a lifetime sitting in a lotus position under a Bo tree, they had come up with the fast-food version of nirvana. Half an hour of puffin' and blawin' and you were on the fast track to Cosmic Consciousness!

After my little trip, it was a bit of a comedown to return to Mimi's world of hurt and pain. She was the kind of woman about whom the saying 'beauty is only skin deep' could have been coined. Despite the lunacy and the lies, our relationship somehow managed to stagger on, until the evening she invited me over for a reconciliatory dinner and tricked me into going into an upstairs bedroom. Once I was in, she locked the door from the outside and went down to the kitchen to pick up a carving knife. From the bedroom window, I saw her walk to my car and slash my tyres before walking coolly back into the house for the exciting climax of the film that was running in the private screening room behind her icy-blue eyes. As I heard her footsteps coming up the stairs, I knew I had to make my escape before she reached the door. By smashing one of the panes, I managed to wrench open the window and scramble out to safety. God alone knows what the neighbours must have thought as I lowered myself down from the window (I knew the hours I spent dreepin' aff wash-house roofs in the Gorbals would come in handy one day), slid off the roof, crash landed on the flower bed and started legging it down the road pursued by a screaming, knife-wielding maniac. They probably thought it was just another film crew making a low-budget slasher movie.

Even though I knew the relationship could only end in tragedy, I was just one more moth drawn to Mimi's deadly flame, and despite having my wings burned again and again, I was in over my head and still held out the foolish hope that one day we would look back and laugh about our early, crazy days – then I thought about Andy Knox.

When I moved into the flat in Belsize Park, the reason there was a room available was because Andy Knox, Steph's friend and flatmate, was in Jersey for a summer season, recreating his role as James Gascoigne in a stage show of the popular TV series *Doctor on the Go*. Andrew had been married to Imogen Hassall, a once famous British beauty, often referred to in the press as 'the Countess of Cleavage' and whose pneumatic charms graced the screen in movies like *The Virgin and the Gypsy* and *When Dinosaurs Ruled the Earth*. When Andy married her, the sultry looks and sensual curves that had made her a star were on the wane, along with, as he discovered to his cost, her sanity. One of the results of Imogen's frequent and uncontrollable fits of fury was the *Doctor on the Go* make-up department working overtime to conceal Andy's latest black eye or split lip. Like me, Andy was a romantic, believing that the power of love would make everything come right again. It was a belief that lasted right up until the night Imogen swallowed a bottle of her anti-psychosis pills and silenced her demons forever. Andy had since remarried, making a new life for himself in Jersey with a woman he had met while working there. One morning, he called the flat to say the marriage was over and asked if he could stay with us until he got himself straightened out. On the night he was due to arrive, I heard a knock at our door and opened it to an officer from the British Transport Police, who asked me if I knew anyone by the name of Andrew Knox. When I said I did and that I was expecting him at any minute, he told me Andy had boarded the ferry in Jersey but hadn't disembarked at Southampton, and the address label on his unclaimed luggage had led the police to our flat. A few weeks later, Andy's body was recovered somewhere off the coast of Normandy.

One evening, after enduring yet another of Mimi's Loony Tunes tirades, I slunk back to the small apartment I was renting in a run-down part of east LA and spent the rest of the night drowning my sorrows in one of the local dives before falling into bed in the early hours of the morning. Whether it was the crash of the rock ricocheting off the wall behind me, or the hailstorm of glass shards from the shattered window that startled me back to consciousness, I don't know, but I was instantly awake, my heart pounding with shock as I heard the screech of tyres as my mystery assailant's car drove off at high speed. It was then I finally realised that if I didn't want to end up like Andy Knox, or poor Peg Entwistle – the would-be starlet who had jumped off the Hollywood sign back in the twenties – I had no option but to get as far away as I could from Mimi and the destructive relationship I had stupidly got myself into.

Salvation came in the shape of a long-distance call from London. My agent told me that Bill Forsyth wanted me for a film he was about to start shooting called *Comfort and Joy*. I accepted gladly and thanked both God and Bill for the lifeline I had just been thrown. Later that day, Mimi called to ask if I wanted to spend the weekend in Laguna. Even though I had no doubt it would end in tears – well, screams and verbal abuse really – I knew it would be our last time together, so I said yes. She picked me up in her car and we set off down the coast road. Laguna is one of the most beautiful and romantic spots in California, and as I stood looking out at the sunset with the warm Pacific Ocean gently lapping around my ankles, suddenly and with complete clarity I saw myself back in London, pedalling my bike up Camden High Street in a drizzle. I couldn't hold back the tears, feeling much as Adam must have felt when he took a last look around before being expelled from the Garden of Eden. I was jolted out of my reverie by Mimi, who had taken a break from sipping her strawberry daiquiri at the beachside bar to join me. 'Oh my,' she said with a smile, 'I do believe you're blubbing.' It was a struggle to stay calm as I told her I would be heading home in a few weeks' time, adding, for good measure, that I had never come across such a poisonous, black-hearted bitch as her in my life and prayed I never would again. A look of puzzlement and hurt came into her beautiful blue eyes. 'Quitter,' she said quietly, and with a toss of her golden tresses marched back to her car and drove off, leaving me to make my own way back to the cheerless apartment with the broken window in the mean streets of east LA.

33

Down in the Dumps

Coincidentally, *Comfort and Joy* was a tale about a chap trying to deal with the aftershock of a broken romance – in this case between hapless radio DJ Alan 'Dicky' Bird, played by Bill Paterson, and his long-term girlfriend Maddy, played by Eleanor David. After being unexpectedly dumped on Christmas Eve, Dicky tries to lose himself in his work, telling his slightly bemused boss (Rikki Fulton) at the radio station that he wants to make documentaries about serious subjects. After stopping to buy an ice cream from the beautiful Charlotte (Clare Grogan), he follows her van and watches aghast as it's trashed by a couple of masked goons who are eventually seen off by Charlotte's driver, Trevor (me). Deciding that this incident will be the subject of his first foray into the world of grown-up programme making, he tracks Charlotte down and finds himself drawn into a bizarre world of rivalries and family feuds, where nothing is quite as it seems. Alison, my old girlfriend, was production assistant on the film (did I mention what a small, slightly incestuous world the Scottish film industry is?) and thankfully we buried the hatchet once and for all as we spent a few evenings having dinner and behaving like the reasonable human beings we should have been when we were together.

One night as I was filming a scene in Possilpark a small group of teenage girls were watching from a distance. During a tea break, one of them came over to me and asked if I was the guy in the

Scampi Fries advert. (I had made an ad for the popular snack shortly before I left for LA.) When I told her it *was* me in the ad, she said, 'Know whit we call Scampi Fries roon' here? "Smell yer Maw's!"' I thought it was hilarious and wondered what the makers of the fishy-smelling snack would think if they knew that! As I autographed the inside of their fag packets for them, they told me they were members of a local girl gang – something I didn't know existed, and was inclined to take with a pinch of salt, until they showed me their impressive display of weaponry. Like Dicky Bird, Bill Paterson's character in the film, I had a notion that maybe I had just stumbled on to something that could make a really interesting project. The thing that really fired my interest, though, was when they told me about the people living on the massive council dump close by. I thought they must be winding me up, but they assured me it was true – they said the dump was inhabited by a community of folk who made a living by sifting through the waste for anything that could be salvaged and sold on. By this point I was completely hooked. Shona, their leader, agreed to meet me the following morning and take me for a guided tour.

To say I was gobsmacked by what I saw at the dump would be an understatement. I had seen images of third-world slum dwellers scavenging through mountains of garbage, but not for a second did I ever expect to see anything like it in Scotland.

I had recently read a book called *Riddley Walker*, which begins with a description of a ragged community digging amid the ruins of an ancient civilisation. It's only when they unearth the rusted body of a car that you realise the book is set in a post-holocaust future and they're excavating the long-buried remains of our present. What I saw that morning could have been a set for a movie version of the book. After the bin lorries had dumped their loads, bulldozers would shove the fresh piles into the canyons of waste, where an army of scavengers waited below to sift through it all and carry their booty back to the homes they had made among the mountains of garbage. They were mainly single men, but here and there were couples working in tandem. I simply couldn't take it in.

Later, as we were heading off, Shona pointed to a puddle of industrial effluent that had leaked from a rusty oil drum. 'Look,' she said, 'a dead rainbow.' Right then I knew *Dead Rainbows* would be the title of the screenplay I was going to write about the lives of Shona and her girl gang, and some years later when Robert Love invited me to write a sixty-minute drama for STV, I thought it was the perfect opportunity to get it made. Unfortunately, for policy reasons, Robert was tied into using the company's studio facilities, so my idea of shooting the piece on location with a handheld camera and a small crew wasn't an option that was open to either of us. Although Robert commissioned my back-up idea, *Extras*, it wasn't the screenplay I was burning to write, and I'll always wonder whether if I had fought a bit harder to get the go-ahead for *Dead Rainbows*, STV might have had a BAFTA to put in its display case, instead of the Television and Radio Industries Best Drama award that *Extras* went on to win.

34

A Meaty Role

A few months after I returned to London, Sally and I met up in a local wine bar and, after telling me in no uncertain terms that our separation had broken her heart, thankfully she forgave my trespasses and took me back without recrimination, without anger and without question. Painful as it had been, I had learned some kind of lesson from my last hurrah in LA, knowing that as I kissed Mimi goodbye, I was also kissing goodbye to my life as a superannuated adolescent. It was time to grow up, and now that I had finally come to my senses (well, most of them), I knew that Sally and I were destined to spend the rest of our days with each other. When I swore I would never forsake her again, she left her bedsit in Primrose Hill and moved in with me. Thirty-one years and three kids later, we're still together.

When Hal Duncan, my friend at STV, called to ask if I would be interested in playing a part in the detective series he was about to direct, I knew things were going my way at last. Created by Robert Love and written by Glen Chandler, *Killer* had created a bit of a stir, and the ITV network had commissioned a second series. Now renamed *Taggart* and starring Mark McManus as the hard-bitten, hard-drinking Glasgow DCI, the show had, at its peak, a staggering eleven and a half million viewers glued to each of its three-part episodes.

Despite my many attempts to get into detective-fiction genre, I found it didn't engage me on any level. I invariably found the characters one-dimensional and with little purpose other than to act as red herrings in a preposterous plot – in short, I didn't really give a toss whodunnit! However, when Glen's scripts for 'Knife Edge' arrived in the post, all my prejudices vanished – I was hooked from the opening scene, where my character, George Bryce, is seen petting his collection of prize pigeons before picking up a butcher's knife and heading into the doocot. As he closes the door behind him, the camera pans down to reveal a naked female wrapped in a polythene sheet. I told Hal I wanted to play George as a real human being – an ordinary man driven by anger and grief to travel down a dark path from which there was no way back to everyday existence. 'Knife Edge' gave me my first real taste of fame, as I couldn't walk down a street in Glasgow without folk stopping me and saying, 'Haw – you're that mad butcher fae *Taggart* that wiz mincin' up women, urn't ye? Oor Ina's no' been able tae look at a black puddin' again since she watched you in that bloody thing.'

Many years later, when I had taken on the role of DCI Burke, *Taggart*'s senior detective, I was on a night shoot in the centre of Glasgow. A few yards along from the location, a lively crowd of patrons were queuing for admission to a gay nightclub. As I waited for my scene to begin, I clocked an interesting couple near the front of the line – one of them was dressed in a straight suit and tie, while his partner seemed to have drawn his flamboyant fashion sense from watching one too many Carmen Miranda movies. Out of the corner of my eye, I saw the straight-looking one point over to where I was standing. 'See that guy ower there?' he said. 'He wiz the butcher in *Taggart*.'

'Butcher?' said Ms Miranda, giving me a swift once-over. 'Christ, ah've seen a lot butcher than him . . .'

35

A Lad o' Pairts

Not long after I finished working on *Taggart*, I got a call from my agent, who asked if I'd ever heard of a director named Bill Douglas. My heart leapt when I heard the name, and I hardly dared to hope what was coming next. By sheer chance, I happened to be channel hopping (there were only three) one night in the late seventies when I caught a film called *My Childhood* on BBC2. From the opening scene I was completely captivated. When it was over, I sat in stunned silence. For the first time I had seen my own background portrayed on the screen with absolute fidelity. The credits revealed that the writer and director was someone called Bill Douglas, and I watched the following two films in his autobiographical trilogy, *My Ain Folk* and *My Way Home*, with deep admiration.

Bill was casting for a film he had written called *Comrades*, and wanted to meet me for a chat. One of the most difficult acting skills to pull off is trying to keep your excitement under control when you meet a director for a job you would sell your granny to get. When I met with Bill, I thought that having seen his trilogy I would be meeting someone with whom I would have quite a lot in common. To my surprise, he turned out to be nothing like the wee boy in his films. Instead, I found myself shaking hands with a well-groomed, smartly dressed man with an urbane manner and just a trace of a Scots accent, who asked me if I knew anything about the Tolpuddle Martyrs. I told him all I knew was that they were a group of agricultural labourers who were sentenced to transportation to Australia for attempting to form a trade union. He outlined the story he had written around this historical event and described the part he was considering me for – an itinerant showman called the Lanternist, who kicks the film off when he turns up in the village of Tolpuddle, drumming up business for his lantern show. Bill explained that the character of the Lanternist was the master of ceremonies, representing the film's director and popping up throughout the story in much the same way that Alfred Hitchcock would often appear in cameo roles in his own films. To be absolutely honest, I didn't really understand the concept, but I was prepared to do anything for the chance to work with this brilliant man.

The next day, Bill's script was biked over to my flat in Belsize Park. It was an offer. Bill later told me that he knew at our meeting I was the right actor to bring the Lanternist to life. As I read the script I was surprised to find that as well as playing the Lanternist I would be appearing as fourteen other characters. Whether my background of playing multiple roles in fringe theatre productions contributed in any way to Bill's decision to cast me, I'll never know, but I'll be forever grateful that he did.[1]

In the late summer of 1985, principal photography began in Dorset, the county where the story of the eight agricultural workers whose cruel and unjust treatment would leave an indelible stamp in the history of the trade union movement originated.

My first day on set could not have been worse. In the first of my fourteen characters, I was to be one of three gentlemen farmers playing a game of cards while deploring the damned impertinence

---

[1] I later learned that *Comrades* had been due to go into production the year before, but that the then producer, Ishmael Merchant (of Merchant Ivory Productions), had trousered the advance production money with seemingly no intention of actually producing a single frame of the film. At that time, the part of the Lanternist was on offer to Albert Finney! Funny how things work out, eh? So thanks, Ishmael – if you hadn't been such a bloody crook, I'd never have landed the part of a lifetime.

of their ungrateful and insubordinate serfs. The main character in the scene was James Frampton, the local magistrate and landowner who would gain notoriety by condemning six innocent men to a living hell on the far side of the world. Frampton was played by Robert Stephens, who, when I first encountered him in the make-up trailer at six o'clock that morning, was polishing off the remains of a bottle of vodka and telling long, rambling anecdotes with no discernible punchline, which were interrupted only by his frequent attempts to stick his fur-coated tongue down the horrified make-up assistant's throat. As we walked on to the set and took our places at the card table for the initial line-up, it suddenly dawned on me that I had absolutely no idea how Bill wanted me to act. I didn't know whether I was meant to be the Lanternist representing the director and playing the role of the gentleman in his own film, or whether I should simply play the character straight without giving a glimpse of the Lanternist behind the performance. Bill clearly had a lot on his mind and I didn't want to interrupt him with unnecessary trifles, so when we started the scene I just went for it without too much over-analysis. Halfway through, I glanced up to see Bill with his head in his hands, staring at the floor and muttering, 'What is he doing? What is he *doing*?' His words were clearly aimed at me and, to my growing sense of dread, he called the rehearsal to a premature halt and motioned me to step outside with him. Bill Douglas, as anyone who has ever worked for him will tell you, didn't often use plain English to describe what he wanted from his actors. He thought first and foremost in pictorial terms and communicated his instructions in purely visual images that he assumed any film actor worthy of the title would intuitively grasp. If I was confused before our little chat, I was completely baffled afterwards. However, even with Bill's furrowed brow and Robert Stephens' belligerent glare, I completed my first scene and was driven back to the little chocolate-box cottage that was my home for the duration of the Dorset shoot – a duration that I thought, as I waited for the phone to ring with the news that I had been replaced, would be extremely brief.

When the phone did ring, it was Sally. 'Hi,' she said, 'just thought I'd give you a ring to see how your first day went.' By the end of what amounted to a twenty-minute monologue from me, her eardrum must have developed calluses. 'Would you like me to come down for a bit and run your scenes with you?' she asked. The following day I picked her up from Dorchester station in my little MG Midget, and for the remainder of the Dorset shoot, my little cottage became our first proper home together.

My next scene was my first appearance as the Lanternist. At our initial meeting, Bill had shown me a nineteenth-century engraving of a tall-hatted travelling lanternist, bent over from the weight of the cumbersome apparatus and boxes of heavy glass slides that he toted from place to place on a wooden frame strapped across his back. I knew it was crucial to get the character absolutely right, and spent a long time at Morris Angels, the theatrical costumiers, trying on stacks of period costumes until I was satisfied that I had captured the look of the shabby showman in Bill's old sketch. As soon as I walked on to the set, Bill lit up like a Christmas tree. 'That's him!' he beamed. 'That's the Lanternist!' From then on I could do absolutely no wrong in his eyes and I learned very quickly how to interpret his unique style of direction. (He would describe the scene as the audience would see it, then allow me free rein to transform his vision into actuality – even encouraging me to improvise, a licence never granted to anyone else in the cast.) I had never worked for a director with such an extraordinary and brilliant sense of the moving image, and under his guidance I think I can say with all due modesty I rose to the occasion, becoming, as he once told his partner Peter Jewell, 'My favourite actor ever.'

Bill had assembled a truly stellar cast for the film and I had the privilege of working alongside some of Britain's best-known and best-loved actors, such as Michael Hordern, James Fox, Freddie Jones, Vanessa Redgrave and the very wonderful Barbara Windsor. Among the relative unknowns that he had cast as the martyrs, Keith Allen (future father of the pop star Lily Allen) and I became buddies during the shoot. I've always found myself drawn to characters who have that 'wild at heart' element about them, and Keith, as anyone who knows him will tell you, is truly one of the profession's bad boys. Of the many tales he told me about his wild life, my favourite was about the time, early on in his career, when he was employed as assistant stage manager at London's Victoria Palace Theatre. The show running at the time was *Singalongamax*, a star vehicle for Max 'I wanna tell you a story' Bygraves. Although he was a popular and well-loved family entertainer, Keith loathed him for what he felt was his phony sentimentality and showbizzy smugness. One evening, as Bygraves was singing a medley of his popular hits to an auditorium packed to the gods with his core audience of pensioners, he became aware of a distinct change in atmosphere: the happy smiles of a moment before had been replaced by frowns and looks of bewildered astonishment. Puzzled, he carried on for a verse or two before turning round to see what it was that the audience were tut-tutting and pointing at. Picture his surprise to discover Keith standing behind him, stark naked and swaying from side to side in time to the music. Scarlet with fury and embarrassment, Bygraves yelled to the stagehands to bring down the curtain. Unfortunately, since he was standing at the very front of the stage, when the curtain fell, instead of hiding Keith from the audience, it came down behind him, leaving Max to wrestle the naked lunatic into the wings while doing his best to cover up his not insubstantial wedding tackle and inadvertently giving a whole new meaning to his hit song 'You Need Hands'.

While I was in Dorset, Hal Duncan got in touch with me. We had worked together on various productions over the years, beginning with *In My Painting Box*, his first production as a fledgling TV director, and whenever he rang me I knew there would be something interesting in store. This time he was calling to say that under the title *Dramarama*, STV were about to commission a series of half-hour plays for a teenage audience and would I be interested in writing one of them?

There's a telling story about a Glasgow actor in days long gone, who was giving of his Hamlet at a Glasgow theatre. Apparently he was so terrible that the audience started booing him. Finally he had enough and, stopping in the middle of the 'To be or not to be' soliloquy, he turned to the audience and said, 'Listen – whit are yiz booin' me fur? Ah didny write this shite!'

I think it's true to say that most actors who turn their hand to writing and directing do so because they've been in so many productions where they've thought to themselves, 'I could do a better job than that useless sod' – a sentiment that's certainly been true in my case. Throughout most of my career I've had a long-held ambition to be an auteur, a French word meaning simply author, but in the film business it's used to describe a writer-director – Bill Forsyth and Bill Douglas being two prime examples. Yet with the scripts I've written and the plays I've directed, I've never yet managed to combine the two. I suppose the closest I've come to realising my ambition was during the 7:84 days, when John McGrath encouraged me to contribute to the writing and staging of the shows. It was the feeling of artistic fulfilment, knowing that our audiences were responding to something that came straight from the heart, that made me want to be like the pavement artists I used to see over the Barras, who would write 'All My Own Work' in chalk next to their upturned bunnets.

I'd first had the notion of trying to make a go of being a writer when I was asked to do a Glaswegian adaptation of Italian auteur Dario Fo's political satire *Can't Pay? Won't Pay!* for the Citizens Theatre touring company. I remember glowing with pride at the first read-through, when everything ground to a halt as the cast went into hysterics over a gag I had written. At one point, the police inspector is lying unconscious on the floor as Antonia and Margherita, the two leading women, try to revive him.

MARGHERITA

Oh my God, Antonia – he's no breathin'. Ah think he
might be deid!

ANTONIA

Well don't jist staun there – gie 'im a kiss.

MARGHERITA

Kiss him? Whit wid Ah want tae kiss a polis fur?

ANTONIA

Tae start him breathin' again. It wiz on the news the
other night – somethin' aboot a man bein' winched tae
safety . . .

The cast of five – Sandy Morton, Maureen Carr, Andy Gray, Anne
Downie and Stuart Hepburn – played their parts to perfection, and
the production went down a storm, so I began to think seriously
that my future just might be in writing and directing, rather than
acting. Like all would-be writers, I found myself constantly mulling
over stories that I could work up into possible productions. One of
the many notions that had been rattling around in my head was the
fact that the only time Elvis Presley ever set foot in Britain was a
brief appearance in Ayrshire on 2 March 1960. At that time, all
USAF flights from Europe to America had to refuel en route, and
when Elvis was discharged from his army service in Germany, his
flight home included a stopover at the US military base attached to
Prestwick Airport. I was ten years old at the time, and I remember
being awestruck when I read about it in the *Evening Times*, and if it
struck me as an extraordinary event, hopefully Hal would think so
too. He whooped with joy when I told him my idea and immediately
gave it the thumbs up. Each day that I wasn't needed on set for
Comrades, I would sit in the back garden of my little cottage and
write. When I nervously sent the finished script off, Hal immediately
rang me back and started singing Cliff Richard's 'Congratulations'

over the phone – he absolutely loved it! I was still busy working on *Comrades* and wasn't able to take any part in the production, but I knew my first telly script was in safe hands, so I was content to let Hal get on with it.[2]

After completing the Dorset scenes for *Comrades*, I boarded a plane bound for Australia. As if a trip to Oz wasn't wonderful enough, as an added bonus there was a one-night stopover in Singapore. And as if *that* wasn't wonderful enough, I was booked into a suite at the world-renowned Raffles Hotel. As I sipped my second (or was it my fourth?) Singapore Sling, lounging beneath a parasol on the immaculate lawn of the very hotel where the famous cocktail was invented, I vaguely recall boarding a train of thought that left from a station called 'My God, I can't believe I'm spending the night in Raffles Hotel!' then clattering over a set of points that diverted it to 'This city has some of the most beautiful women I've ever seen!' before finally trundling along a branch line that led to 'I've always wondered what it would be like to . . .' A couple of gin slings later and I found myself assuming a character from a novel, probably by Graham Greene, and probably called something like *Our Man in Singapore*. 'Donning his crumpled Panama hat and fastening the buttons of his well-travelled linen jacket with the slightly frayed cuffs, Our Man in Singapore downed his fifth gin sling before strolling nonchalantly out of the hotel gates to sample the legendary pleasure of the Orient . . .'

As I stood swaying gently by the roadside, an ancient trishaw driver pedalled over to me. 'You wan' see Singapore by night, sir?' he enquired.

---

[2] Which he did superbly, casting Valerie Gogan, Sandy Morton, Douglas Sannachan (Billy the window cleaner in *Gregory's Girl*) and Jeni Maxwell in the principal roles, while set designer Marius Van Der Werf brilliantly transformed STV's main studio into Prestwick Airport's passenger lounge circa 1960. 'Waiting for Elvis' topped the viewing figures for the entire *Dramarama* series and went on to win the Silver Medal at the prestigious New York Film and Television Awards ceremony. Thanks for having faith in me, Hal.

'Certainly do, my good man,' I replied, as the gin and the jet lag shook hands before taking over the controls and swiftly replacing the dull and boring old me with a suave, urbane and devil-may-care new me, who thought a little Oriental encounter could not by *any* means be classed as infidelity. As the trishaw rattled along in the jasmine-scented dusk, the transfiguration was complete and Our Man in Singapore was up for anything.

After about ten minutes, my driver pulled up outside what appeared to be a run-down council tower block. 'You wan' girl, sir?' he asked.

'Oh, I think I just might,' I replied, in the louche drawl my new character seemed to have affected.

'OK. You stay here. One minute,' said my driver, scuttling up the stairs that led from the heavily graffitied entrance. Glancing round at the dark and forbidding streets of a neighbourhood that made the Gorbals of my childhood look like Park Lane, Our Man in Singapore felt that first small pang of unease that is, alas, so often the harbinger of doom.

My driver reappeared, flanked by two huge, scary-looking bastards who looked like they had just stepped off the set of a Steven Spielberg movie called *Indiana Jones and the Two Huge, Scary-Looking Bastards*. 'OK,' he said, 'you go now with my friends. I come back soon.' And with that he pedalled off into the Stygian darkness, taking Our Man in Singapore along with him and leaving me to sober up with a rapidity that should have got me a mention in the Guinness Book of Records. The two heavies from Central Casting didn't look like they would be the sympathetic type if I said there had been a slight misunderstanding, and if they would be so kind as to point me in the direction of Raffles Hotel, I'm sure we would all laugh about it in the morning. Alarm bells were clanging in time to the pounding of my heart as I followed them up to a courtyard, somewhere around the fifth or sixth floor.

'You wan' drink?' said the more menacing of the pair, gesturing for me to sit down. 'Beer, whisky, vodka? Wha' you wan'?'

'Thank you, no,' I answered in a weirdly high voice.

'You no' wan' drink? OK. No problem,' he said, in a way that seemed to imply that perhaps it might be.

'You pick girl now,' growled the other heavy, clapping his hands together a couple of times. This was the signal for about a dozen girls to appear from round the corner and line up in front of me. As they stood there posing and pouting like they were auditioning for an amateur production of *Cabaret*, my autonomic nervous system kicked in and told me to get the hell out of this place right now.

'Sorry,' I said as I stood up. 'They're all very nice, very sweet, but not really my type I'm afraid. So I'll just be—'

'SIT DOWN!' roared heavy number one. I sat down. 'You no like? No problem – I get more girl.' Dismissing the first lot with a wave of his hand, he turned to me and asked, 'Where you from? America? Australia?'

'No,' I answered in a chatty tone that I hoped would mask my terror, 'actually I'm from Glasgow.'

'Glesca?' he said, breaking into a big grin. 'Hullawrer Jimmy – howzitgaun?' His surprisingly accurate impression led me to believe that I may not have been the first Glaswegian to set foot in the premises.

A fresh set of girls appeared before me and began the same hip-swivelling routine as the previous line-up. Realising that my chances of leaving without some kind of financial transaction taking place were minimal, I singled out a petite, almond-eyed beauty with a demure, slightly shy air about her. 'This girl?' said heavy number two. 'OK. One hour – fifty dollar.' In truth I would have signed all my future earnings over to him in return for a pledge to let me leave in one piece. Instead, I continued to play the seasoned roué, hoping my feigned nonchalance would prevent him from seeing me as a lamb to be fleeced before a swift visit to the abattoir. 'Half-hour,' I said. 'Twenty-five dollars.'

He gave it a moment's thought. 'Thirty dollar.'

'OK,' I said. 'Thirty dollars.' I was relieved to think that in thirty minutes I would be far away from the nightmare Our Man in Singapore had stupidly got me into. My hostess beckoned me to follow her along a grimy corridor and into a windowless room so disgusting it could have been the set for a post-apocalyptic zombie movie. As soon as the door closed behind us, she dropped the coquette act along with her sarong. The first thing I noticed, as she waited for me to make a move, was the complexity of the tattoo that covered most of her right thigh. It wasn't, as you might expect, an Oriental dragon or something similar; instead it was a long scroll of densely packed Chinese letters. It was the second time in my life a tattoo had made me gasp. The first was when I took some of my shirts into a little neighbourhood laundry in Hollywood. The elderly owner asked me if I was an actor, and as I was leaving he shook my hand and wished me luck with my career. That was when I saw the numbers tattooed on his forearm and realised with a jolt he was someone who had lived through the hell of the Nazi death camps. It was a handshake that touched my soul. The tattoo on this girl's thigh had the same effect on me – it was clearly a certificate of ownership, and she was someone's piece of property. As she lay back on the stained mattress, the second thing I noticed was the mass of livid scar tissue running the entire length of her right arm. It was obvious that someone had taken a blowtorch to her, probably as punishment for some misdemeanour, like trying to escape maybe. Any feelings of relief that I would soon be out of this awful place turned to shame and disgust.

'You lie here,' said the girl, patting the space next to her.

'No,' I answered quietly. 'I leave now.'

She sat up like a startled animal. 'You no like me?' she asked.

'No – I mean, yes – yes I like you, but I have to go.'

She grabbed my wrist, her eyes wide with fear. 'No, you no go – if you go, is big trouble for me.' I understood her concern – the two heavies would be far from happy with her if they thought she had failed to satisfy a paying customer.

'OK,' I said, 'I'll stay.' I handed her back her sarong and told her to get dressed. Not from any sense of gallantry on my part; I just couldn't bear to see the graphic evidence of how low the human race could sink. We sat together in silence on the bed for twenty minutes or so, before I rose to leave. Thankfully there was no sign of the Chuckle Brothers as I made my way back down the stairs and climbed into the waiting trishaw.

Psychologists speak of 'adult knowledge', the wisdom that only comes from experience and supersedes the beliefs we held as adolescents. With all the naivety of youth, I went in search of an experience that I thought would provide an illicit and exciting thrill, and returned with adult knowledge of the misery and degradation prostitutes are forced to suffer. It was my experience in Singapore that prompted me, years later, to write my award-winning TV drama *Extras*, a story about a group of women working as prostitutes in a Glasgow massage parlour. In a way it was a measure of atonement: my way of expressing some of the disgust I felt, both then and now, about the night I bought half an hour of a young girl's tragic life for thirty dollars.

A few days after arriving in Sydney, I travelled to Broken Hill, a mining town in the middle of the Australian outback, to shoot the sequence where one of the Tolpuddle Martyrs is on a chain gang, breaking rocks to build a road through the desert. I played their overseer, a brutal whip-wielding thug named McCallum. Bill wanted him portrayed as a disgusting degenerate and had written a sequence where he has carnal relations with his guard dog in the darkness of his hut. Bill told me to improvise the scene and, as the camera rolled, I began by feeding the slavering animal a tasty bit of chicken and encouraging it to lick my face before giving it a full-on snog. Since boyhood, I had cherished a secret hope that my first screen kiss might be with Hayley Mills – but hey, beggars can't be choosers, and at least I didn't have to worry about whether or not my breath was a bit off . . .

After we wrapped in Broken Hill, we travelled to Kinchega National Park in New South Wales to film at a surreal-looking landscape called Lake Menindee. Bill had cast a pure-blooded Aboriginal boy in the sequence, who had a tendency to go walkabout whenever the fancy took him, so a well-known

Aboriginal actor named Ernie Dingo was employed as his minder and, if necessary, tracker. Ernie turned out to have an encyclopaedic knowledge about his beloved country and gave me a fascinating insight into the culture of his ancestors. I was astonished to learn that up until legislation was passed in the 1970s, Christian charities were entitled to march into Aboriginal settlements, take children from their mothers and bring them up in institutions as good, God-fearing folk like themselves. They may have been acting out of sincerely held principles, but they had simply no idea of the cultural genocide they were perpetrating. For example, to the white European immigrants, many of them Scots, land was a commodity to be bought and sold in massive tracts and turned over to the rearing of vast flocks of sheep. To the Aborigines, on the other hand, the land was a living entity that could only be quantified in the abstract. Using songlines from the mystical dreamtime, an Aborigine boy on the rite of passage known as walkabout could travel thousands of miles through featureless outback terrain, living off the land, and finding his way to sacred sites with a precision that a modern GPS system would have difficulty matching. I only scratched the surface of Ernie's profound knowledge of his heritage and his culture, and if time and circumstance had allowed, I would dearly love to have spent a lot longer in both his wonderful company and his fascinating homeland.

My dad's brothers had all emigrated to Australia in the early fifties, and he had been hinting for some time that he would dearly like to see them while they were still around. Thanks to the decent fee I was getting for the film, I was able to make his wish come true and fly him out for a reunion. We had a week's break over the Christmas and New Year period, so I booked a flight from Sydney to stay with my Dad and the 'Rellies' (Aussie slang for relatives). My cousin John collected me from the airport and drove me to my uncle Bob and aunt Yvonne's house in the small town of Traralgon. It was great to see my dad reunited with his brother once again, and the hospitality and friendliness shown to me on that visit will stay with me always. My dad and I had long reconciled our differences, although in typical Glasgow fashion, the only time our once-troubled relationship was mentioned was the night he came to see me in *Writer's Cramp*. Over a pint at a nearby pub, he told me how good he thought I had been in the production, adding tersely, 'I know when you were younger, we had our disagreements about you wantin' to be an actor. Well, I just want to say I was wrong. You're doin' well for yourself and you were right to stick to your guns.' The impact of what he said didn't really hit home until later that night when I realised how often I had thought to myself, 'I'll bloody show him I've got it!' But no longer; I had finally proved myself to my father. It made a huge psychological difference to me and from that night on I felt free to work for my own satisfaction.

Shortly before *Comrades* was due for release, I was invited to a press screening in London's Wardour Street. Pitching up at eleven o'clock on a drizzly Tuesday morning, I spotted among the assembled pressmen in the foyer the familiar face of Barry Norman. I had spent a pleasant half-hour or so chatting to him about classic Hollywood films when I'd met him at a party a few years previously and I was glad to see him again. Thanks to his high-profile series *Film*, he was arguably the most influential of all the British movie critics: a good review on his show would have the public queuing round the block, while a thumbs down could spell box-office disaster. As a regular viewer of the show, by and large I agreed with his opinions, but as he stood there in his damp trench coat waiting for the screening to start, I sensed that he wasn't in the best of moods. 'Good to meet you again, Barry,' I said affably as we made our way into the tiny auditorium. 'I hope you enjoy the film.'

'It's three bloody hours long,' he snorted derisively. 'If John Ford can make a masterpiece like *Stagecoach* in ninety-six minutes, why can't Bill Douglas?'

My heart sank, as it seemed to me that he might not be in exactly the right frame of mind to assess the film he was about to sit through.

My doubts seemed to be confirmed when a few weeks later on

Film '86 he began his review of *Comrades* with the words, 'Well, if John Ford can make a masterpiece like *Stagecoach* in ninety-six minutes, I don't see why Bill Douglas can't,' before disparaging the film in no uncertain terms. Although the majority of critics considered *Comrades* a triumph, *Film '86* was watched by millions of viewers, and I'm convinced it was the thumbs down we got from Barry Norman that scuppered any chance of success *Comrades* might have had at the box office by ensuring audiences stayed away in their droves.

Thanks largely to the release of the British Film Institute's DVD, *Comrades* is now seen as something of a minor miracle in the history of British cinema. Bill Douglas's refusal to compromise his artistic vision led to problems with the distributors: from the original running time of just under four hours (Bill wanted to screen it as a two-parter), it was re-edited – with Bill shamefully locked out of the cutting room – to its present length of around 180 minutes. Many, if not most, of Bill's carefully considered and beautifully realised narrative sequences that drew the threads of the story together were gone. The result of this shameful butchery was that the version of *Comrades* that was finally released was nowhere near the masterpiece it could have been, and after Barry Norman's scathing and ill-judged review, it soon found itself on the bottom shelf of Blockbusters. I had been praised to the rafters for my performance in the film and I really thought it would be my breakthrough – alas, there's nothing to be gained from giving a good performance in a film that nobody goes to see, and my movie career failed to make the great leap forward I had so hoped for. As for Bill Douglas, although none of us could have predicted it at the time, *Comrades* was to be his final film. We last met back in the late nineties, when he told me that he had completed a screen adaptation of one of my all-time favourite novels, *The Private Memoirs and Confessions of a Justified Sinner*. He said he had written one of the leading roles for me – Gil-Martin, the mysterious and enigmatic charmer who, as the hero begins belatedly to realise, may actually be the Devil in human form. I loved the book and knew that if anyone could successfully bring James Hogg's Gothic Scots horror story to the screen, it would be Bill Douglas. Less than a year later, Peter Jewell rang to tell me that Bill, his lifelong friend and partner, had died of cancer. And so, gathering dust on some producer's shelf somewhere in Soho, sits a brilliant screenplay that I have no doubt, if Bill had lived to direct it, would have been the jewel in the crown of both our careers.

36

Notes on a Scandal

I was just thirteen when John Profumo, the Tory MP, resigned his position as the Conservative government's Minister for War over his relationship with a showgirl named Christine Keeler. I was a bit too young to understand the full ramifications of the whole sordid saga, but since it was headline news every day, I was certainly very aware of it. Profumo had met Keeler at a party hosted by Lord Astor at Cliveden, his ancestral home, and embarked on a torrid affair with her. However, when Fleet Street got wind of the dirty doings and discovered that Keeler was also sleeping with Yevgeny Ivanov, an attaché at the Soviet embassy in London, they had a field day. This was a story that had everything – sex, politics and corruption in high places. Profumo's denial of the affair to the House of Commons led not only to his resignation, but also to the defeat of Harold Macmillan's Conservative government in the 1964 general election. Twenty-five years later, in 1989, Palace Pictures started production on *Scandal*, the film of the affair that brought down the British government.

I had worked with the film's director, Michael Caton-Jones, a year before, in an excellent TV film called *Lucky Sunil*, a story about a naïve young Indian lad who is sent by his doting parents to be privately educated in London. Through a series of misunderstandings, he finds himself playing Huree Jamset Ram Singh in a low-budget porn movie called *Billy Bunter Goes to Roedean*.[1] The seedy director of the porn movie was, of course, yours truly. In *Scandal*, Michael cast me as the police inspector responsible for rounding up and questioning the witnesses in Stephen Ward's forthcoming trial. Brilliantly portrayed in the movie by John Hurt, Ward became the scapegoat for the British upper class's venal indiscretions. He was a Harley Street osteopath, a grammar-school boy who had wormed his way into the elite ranks of the British Establishment by organising sex parties, where his young and pretty protégées, like Christine Keeler and Mandy Rice-Davies, would liven up the proceedings with their readily available charms. The first character I had to arrest was high-class hooker Mariella Novotny. As I sat in the make-up truck, making the usual small talk with my make-up girl, I didn't really pay much attention to the short middle-aged lady in the adjacent chair, with no make-up and her hair tucked into a stocking cap. My make-up girl told me she had recently read an article about Elizabeth Taylor losing a serious amount of weight. 'Really?' I said. 'I wonder how she did it?'

'I'll tell you how she fugging did it dahling,' said a strongly accented voice beside me. 'She had it all sugged out – that's how she fugging did it!' That was my first introduction to sixties screen goddess Britt Ekland, who had played a major role in quite a few of my adolescent fantasies. What a treat then to find myself a few hours later wrestling her, kicking and struggling, into the back of a Black Maria.

A few weeks before the production was due to begin, Michael Caton-Jones rang me to ask if I would be interested in 'reading in' for the screen tests he was about to make of the final few hopefuls who were being considered for the part of Mandy Rice-Davies. When I pitched up at Shepperton Studios I was taken to an empty sound stage where a solitary witness box stood in front of a set of black drapes. Michael handed me the scene where Mandy puts up a spirited defence (including her oft-quoted reply when told that

---

[1] With a young Michelle Collins as a *very* naughty schoolgirl.

Lord Astor had denied any impropriety with her: 'Well, he would, wouldn't he . . .') and I read in the part of the prosecuting council while the camera rolled on a succession of hopeful Mandys. Although most of them were perfectly good, in the end the part went to Bridget Fonda, a young American actress who made her first screen appearance aged five as a hippie kid in her father Peter's seminal sixties movie *Easy Rider*, and had just finished her first starring role in a film called *Shag* – appropriate really for someone taking on the role of Ms Rice-Davies.

After the screen tests were over, Michael had one more thing to take care of before we headed back to London – a group of extras had been assembled for his approval. He gave them the once-over before selecting around twenty or so he thought had the most upper-class appearance. Gathering them together, he said, 'Now, I need about a dozen of you to take part in an orgy scene. There will be nudity and simulated sex, so . . . any volunteers?' We both hooted with laughter as every one of the men sprang eagerly forward, while all of the women took a step back.

One of the highlights of working on *Scandal* was the opportunity to play a scene with John Hurt. I had met him a couple of times before when, like me, he frequented the Vault, a shady and now sadly defunct drinking club in Primrose Hill that was owned by a notorious Glasgow villain.[2] To watch him prepare for a take was a rare privilege. Before the camera started to roll, he would begin quietly talking to himself, improvising dialogue that would lead into the mood of the scene we were just about to shoot, so that when action was called he would be completely in the moment. Over lunch one day I told him how brilliant I thought he was in *The Elephant Man*. He smiled and thanked me for the compliment, agreeing that the film was a fine piece of work. 'And will you be doing any of the follow-ups?' I asked.

'Follow-ups?' he said with a perplexed look. 'What follow-ups?'

---

[2] Who I would later channel for the character of Malky Mulherron in the comedy series *Bad Boys*.

'You know,' I said, '*Return of the Elephant Man. Bride of the Elephant Man, Abbott and Costello meet the Ele*—' I stuttered to a halt as his smile vanished like snow off a dyke, and I felt like I had just farted in church. Apart from our scripted dialogue, we never exchanged another word on the set, and he totally blanked me the next time we met in the Vault when he dropped in to buy a little something for the weekend. Ach well. To quote Anthony Hopkins, 'Don't take it so seriously; it's only acting!'

37

Idol Chatter

Like Marmite, you either love Tom Waits or you don't. As a major fan from his early days at Asylum Records, it was a huge buzz for me to work with him on *The Bearskin* – one of those strange eighties 'Europudding' films that were financed by several European production companies with their snouts deep in the trough of EU film subsidy. The plot was about a young snooker hustler who owes money to a gangster and is on the run through London's dark underworld. Chased by a couple of gun-toting heavies (Mark Arden and myself), he ducks inside a Punch and Judy booth for safety. The puppeteer (Tom Waits) hides the boy and later gives him sanctuary at the disused warehouse where he lives, surrounded by old props, costumes and scenery. We later discover the reason he decides to help the boy is because he too is on the run – a fellow fugitive, forced to adopt a new identity due to some misdeed in his shady past.

I could see the potential in the script, and it might have made a creditable film-noir-type thriller if Tom hadn't decided to play the Punch and Judy man in the style of a Japanese kabuki actor. In the script, the character was written as a shabbily dressed London street entertainer and Tom's Toshiro Mifune tribute made absolutely no sense whatsoever. I sensed that the film's Portuguese writer and director, Eduardo Guedes, was as bewildered by this bizarre performance as we were, but as a mere actor you have absolutely no influence over how a film is going to turn out. But no matter how big a stinker I've been in, I've invariably come away with some unforgettable memories of people I would never otherwise have met and places I would probably never have seen. For instance, on *The Bearskin*, apart from the opportunity to hang out with Tom Waits, I got to spend an unforgettable week on location in Lisbon, where, on our last night, Mark Arden and I went on the lash, drinking absinthe in a transvestite bar (it was only after our second or third glass that we noticed all the gorgeously dressed and heavily made-up ladies had rather large hands and feet) before heading down to the waterfront, where we stumbled across a seedy-looking pub called the British Bar and fell in with an equally pissed merchant seaman from Wishaw who took it upon himself to introduce us to a whole other side of life by shepherding us around the Rags, as Lisbon's red-light area is known by the legions of sailors who frequent its colourful bordellos and know the password that will get them past the door of its illegal drinking dens.

Another indelible memory of *The Bearskin* is sharing a bottle of gin with Michael, the flamboyantly camp wardrobe designer, as we waited for the rain to stop so we could continue with the night shoot in Camden market. As the night wore on and a second bottle was produced, he became wonderfully indiscreet about his former occupation as Peter Sellers' valet and general life sorter-outer. Some of his tales of Sellers' bizarre lifestyle were almost beyond belief – like the time he and Britt Ekland were travelling to Los Angeles from their home in Switzerland. Michael had been instructed to charter two Lear jets for the trip – one for Peter and Britt, the other for their luggage. Halfway across the Atlantic, Sellers realised he had left his favourite pair of jeans behind, and when they landed he instructed Michael to go straight back to Switzerland in one of the Lear jets, pick up the jeans and fly directly back to LA. On another occasion, following a lovers' tiff ('a total fucking Donnybrook' was how Michael actually put it), Britt had stormed out of their Swiss home, boarded the first flight to America and barricaded herself in their Beverly Hills mansion. A few days later, Sellers told Michael that Britt wasn't picking up the phone when he called, and would he charter a private jet and go out there to ask her why. 'Hello Britt,' said a jet-lagged Michael when she finally answered the door to his insistent knocking. 'Peter says he's very sorry, and would you please answer the phone.'

'No!' said Mrs Sellers, slamming the door and leaving Michael wondering whether he should get a mention in the Guinness Book of Records as the man who made the world's longest journey for the world's shortest reply.

Michael clearly adored his former boss and desperately missed the privileged lifestyle he knew would never come his way again. He told me that when Sellers died, he left Michael a sizeable bequest on condition he never wrote his memoirs or sold his story to the newspapers. When I mentioned that I had recently read Roger Lewis's biography of Sellers, Michael exploded. 'I fucking hate that book!' he shrieked. 'That bastard had the effrontery to suggest my relationship with Peter was more than just platonic!'

'And was it?' I asked. Michael smiled enigmatically and mimed zipping his lips together.

'That's a secret I'll take to the grave,' he said – I leave you, dear reader, to make of his words what you will.

As it turned out, neither the considerable talents of Bill Paterson and Ian Dury, nor even a panicky, last-minute title change from *The Bearskin* to *Bearskin: An Urban Fairytale* could save this dog of a movie from being tried, convicted and sentenced to a single three o'clock in the morning screening on Channel 4 followed by a short stretch on Blockbuster's bottom shelf. Ah well, at least it had *Comrades* to keep it company.

38

Dirty Harare

Why Clint Eastwood cast me as Zibelinsky in the movie he was about to start shooting in Africa, I'll never know. *White Hunter Black Heart* was the thinly disguised story of legendary Hollywood director John Huston's efforts to make the classic Humphrey Bogart/Katharine Hepburn vehicle *The African Queen*. Apparently, Huston was one of Eastwood's heroes and he had commissioned a screenplay based on Peter Viertel's 1953 novel about his difficult relationship with Huston while working with him as *The African Queen*'s scriptwriter. In the book, he rechristened Huston 'John Wilson' while his own character became 'Pete Verril'.

Mary Selway, the casting director, had auditioned me on video-tape at her office in Soho for the character of Ralph Lockhart, John Wilson's assistant director. An unpleasant, racist drunk, Lockhart was a gift of a part, so when my agent called to say I was in the movie, I whooped with joy. 'It's not the part you went up for, though,' she said. 'It's Zibelinsky, the Russian big-game hunter who owns the safari lodge and takes Wilson out shooting elephants.' I was a bit taken aback, to say the least. On a theatre production costing a few thousand quid there is likely to be a long and meticulous process of auditions and workshops before the suc-cessful candidate is selected and cast. On a mega-budget Hollywood movie like this, though, Clint Eastwood cast me in a role that he hadn't even auditioned me for! Nevertheless, I wasn't going to turn down the chance of working with one of the greatest screen icons of my generation, so I accepted without hesitation.

My first day's filming almost turned out to be my last. The previous evening a limo had picked me up from Zimbabwe's Harare airport and driven me out to the hotel complex on the shores of Lake Kariba that would be my home for the next month or so. Filming had started a few weeks before, and Alun Armstrong (who had landed the part of Lockhart) and Timothy Spall welcomed me in to their company with an ice-cold beer, quickly followed by a visit to the hotel's casino. Since the Zimbabwean dollars I had been given for living expenses were worthless outside the country, I didn't feel too bad about losing most of them on the roulette table that night.

Early next morning, I joined the cast and crew at the hotel's jetty, where a flotilla of speedboats were waiting to ferry us over to one of the lake's islands that served as the location for Zibelinsky's hunting lodge. That first journey across Lake Kariba as dawn broke and the huge, African sun rose in the gold and scarlet sky is a sight I'll never forget. After breakfast, one of the assistants showed me the vehicle I would be driving later in the day. It was an original 1940s open-top Land Rover with the doors removed. 'I've never driven one of these before,' I told him. 'I'll really need to have a practice.'

'Of course,' he said. 'I'll get that organised for you – no worries.' *No worries?* I should have known that when anyone uses that stupid phrase it's time to reach for the tranquillisers.

A few hours later as I sat on a folding chair, waiting for Mr No Worries to arrange my try-out with the Landy and marvelling at the fact that I was really here in the heart of Africa, I was jolted out of my reverie by a husky voice saying, 'Hi Alex, I just wanted to come over and say hello and thanks for being in the movie. I thought your tape was really excellent.' Actually, I've just invented most of that conversation because the only bit I really heard was 'Hi Alex.' Whatever else Clint Eastwood might have said to me became a meaningless jumble as my brain was too busy going,

'Jesus Christ – it's Clint Eastwood! Clint Eastwood's just called you Alex! Clint Eastwood knows your name!'

'Hi Clint,' I replied. 'Pleasure to meet you.' I may have said something else as well, but all I remember is thinking 'Oh my God, I've just said "Hi" to Clint Eastwood – and no' only that, I've just called him Clint!' It was only after he'd gone and I stood up to stretch my legs that I noticed the name CLINT EASTWOOD stencilled across the canvas back of the seat. This time my brain didn't seem quite so excited as it went: 'Oh shit – all the time he was talking to you, you were sitting in his bloody chair!'

Twice more I asked Mr No Worries for a go in the Land Rover, and both times he assured me a practice drive was being organised. It probably goes without saying that I never got into the vehicle until the moment I had to drive it. I was taken out to the location – a narrow dirt track that ran through a dense stretch of jungle, where the Landy was already in position with Clint and Jeff Fahey on board. Clint was in the passenger's seat and Jeff, the film's handsome young leading man, was perched on the tailgate. I clambered into the driver's seat, only to discover that it was so low I couldn't see over the top of the bonnet-mounted spare wheel. I wondered whether I should mention this to Clint, but as he was busy running through the words with Jeff, I decided to say nothing – after all, what was the worst that could happen?

As I waggled the floppy gear lever, trying to discover where first gear was, Clint said to me, 'We're gonna go straight for a take on this – so, when we're rollin', maintain your speed at around twenty miles an hour, make sure you stay about ten yards behind the camera car, and keep goin' straight along the track.' To our right, the camera car was sitting on a smooth tarmac road that ran parallel to our jungle path. 'All set?' he called to the cameraman and got a thumbs up in reply. 'OK, Alex – start her up.'

I turned the key in the ignition and the Land Rover lurched forward and stalled – the bloody thing had been left in gear. Hauling the gear lever back to neutral, I turned the ignition key again. *Wowowowowow* went the engine. I turned it again.

Wowowowowowowowow. As Clint stared at me with just a hint of concern, I pressed the accelerator and gave the key another turn. *Wowowowowowo-rrroooooooaaaarrrrr!* Thank God, the engine fired up. Relieved, I pressed the clutch and tried to manipulate the gear lever. *Grrrrrrrrrraaarrr* went the gearbox. I tried again. *Grrrrrrrrrraaarrraaaaarrrr.* 'Oh God,' I silently prayed. 'Please, please just get into bloody gear.' *Grrrrraarrrrr – kachunk* went the cogs as they finally meshed. 'ACTION' called Clint, and as the camera car started to pull away, I revved up the engine and released the clutch. Picture my surprise when the car took a mighty leap backwards: in my panic I had selected reverse by mistake. 'OK,' said Clint testily. 'Everybody back to first positions.' The camera car went back to its starting point and the assistant cameraman held up the clapperboard with 'TAKE 2' written on it. Nervously, I turned the key and offered up a silent prayer. *Wowowowowowoworrrrrooooaaaarrrrr.* OK, engine fired up, now, carefully slip the gear lever into first. *Grrrrraaarrrrr – kachunk!* Somebody up there must have had heard my plea – we were in gear. Clint called 'action' again and I gently increased the revs while slowly slipping the clutch. To my relief the Landy began to move slowly forwards. When the speedometer hit twenty, Clint turned around in his seat and started his dialogue with Jeff Fahey. Despite my worrying lack of forward vision, I managed to keep the car at speed, on the track and at the right distance behind the camera car while acting like driving through the jungle was something I did on a daily basis. As I started to relax, something – I couldn't tell what because of the spare wheel, but *something* – in the distance caught my eye. As we drew closer, I could see there was a fallen tree branch lying across the track. Clint and Jeff were still in the middle of the dialogue, so I couldn't just stop. Instead I turned the steering wheel and drove around the obstruction.

'Hold it,' said Clint. 'Cut!' I stopped the car. 'What are you doing?' he said angrily. 'I told you to go straight!'

'I – I couldn't,' I stammered. 'There was a big log lying across the—'

'Just keep goin' straight ahead,' Clint snapped. 'Goddamn it! Now we gotta go again.'

'Right, everyone,' shouted Mr No Worries, the assistant director. 'Back to first positions please.'

'Never mind goin' back to first position,' said Clint. 'We'll just carry on from here.' Once again the clapperboard clacked, once again Clint called 'action', once again the engine misfired and once again the gears whined and crunched as I manipulated the gear lever into first and pulled away (thankfully) in the right direction. As we reached twenty miles per hour, all seemed to be going well. Clint and Jeff started their dialogue again as I kept one eye on the speedo and the other on the track, while maintaining my distance behind the camera car. Halfway through the scene, my heart missed a beat. Again, I glimpsed something ahead – about a hundred yards away, a dark shadow lay across the track – what it was I couldn't tell. I had to make a rapid decision. Bearing in mind Clint's ire when I went off route on the previous take, I decided to do what I had been instructed and keep going straight. The moment we reached the shadow, I knew I had made the wrong choice – the damn thing was a ditch about two feet deep and three feet wide. There was nothing I could do – the Landy plunged down one side and bounced up the other. I looked to my left to see Clint sprawled halfway out of the car, the soles of his boots level with my head, and his hands scrabbling frantically at the door pillars in a desperate effort to stop himself being pitched on to the track, while a glance in my rear-view mirror showed Jeff Fahey's khaki-clad backside as it disappeared over the tailgate.

I drew to a halt and Clint hauled himself back into the car. He was shaking, his face a mask of shock and fury. 'What the *fuck* did you do that for?' he roared. 'You coulda killed me – can't you do anything as simple as drive a goddamn car?'

With a vivid picture in my mind of a sorrowful wee Glaswegian travelling home on the first available plane, I knew I had nothing to lose by staying silent. 'Don't fucking blame me!' I yelled. 'I asked for a practice run in the fucking thing and didn't get one – and somebody should have scouted this fucking track before I drove along it. You told me to go straight on, so I went straight on – what the hell else was I supposed to do?' The crew held their breath as Clint fixed me with the same narrow-eyed squint that made his name in Sergio Leone's *A Fistful of Dollars*.

'OK,' he growled, 'let's get back to first positions.' And glaring at Mr No Worries, he added, 'And somebody get this goddamn track checked right now.'

Much to my relief, I didn't get sacked that day. My guess is that as a movie star Clint wasn't used to being bowfed at by some two-bit supporting player, but as someone who had worked his way up to international stardom from his first role in *Revenge of the Creature* (one of the Z-grade movies I remember watching in the mid fifties at the local fleapit in Pollokshaws), he respected a fellow actor who had the balls to stand up for himself.

I don't know whether the fates were testing Clint's mettle, but that wasn't the only time he almost came a cropper during the shoot. While he was filming a scene on the Liwunga River aboard the purpose-built steam launch that doubled for the *African Queen*, Bogart's boat in the original John Huston film, its diesel engine unexpectedly packed up. Clint used his hand-held transmitter to call for assistance from the support vessel, only to find that its two crewmen, who were supposed to stay within range of Clint's boat at all times, had taken an unscheduled break and couldn't be contacted. With Clint yelling impotently into his walkie-talkie, the film crew watched in horror as the *African Queen* began drifting downstream to where, a few hundred yards further on, the Liwunga plummeted over the edge of the mighty Victoria Falls. Fortunately, the skipper of a tourist boat, alerted by Clint's frantic waving and shouting, realised something was seriously amiss and towed the *African Queen* to safety. Knowing how irate Clint was after our near disaster, I'm glad I wasn't around when he got hold of the pair of idiots from the safety boat . . .

Clint wasn't the only one who had a close call during the shoot. One evening, after a long, hot day on location, Alun Armstrong,

Tim Spall and I made a beeline for the hotel's palm-fringed bar at the edge of the swimming pool. My tongue was hanging out as I stood in the welcoming shade, waiting for the barman to pour me a glass of ice-cold lager. As I took my first delicious sip, I felt something wriggle on my tongue. Tim Spall must have got the surprise of his life when I sprayed a fountain of lager over his shirt. I looked down in time to see a small black spider with tiny red dots scuttle away across the tiles and vanish into the undergrowth, seemingly none the worse for its ordeal. I learned later just how lucky I had been as, despite its tiny size, the African button spider is one of the most deadly in the entire continent and if it had bitten me, I would probably have choked to death on my massively swollen tongue, long before its venom stopped my heart beating.

Eleanor David, who I had worked with in *Comfort and Joy*, played Dorshka, my wife. Since our filming schedules were more or less identical, we found we both had an upcoming weekend free, so we decided to have a splurge and charter a small plane to fly us to Bumi Hills, a five-star safari lodge on the far side of Lake Kariba. After asking around, I managed to get a good deal from a local pilot while Eleanor managed to negotiate a healthy discount on the lodge's standard rate. The place was beautiful beyond words. Our rooms had balconies that overlooked a waterhole, where at dusk the animals gathered to drink from the life-giving spring. That evening, as we sat in the dining room, toasting our good fortune with vintage champagne, the head waiter came over to say there was an urgent phone call from the production office asking if they could speak to us right away. We both guessed what the call was about, and we were right – they wanted us back on set the following morning. Apparently the scene Eleanor and I had filmed a couple of days before would have to be reshot due to a technical problem, and that was the only time they could fit it in to the schedule. 'How will we get back?' I asked. 'Our return flight isn't until Monday.'

'Don't worry,' said the PA. 'We'll send someone to pick you both up tomorrow morning.'

Oh well, no point in moaning – it would have been nice to stay a few more nights and join one of the wildlife safaris that left at dawn each morning, but since the film was the reason we were in Africa in the first place, business would have to come before pleasure.

The following morning, as Eleanor and I ate our breakfast at a table overlooking the lodge's sweeping front lawn, we became aware of a distant thrumming sound. A few minutes later the flowers were being blown off the tables of the astonished guests as a helicopter set down on the front lawn. Picking up our luggage, we strolled over, climbed in and, like a couple of Royals, waved graciously to our fellow guests as we lifted off and disappeared over the sun-tipped treetops. As far as perfect moments go, that was certainly one of them – the only time in my life I can honestly say I knew what it felt like to be a genuine movie star.

Despite the excitement of working on an exotic location in a big-budget Hollywood movie, when I finished my scenes in Zimbabwe I was glad to get back to London again – after several years of trying to start a family with no result, Sally and I were about to become parents. When she came to visit me on the set at Pinewood Studios, where I had a few pick-up shots to complete, Clint took a real shine to her, wishing her well with the birth and giving her 'bump' a pat for good luck. A month later, Jock, our first child made his welcome debut. Years later, he seemed really pleased when I told him Clint Eastwood had patted him on the head while he was still in the wrapper – 'At least,' I added, 'I *think* it was your head he patted . . .'

39

Midnight (Cowboy) in Moscow

Jon Voight was an actor I admired tremendously. Back in the sixties, he served his time in episodes of forgettable TV series before exploding on to the big screen as one of the most memorable characters in modern American cinema: Joe Buck, the would-be gigolo in John Schlesinger's brilliant *Midnight Cowboy*. Our paths crossed when I travelled to the USSR to work on an American TV movie called *Chernobyl: The Final Warning*. In 1986 the nuclear reactor at Chernobyl, a small town in Ukraine, went into meltdown, spewing a plume of radioactive particles high into the atmosphere. Instead of the country's usual culture of secrecy, President Gorbachev decided to implement a policy of glasnost (openness) and tell the world the truth.

The screenplay of *Final Warning* was based on the story of Dr Robert Gale, an American bone-marrow transplant specialist who was one of the millions in the USA who watched the footage of the tragedy on NBC news. He was so moved by the heroism of the local firemen who elected to stay and fight the out-of-control inferno that he immediately volunteered his services to do what he could to help the heavily irradiated survivors. Jon played Dr Gale, while I was cast as Dr Andreyev, his Soviet counterpart.

Growing up in the fifties and sixties, you couldn't be unaware of the growing tension between the planet's two major superpowers at the time. The menacing atmosphere of the Cold War, as it was known, loomed over my childhood like a distant storm cloud, growing ever larger and more threatening before reaching critical mass in October 1962 when America and the Soviet Union went head to head over Nikita Khrushchev's decision to site nuclear missiles in Cuba. A Third World War seemed inevitable, and we all held our breath as we waited for the angry cloud to burst and release an atomic deluge.

I had always been fascinated and frightened by the USSR in equal measure, even though most of what I knew about the country and its people had been gleaned from the right-wing press and newsreels that looked as though they could have been funded by a covert propaganda department in MI6 (given what we know now about the British Security Services, that might not be too far from the truth). Although I had strongly held opinions about the evils of totalitarianism, I always wondered whether I was being given an accurate picture of the Soviet way of life, and now, as I fastened my seatbelt in preparation for landing at Moscow's Sheremetyevo airport, I felt a real tingle of excitement, knowing that finally I would be able to gain a first-hand impression of the bogeyman, aka 'The Red Menace', that haunted my childhood.

My first introduction to the Soviet way of life was when I checked into my Stalinist-era hotel round the corner from Red Square. Originally built to provide luxury accommodation for visiting dignitaries and party apparatchiks, now everyone and anyone who could settle their bill in US dollars were welcomed into its cavernous marble and gilt lobby. The interpreter provided by the production company guided me through the sheaves of forms at the check-in desk, and a stout matron showed me to my room. Sorry, did I say room? What I meant was my very own mini Versailles, complete with a grand piano and a dining table that would have comfortably seated the chorus of the Bolshoi Ballet. Impressive as it was, I quickly discovered it was all for show – the piano was hopelessly out of tune, there were no cutlery, plates or glasses for the table and, despite the neo-baroque splendour of my en-suite facilities, with a tub roughly the size of the swimming baths back in

Pollokshaws and a marble wash-hand basin, there was neither towel, toilet paper nor a bath plug – and yes, in case you're wondering, I *did* check the room for hidden microphones. James Bond has a lot to answer for.

The following morning I filmed my first scene with Jon Voight in the Moscow hospital where the heroes of the Chernobyl fire brigade were treated for the effects of radiation poisoning. I know our NHS hospitals come in for some stick when they fail to meet the high standards we rightly expect of them, but this place took the biscuit – the wards were dismal and dank, and most of the staff seemed to have had a compassion bypass. In fact, the best thing you could say about Moscow's Hospital Number One was that, regardless of wealth or social standing, every patient was treated with equal disregard.

We began with the scenes where Jon and I are speaking to two of the burned firemen as they lie in their beds, isolated from air-borne infection by thick vertical drapes of clear plastic sheeting. The make-up department had really gone to town, and Vince Ricotta and Steve Hartley's faces were covered with suppurating sores, angry-looking boils and weeping radiation burns. Unlike the UK, where hospital scenes are always filmed in either a studio or a disused ward, we were filming in an active burns unit, and the patients – at least those who were well enough to leave their beds – were watching the scene from behind the camera. Vince and Steve confessed they felt a deep sense of shame knowing that, unlike the rest of the unit's residents, when the day's filming was over they could simply wash off their facial disfigurements and walk down the street without being stared at with pity or revulsion.

On my days off, I liked to walk around the city and try to get a feel for the place. It might seem strange to say, but I felt a real affinity with Moscow, whose people reminded me very much of Glaswegians – although growing up in Glasgow, I thought I had seen my fair share of drunks, but nothing like the number of respectably dressed men I saw in Moscow, clutching bottles of vodka and bouncing off walls, or lying spread-eagled on the pavement as people stepped over them without batting an eyelid.[1]

On one of my rambles, I came across a line of people queuing outside what looked like an entertainment venue. With a little help from my phrasebook, I managed to translate the Cyrillic lettering on the sign above the entrance. It read 'Variety Theatre'. The doors opened and the line began to move forward – this was an opportunity I couldn't miss. The show's leading performer was a man named Yuri Kuklachev, whose act consisted of getting a troupe of cats to do the most astonishing tricks – they walked across tightropes, performed acrobatics and, for the grand finale, one of them ran up a pole and dived head first into his upturned hat. Normally, clowns make me want to run screaming to the nearest exit, but Yuri Kuklachev was like nothing I had ever seen. At one point he walked on stage while struggling to put on a jacket. No matter how hard he tried, somehow he just couldn't manage to get it on properly – it would end up either inside out or upside down. Sleeves and pockets began to take on a life of their own until finally the whole thing became an all-out war between him and the jacket. The payoff came when, in disgust, he threw the jacket down on one end of a small see-saw, jumped on the other end and stood with his hands in the air as the jacket flew upwards, unfolded itself in mid air, and draped itself perfectly over his upstretched arms. In that moment, I understood the difference between genuine clowns and the woefully unfunny gits who used to bore me stiff at the Kelvin Hall circus each Christmas. Yuri Kuklachev is in the tradition of legendary performers like Grock and Joseph Grimaldi, and thanks to stumbling across a tiny theatre in the heart of Moscow, I learned what clowning was really all about. You can catch parts of his act on YouTube – I urge you to check it out.

---

[1] As part of his perestroika (reconstruction) policy, Gorbachev tried to clamp down on the national pastime of swilling vodka until you passed out. For most Soviet citizens this was a step too far and played a major part in his swift fall from grace.

Dining out in Moscow was a novel experience. I discovered there were two types of restaurant – the massive, state-owned restaurants where the prices were laughably cheap but the food and service was bloody awful, and the recently sanctioned private bistros where the food was decent but the prices, although still low by Western standards, were way beyond the reach of most Muscovites. It was such a palaver to book tables in the private bistros that most nights the cast ate in one of the big state-run restaurants, where there were usually no more than a few dozen people at most gathered in the cheerless atmosphere, swilling vodka, making endless toasts and chewing on the lumps of lukewarm gristle that passed for beef stroganoff. Yet despite the scarcity of patrons, every time we would ask the maître d' for a table, the answer was always a none-too-friendly, 'Nyet – fully booked.' We soon discovered the trick was to simply stand there and wait, until eventually we would be grudgingly seated at one of the hundred or so empty tables. A standing joke among the cast was to walk up to a maître d' and say, 'Good evening, I'd like a long, blank stare please.'

Before we set off for Kurchatov, the town whose nuclear reactor was the double for the one at Chernobyl, I had one final scene left to shoot – a long two-hander in the back of a limousine, with Jon Voight and myself discussing medical procedures. All of Moscow's main roads had a centre lane reserved solely for government vehicles, with a watchtower at the corner of every junction. When the traffic guard got the word that an official car was approaching, he pressed a button that instantly turned the traffic lights green, allowing party bigwigs to speed through the city without the bothersome nuisance of having to stop at a red light like the rest of their comrades. We had been filming for an hour or so in this private lane when, in the middle of one of the long takes, our driver suddenly veered to one side and stamped on the brakes, causing momentary chaos as cars and lorries swerved around us, angrily blowing their horns. Jon and I were pitched forward in our seats while the cameraman was sent sprawling on to the floor. 'Sorry. Sorry,' said our driver. Pointing to his earpiece, he said, 'Government car coming – I have order to let pass.' I turned around to see a sleek black stretch Mercedes travelling towards us in the centre lane. It slowed down momentarily as it passed, and Jon and I peered into its rear windows, curious to see who was important enough to have ruined a perfectly good take. There, staring back at us with equal curiosity, were the sombre faces of Mikhail Gorbachev and his soon-to-be successor, Boris Yeltsin.

I discovered that Jon and I were both passionate about ecology – in particular, the growing threat to the planet's endangered species. One day, when we broke for lunch, we were taken to one of Moscow's privately owned restaurants – a homely little bistro specialising in traditional cooking from the Caspian region. The first course was a plate of what looked like cured fish, thickly sliced and served with a sweet, mayonnaise-type sauce. Although it was a little too chewy and oily for my liking, it was tasty enough.

'That wasn't bad,' Jon said to me as the waitress was clearing our plates. 'What do you think it was?'

'Some sort of smoked salmon?' I guessed.

Jon wasn't convinced and asked our interpreter what we had just eaten. Our green credentials went straight out the window when we discovered we had just polished off two hearty servings of whale.[2]

After a white-knuckle ride on one of Aeroflot's decrepit planes, we landed at Kursk – a town about four hundred miles south of Moscow and site of the greatest tank battle of the Second World War. From Kursk we were taken by minibus to Kurchatov, our location for all the Chernobyl scenes. Named in honour of the nuclear physicist who had designed and built the USSR's first atomic bomb, Kurchatov had been constructed to house the workforce of the nuclear reactor that dominated the town's skyline. As we bumped along the potholed road that led to our hotel, my heart sank: there were no signs of life on the drab streets, no shops

---

[2] Whenever I tell anyone that story, they invariably ask me what whale meat tastes like. I love to watch their delayed reaction when I tell them it's a bit like dolphin . . .

THERE'S BEEN A LIFE!

that I could see, no bars, restaurants, cinemas or friendly cafés – just row after row of ugly, unloved breezeblock apartments. I began to suspect I was in an episode of *The Twilight Zone* and was being taken to the place where the souls of the damned spend eternity. By the end of my first week there, I was convinced I had stumbled on the truth. If you want to know how badly I was affected by the soul-sapping bleakness of Kurchatov, you should see the photo of me splashing around in the local lake, brandishing a half-empty bottle of vodka and grinning inanely at the camera with a slightly glazed look in my eyes. Although the weather was a little on the chilly side that day, the water was pleasingly warm – hardly surprising, I suppose, since it had come straight from cooling the uranium fuel rods in the reactor chamber! But by that point I was past the stage of caring – any distraction was welcome, and to hell with the consequences. As Bill Paterson said when I showed him the photo, 'By God, you must have been positively glowing with health after that swim.'

When my final day of filming was over, I couldn't get to the airport at Kursk quick enough. As I was about to board the Moscow flight, Pavel, the young interpreter whose duty was to shepherd me back to Moscow and see me safely on to the BA flight to London, said the captain had invited us to sit in the cockpit with the flight crew. I did briefly wonder why they would have made such an unusual offer, but as a diversion it certainly beat a drunken dip in the reactor lake, so I jumped at the chance. Once we were underway, I realised why I had been invited to the cockpit – the crew wanted to quiz me about how much a pilot or a navigator might earn in the West. Of course I had no idea what flight personnel earned, but I said it was probably sixty-odd thousand a year. As Pavel translated my answer, the plane gave a lurch as the captain involuntarily yanked the wheel in shock. The three of them began talking excitedly among themselves while Pavel told me about how, under the communist system, highly qualified personnel such as anaesthetists, architects and airline pilots were paid not much more than bin men or street sweepers, with the result that, with no financial incentive to spur them on, droves of skilled professionals had quit the long hours and stressful working conditions of their former vocations for jobs as subway guards or bus conductors. I glanced nervously back at the pilot and his crew, who were still murmuring to each other, and wondered if they were working out whether they had enough fuel on board to make it to Helsinki.

During the shoot, I had become good friends with Yuri Petrov, one of the Russian cast who, as well as being an accomplished actor was also a presenter on Moscow Television's news channel. One evening, at a get together in the hotel bar, someone mentioned a story they had seen on the BBC news about a Soviet Mars probe that had mysteriously vanished. Apparently the Russian government had imposed an information embargo, and scientists in the West were in the dark as to what could have happened to it. Yuri said he had been in the newsroom when the story came in.

'Why was it such a big secret?' I asked.

'Because of the final images sent back by the probe,' he said. 'One showed what looked like the outline of a city – a grid system, clearly not a natural formation. Another looked like some sort of sculpture.'

'And you saw these pictures?' I asked.

'Oh yes,' he answered. 'The last image the probe transmitted before contact was lost showed a huge circular shadow on the planet's surface, then *pfhhttt*! No more pictures, no more probe – the cosmologists had no rational explanation for what might have cast the shadow; they could only say it was something that should not have been there.'

'We're not talking about a UFO here, are we, Yuri?' I asked incredulously.

Putting his finger to his lips in the universal 'I shouldn't be telling you this, so keep it to yourself' sign, he said the Soviet Air Ministry firmly believed in the existence of UFOs, to the extent of providing all military and civilian flight crews with special forms for the purpose of recording any sightings. He said that the process of filing a report was so complex and time-consuming that most pilots simply kept quiet and said nothing about any 'close encounters' they might have experienced.

Yuri's extraordinary revelations came into my mind as I sat with the three airmen in the Aeroflot plane's cramped cockpit. I knew I would never have an opportunity like this again, and decided it was worth risking ridicule to discover if the truth actually *was* out there. Through Pavel, I asked if any of them had ever seen a UFO. As Pavel translated my question, the co-pilot and the navigator both looked towards the captain, who hesitated for a moment before telling me that while on a routine flight, a massive, disc-shaped craft had appeared above his cockpit window, keeping pace with the plane for several minutes before banking sharply and vanishing over the horizon at lightning speed. He said that because the mystery craft had been tracked by a ground-based radar station, he had no option but to go through the laborious process of filing an official report. Even though I could tell he was really uncomfortable about disclosing the story, I thought it might have been a leg-pull, and told him so. He said something to the navigator, who reached into his flight case and showed me the official Air Ministry form that was to be completed in the event of a sighting. Even though it was in Russian and for all I knew might have been his granny's recipe for making vodka out of old potato peelings, there was no mistaking the depictions of UFOs, from the classic disc shape to sinister-looking black triangles with clusters of lights at their centre. I've been a lifelong sceptic about all that 'flying saucer' stuff, but after speaking with both Yuri and the Aeroflot pilot, I ain't so sure no more.

During my stay in the USSR, I had developed a wee bit of a taste for caviar. It was cheap as chips, but considerably tastier, so before I headed out to the airport, I had a quiet word with the hotel's Maître d', with the result that for eighty quid in cash I left with a dozen large jars of Beluga caviar that would have cost a small fortune back in London. Naively, I had no idea that taking caviar, particularly black-market caviar, out of the country was a criminal offence, and that if the stony-faced customs officials at Sheremetyevo airport had opened my suitcase, this chapter would probably have been written on a roll of shiny toilet paper during a lengthy sojourn in Lubyanka jail.

As I flew thankfully homeward, I reflected on the unique opportunity I had been given to experience life in Russia at the tail end of the communist era. Any youthful notions I might have had about communism as the answer to the ills of mankind were dispelled forever: I had seen how the Soviet system perpetuated the same old system of haves and have-nots, and after witnessing the soul-sapping misery of life there, I swore to myself that I would never again complain about bad service or moan about the trivialities we in the West feel constantly bothered by. As my granny used to say, 'Ye don't know ye're born.'

40

The Moore of Venice

Bill Paterson rang me one morning. 'Are you listening to Radio Four at the moment?' he asked.

'No I'm not,' I answered. 'Why?'

'Because Dudley Moore's being interviewed about that film you did with him and he's just said you're the funniest actor he's ever worked with.'

The offer of a part in *Blame It on the Bellboy* came out of the blue – no interview, no screen test, just a straight offer from the film's writer/director, Mark Herman. I loved the script, and even though the part of Alfio, one of the Mafia boss's two henchmen (Jim Carter, in pre-*Downton Abbey* days, was the other) wasn't all that big, it meant I would be spending six weeks in Venice, working with a cast that included Dudley Moore, Bryan Brown, Richard Griffiths, Patsy Kensit and Alison Steadman.

On my first visit to the city, I had stayed at a tiny *pensione* in a narrow back street, courtesy of Arthur Frommer's *Europe on $10 a day*, an indispensible guidebook for the seriously skint. Now, courtesy of the film company, I was occupying a suite in one of the city's grandest hotels.

To explain the plot of *Bellboy* would take far too much time – suffice it to say that mistaken identities lead to misunderstandings and mayhem as the main protagonists dash round Venice at the gallop, getting their wires crossed in their efforts to achieve their individual aims. Dudley was Melvyn Orton, a mild-mannered clerk from London; Bryan Brown was Mike Lawton, a professional hitman; and Richard Griffiths was Maurice Horton, a North Country mayor who, unknown to his wife Rosemary, played by Alison Steadman, has booked a holiday through a dating company in hopes of some illicit nookie. Throw in Bronson Pinchot as the eponymous bellboy who, due to his almost impenetrable Italian accent, manages to mix up the names Lawton, Orton and Horton, and you have all the ingredients of a classic farce.

To say *Bellboy* was a dream job would be an understatement. I had an instant rapport with Dudley, a performer I had admired hugely since his *Not Only, But Also* days with the great Peter Cook. Under the job description of 'personal make-up assistant', Dudley had brought along his then-wife, Brogan Lane – a big Californian gal who was so tall that whenever she and Dudley strolled arm in arm it looked like she had him under arrest. Since most of my scenes were with him, I had the great fortune to spend a lot of time in his company. Over the course of my career I've worked with some professional funny men who, when the cameras stop turning, are anything but. Dudley, I was delighted to discover, wasn't one of them. He was warm, open and extremely generous, on one occasion treating Jim Carter and me to a dinner at the Cipriani Hotel that must have cost at least a combined week's wages for the two of us. He spoke candidly about his days at Cambridge University, where he joined the famous Footlights Company. When I asked him what it was like to work with the brilliant cast of *Beyond the Fringe*, the sixties revue show that changed the face of British comedy forever, he surprised me by saying that he had always felt like the idiot son of the family. Because of his precocious skill as a keyboard player, he had got into Cambridge through the back door on an organ scholarship, while his contemporaries like Peter Cook, Jonathan Miller and Alan Bennett were there because of their academic brilliance.

Like me, Dudley loved a good rude joke – and like me, the ruder the better. An image that will stay with me always is the day we spent filming in the grounds of a millionaire's villa on the Venetian lagoon. We had broken for lunch and were sitting around on the lawn when Dudley asked me to tell the others a joke I had told him the day before. Now, I'm sure most of you have had at least one time when you tell the right joke, at the right moment, in the right company, and it goes down a storm – well, never in my life has any joke I've ever told had the same effect as that particular one on that particular afternoon. The joke in question was about ... well, should I repeat it at the risk of offending any of my more sensitive readers who have stuck with the book so far? What was that? Did I hear a resounding YES? Oh well, all right then, but only for the purpose of illustrating what happened when I told it on that afternoon. Readers of a sensitive nature should probably skip the following paragraph.

A little specky guy is convicted of some minor fraud and sentenced to six months in jail. As the cell door clangs shut behind him, he stands there and looks around at the graffiti-covered walls. Blinking in the dim light from the small barred window he sees there are two bunk beds in the cell; the bottom one is empty, while the top one is occupied by a huge, sweaty, shaven-headed hulk covered in tattoos.

'Hello,' he growls.

'Hello.'

'I'm your cell mate.'

'Very pleased to meet you,' the little chap replies politely.

'Do you like games?'

'Er, yes, I'm quite fond of a hand or two of cribbage or the occasional rubber of bridge.'

'We're gonna play a game.'

'Oh, are we?'

'Yeah. We're gonna play a game called Mummies and Daddies.'

'Oh dear,' gulps the little fellow, 'I thought it might be something like that. And who will you be?'

'I'll be Mummy.'

'Mummy?'

'Yeah, Mummy.'

'I see. And I'll be . . .'

'You'll be Daddy.'

'Daddy, yes, yes of course. So, er, what is it exactly that I have to do?'

'Come over 'ere and suck Mummy's cock.'

The place erupted. Dudley, even though he had already heard the joke, was screaming with laughter. Bryan Brown had crumpled to his knees and was making weird whooping noises, his face a shade of maroon normally reserved for heart attack victims. Richard Griffiths bellowed like a bull moose and shook so violently with laughter that the wooden garden swing he was sitting on broke, sending him sprawling on the grass, which on its own would have been enough to increase the general level of hilarity, but as his ample backside hit the lawn, he let out the loudest fart you've ever heard. I'm afraid it's completely outwith my powers of description to describe the hysteria that ensued. As poor Richard struggled in vain to salvage what was left of his dignity, Dudley lay curled in a foetal ball, heels drumming on the gravel and sounding like a hyena with the whooping cough. Bryan, meanwhile, seemed to have lost control of his motor functions as he convulsed helplessly, his eyes bulging from their sockets and the tendons on his neck standing out like something from the transformation scene in a werewolf movie, while the pitch and volume of Patsy Kensit's shrieks must have shattered most of the day's output at the nearby Murano glass factory.

It was during the final week of the shoot that I had one of life's perfect moments. We were filming some scenes in what was supposed to be the big Mafia boss's headquarters. In reality the house was a seventeenth-century palazzo on the banks of the Grand Canal that now served as a music conservatory. Over lunch, I had been telling Dudley how I had wanted to learn the piano when I was a kid, and how much I enjoyed listening to classical music. 'Do you like Bach?' he asked. I told him my knowledge of Bach was a bit limited, but I loved the few airs I was familiar with.

'Want to hear a couple of his piano pieces?' he asked.

'Sure,' I said.

He led me to a small chamber on the top floor of the palazzo where a beautiful grand piano took up most of the space, and I spent the next thirty minutes or so listening entranced as Dudley played selections from 'The Well-Tempered Clavier' while the sunlight, reflecting from the ripples on the Grand Canal, sparkled and danced across the room's ancient frescoes. Believe me, perfect moments don't get much more perfect than that.

Between takes one day, we were talking about his well-documented relationships with some of the most glamorous women on the planet. I nearly fell off my chair when he told me about how his ex-wife, the sixties movie star Tuesday Weld, had once been proposed to by Freddie March the Third, grandson of the 1930s film star Fredric March. He said she turned poor Freddie down when she realised that if she said yes, she would become Tuesday March the Third. The conversation moved on to his breakthrough film *Arthur*. When I told him how good I thought his 'drunk' performance was, he said, 'I'll tell you where I got that from – have you ever heard of Jack Radcliffe?' Had I heard of him? Jack Radcliffe had been one of Scotland's biggest variety stars of the forties and fifties, famous for his brilliant characterisation of a Glasgow drunk. I told Dudley I had never seen him on stage, but I had worked with Nellie Norman, his one-time comic feed. Dudley said that as a youngster he had spent many summer holidays staying with relatives in Glasgow who would often take him to the variety theatre, and it was Jack Radcliffe's 'drunk' at the Alhambra that inspired his performance in *Arthur*. Jack Radcliffe inspiring an Oscar-nominated performance in a big Hollywood movie – who would have guessed it?

When *Bellboy*'s interior scenes were being shot at Shepperton Studios, Sally called to say that our second child, who wasn't supposed to be due until the week after filming had finished, had decided to jump the gun and make a surprise appearance. Thankfully, the production company gave me a day off and I was able to be at the birth of my new baby boy, who was absolutely adorable and couldn't have been more welcome. I wanted to name him Roddy, after Roddy McMillan, but when I thought of him going through his schooldays being called 'Rod' or, worse, 'Rodders' (after Nicholas Lyndhurst's character in *Only Fools And Horses*), I named him Rory after two of my boyhood heroes: 'Red Rory of the Eagles' from the pages of *The Dandy*, and Rory McEwen, a handsome and charismatic troubadour from the early days of the Scottish folk music revival. Great lineage, if a bit of a challenge to live up to . . .

At its London premiere, Mark Herman, the film's writer and director, told me the producers had previewed *Bellboy* in a handful of cinemas in the American Midwest, with audience members being asked to fill in a form saying what they thought about it. He said the best response he got was in reply to the question 'What was your favourite moment in the film?' Referring to the scene where Richard Griffiths beds Patsy Kensit, a member of the preview audience had written: 'When the fat fuck fucked the bitch!'

Although Dudley seemed pleased to see me at the party after the premiere, I could tell he wasn't in the greatest of spirits. His one time partner Peter Cook was at the far end of the room, and I asked Dudley what he had thought of the film. 'I've no idea,' he answered. 'Peter hasn't said a word to me all evening.' He told me he loved Peter Cook and had always considered him a true comic genius, but since Dudley's meteoric rise to stardom, Peter, who thought he should have been the big Hollywood star, had become so embittered by Dudley's success that he couldn't bring himself to speak to the man he had known and worked with since the early sixties. A successful double act is not unlike a successful marriage, but if one partner seeks to be free from the other, love can turn to hatred in the blink of an eye.

The night of *Bellboy*'s premiere turned out to be the last time Dudley and I would meet. My heart sank when, some years later, I read that he had been sacked from a Barbra Streisand film for being drunk on the set. His 'drunkenness' turned out to be the early signs of progressive supranuclear palsy, a degenerative disease that would take his life within a few years. Apparently his final words were, 'I can hear the music all around me.'

One of my life's greatest privileges is to have known Dudley Moore – he was the funniest, warmest, most generous and brilliant man I've ever met, and when my thoughts drift back to a sun-dappled afternoon in a Venetian palazzo, I too can hear the music all around me.

41

Biting the Bullet

I guessed, since Harrison Ford had been signed to play Jack Ryan, that the film of Tom Clancy's novel about a CIA operative inadvertently caught up in an IRA attempt to assassinate members of the Royal Family would be something of a box office hit. I wasn't far wrong – on its release in 1992, *Patriot Games* proved to be one of the highest-grossing movies of the year.

The part I had been offered was Dennis Cooley, a dealer in rare books whose bland exterior masked a dark secret. Normally, I would have bought Clancy's novel in order to acquaint myself with the character, but when I read the screenplay I felt there was more than enough there for me to slip into Mr Cooley's skin without hampering myself with too much excess baggage. I based my concept of him on a composite of several people I had come across over the years, the principal one being an Irish chat show host I had met in Dublin when I was one of his interviewees. Although he was friendly enough, there was something a bit prim and proper about his manner that I found interesting, sensing that beneath the professional persona there was an alter ego being kept tightly under wraps, so I used my observations to try to convey a sense of something hidden beneath Cooley's neat, fussy exterior.

I had completed the scenes at Piccadilly's elegant Burlington Arcade, where Cooley flees for his life after realising his cover has been blown.[1] The interior scenes were to be filmed at Pinewood Studios, where, a few weeks later, I tiptoed into the vast, unlit soundstage to familiarise myself with the set before the crew arrived. As I stood in the heart of Cooley's shop, a voice from the shadows said, 'Sorry to interrupt, Alex, I just wanted to say I saw a rough cut of your scenes last week – they look terrific. Well done, you're doin' a great job.' I wish I had some good tales to tell you about working with Harrison Ford, but in truth that was the one and only time our paths crossed during the entire shoot. Still, no' bad gettin' a wee pat on the back fae Indiana Jones, eh?

My final scenes involved a trip to LA. Sally was keen to visit Hollywood and the production office at Warner Brothers generously agreed to swap my first-class air ticket for four coach-class returns (since our two sons were only toddlers at the time, we brought them along too). When the studio limo picked us all up from the airport and chauffeured us to our swanky hotel on the seafront at LA's Venice Beach, I realised that going back to Hollywood as a featured player was a whole lot different from the time before, when I was a complete unknown.

The scenes where Cooley comes to a sticky end were to be shot in southern California, so Sally and the boys stayed on in LA while I joined my fellow actors on a private jet bound for the dune-covered National Park near the Mexican border that would stand in for the Libyan Desert. During the shoot, one of the studio execs invited a few of us to join him at a Mexican restaurant for dinner one night, and as the tequila cocktails flowed, so did his endless fund of tales about life in the Hollywood movie business. One of my favourites was about *The Hunt for Red October*, another Tom Clancy story Paramount had produced some years previously. Largely set on board a Soviet nuclear submarine, it starred Sean Connery as

---

[1] Those of you who like to spot movie 'bloopers' may have noticed that when Cooley flees to the nearest tube station after realising his cover has been blown, instead of dashing round the corner to nearby Green Park, he crashes through the barriers of Aldwych station, a good half-mile away. The reason being that Aldwych station is closed at the weekends, making it an ideal location for film companies.

Captain Marko Ramius. According to our host, part of Connery's contract included 'rushes approval', meaning that he had the final say on which of his scenes' takes were chosen for inclusion in the finished film. He said he was sitting with Connery at the back of the studio's screening room, watching the scene that introduces Captain Ramius. It was a long Steadicam shot that travelled the entire length of the submarine before finishing on a huge close-up of Connery as he looks up from his navigational charts and gives the order to set sail. After watching the first take, Connery gave an approving nod. At the end of the second take he said quietly, 'That's the one.' After the third take, he made a so-so gesture. From the front of the screening room, the film's director John McTiernan called back, 'We'll use take three.' At this, Connery's impressive eyebrows shot up. 'Take two was the one,' he said tersely.

'Yes,' said the director, 'but if you notice on take two, just before the camera enters your cabin there's a little bit of a bump, so we'll go with take three.'

Connery leapt to his feet. 'Fuck yer bump!' he roared. Pointing to his face, he said, 'This is what they're paying to look at, no' yer fuckin' bump – we'll go with take two!'

The other story I got that evening was about the Soviet trade delegation who were visiting Los Angeles shortly before principal photography on *Red October* was due to start. Apart from the obligatory trip to Disneyland (apparently every visiting Soviet delegation insisted on a trip to Uncle Walt's Magic Kingdom), Paramount gave the party a guided tour of their studios, the high-light being a look at the multi-million-dollar submarine set they had just finished building. The party were spellbound as the film's producer, Mace Neufeld, proudly ushered them into the soundstage where the full-size submarine sat on top of the massive hydraulic pistons that would enable it to be tilted in all directions. The group leader's look of awe changed to one of puzzlement, however, when he climbed inside and took a closer look at one of the signs that were screwed to the sub's interior bulkheads. 'What does this say?' he asked Mace.

'It says "Emergency Alarm",' said Mace, slightly bewildered by the fact that the man seemed incapable of understanding his own language.

'No it does not,' he said. 'I do not know what it says, but I assure you it most certainly does not say "Emergency Alarm".'

It was when he inspected the rest of the signs that the penny finally dropped. In order to make the set as authentic as possible, Mace had hired a translator who advertised himself as a specialist in Russian technical terminology. For a hefty fee, he provided Mace with a Russian translation of all the signage likely to be found on board a Soviet sub. At huge cost, Mace had then commissioned a leading Hollywood prop company to have all the signage fabricated in brass and steel. It wasn't until the visit of the Soviet delegate that Mace realised the so-called specialist in Russian technical terminology was a con artist who had simply written the signs in English before substituting each letter with its Cyrillic equivalent, so a notice such as 'EMERGENCY ALARM' was rendered as 'ЕМЕРЪЕСНЦ АЛАРМ' – and since the actual Russian term for emergency alarm is аварийный тревояа, the exquisitely engraved sign made no linguistic sense whatsoever. Here's the kicker, though – when Mace refused to pay the balance of the scammer's fee, he had the barefaced cheek to threaten to sue for breach of contract. In a terse response, Mace employed the same letter-for-letter substitution the phony linguist had employed. It read: 'Го фнд юоусефл! Can you work it out? Here's a hint: the first word is "go" and the last word is "yourself".'

In my final scene, Sean Bean's character realises Cooley has become a liability and cold-bloodedly executes him. However, on the day we were due to film the scene the director, Phillip Noyce, clandestinely shot an alternative version. Apparently the studio heads wanted Cooley to remain alive, while Phillip was adamant that Sean should put a bullet through Cooley's head before making his escape. Although Phillip finally won the toss during the film's editing stage, the reason you don't actually see Cooley taking the hit onscreen was that the studio had refused to provide the SFX prosthetics and exploding blood bags required to simulate a bullet strike in the forehead. If you watch my death scene in the film, you'll see Sean Bean raise his gun and point it towards the camera. Then there's a quick shot of Cooley's startled face before the camera cuts back to the gun as Sean calmly pulls the trigger. Off camera, there's a muffled 'uuurrgghh', followed by a 'whump' as Cooley bites the dust: not one of the most memorable death scenes an actor could wish for – especially after all the practice I put in playing at 'best fall' when I was a kid . . .

42

Argie Bargy

I thought Aeroflot was probably the world's least passenger-friendly airline until the day I boarded an RAF plane at Brize Norton airfield. It was 1992, and I was bound for the Falkland Islands to make *An Ungentlemanly Act*, a BBC drama about the Argentinian invasion ten years earlier. Other than our cast and crew, the big 737 was virtually empty, but when I asked the stewardess, who could have won money in a Rosa Klebb look-alike contest, if I could take one of the vacant rows in the centre, she barked at me to sit in the seat that had been assigned to me. Even as a civilian, I had a notion that disobeying her order would have been a very bad idea. The plane was, to say the least, spartan – no booze trolley, no duty-free gifts and no in-flight entertainment of any kind. The one magical moment that made the whole bum-numbing experience worthwhile was as we approached Falklands airspace, and a pair of fighter jets suddenly appeared on either side of the plane, flying so close you could see the pilots' faces. As we began our final descent, we all gave a spontaneous cheer as, with an ear-splitting roar, both jets veered off in perfect sync. It was one of the most thrilling sights I'd ever seen, and a memorable welcome to one of the British Empire's last remaining outposts.

I had my first inkling of just how peculiar life in the Falklands was as we travelled across the stark, treeless camp[1] from RAF Mount Pleasant to Port Stanley. You could be forgiven for thinking you were in one of the more remote Hebridean islands if it weren't for the long stretches of tape bearing the word 'DANGER' in large letters, along with images of skulls and crossbones. These, we learned from our driver, were the areas of the camp that hadn't yet been cleared of explosives. When I asked about the herds of sheep that were still happily grazing in the danger zones, he told me they were used as bomb detectors, and every time another one went bang, it meant one less Argie landmine to worry about.

If I thought my first glimpse of life in the Falklands was odd, I soon realised that exploding sheep was the very least of it. In *An Ungentlemanly Act* I played Ronnie Lamb, the Scots-born Chief of Police at the time of the Argentinian invasion. Inspector Lamb had retired to Drumnadrochit some years before, but his old police station in Port Stanley was still in daily use. Attached to the back of it, like the Sheriff's office in an old cowboy movie, was the town jail, which was home to Port Stanley's only prisoner – Kevin, a New Zealander with a missing leg. It seemed Kevin got drunk one night and stole a yacht and, with little or no knowledge of seamanship, headed off into the wild blue yonder. Somewhere off the Falklands he found himself caught in a raging storm and managed to fire off a couple of flares. The local coastguard came to his rescue and towed him back to Port Stanley, where he was promptly arrested, tried and sentenced to seven years in jail for piracy. However, this being the Falkland Islands, nothing was quite as it seemed at first glance. The islands' entire police force consisted of just three cops, and if they were ever called out at the same time, Kevin the one-legged pirate cheerfully manned the station until they got back.

Since the war, the camaraderie between the British occupational force and the locals was somewhat strained, to say the least, and

---

[1] An abbreviation of 'campo', the Argentinian word for countryside. Don't forget that a century before Thatcher's war, Argentina was defending the islands against a British invasion . . .

one of the stories I heard that summed up the relationship was about the young officer who overheard his men referring to the male islanders as 'Bennys'. When he asked the meaning of the nickname, he was told it was because most of the locals wore knitted bobble-hats like Benny, a character from the then popular soap opera *Crossroads* and, like Benny, they were all as thick as pigshit. The young officer was outraged and lectured his men on the importance of maintaining good relations with the islanders, telling them that from then on, anyone calling them Bennys would be dealt with severely. Some weeks later, he overheard one of his squaddies referring to the civilians as 'stills'. Puzzled, he asked why on earth he called them stills. 'Because they're still Bennys, Sir,' he replied.

We had a military adviser attached to the film unit – Mike Norman, a Royal Marines commander who had taken part in the conflict, and whose tales of courage and endurance under fire held me spellbound.[2] He said he was planning a visit to the hills above Goose Green, where he and his men had fought alongside the legendary Lieutenant Colonel 'H' Jones, and asked if any of us would be interested in joining him. Like many others of my generation, I had demonstrated against the Falklands war, seeing it as little more than Margaret Thatcher's opportunity to show her devotees she had bigger balls than Churchill. Personal feelings aside, I realised the opportunity to visit the site of a major event in British military history was not to be missed.

Fearing the swift and decisive victory they had predicted wasn't exactly going to plan, on 25 May 1982 the British government ordered the army to attack the Argentinian forces entrenched around the East Falkland settlements of Darwin and Goose Green. What intelligence reports estimated were no more than five hundred or so draftees who would, in all probability, surrender at the first opportunity, turned out to be 'Task Force Mercedes' –

---

[2] Unlike the lies and misinformation we were fed at the time, the Argentinian troops were very far from a ragtag army of poorly trained and terrified farm boys.

about twelve hundred well-equipped crack Argentinian troops who were dug in on the higher ground and fought like fury to defend their positions. After an affray lasting a day and a night, 119 men from both sides lost their lives with around 190 badly wounded. As I stood on the bleak, windblown slope, looking around at the shell casings, ammunition clips and abandoned detritus of war that, ten years after the battle, no one had thought worth the bother of clearing up, like most of the others who were with me that day, I found it difficult to be unemotional. In the seventy-four days the war lasted, there were 907 deaths in total – including three local women who were killed by 'friendly fire' – and 1,965 were maimed and wounded, and for what? To maintain sovereignty over a tiny scrap of land in a remote corner of the world that few of us knew existed, much less being able to point to it on a map? From talking to a local historian, I learned the war was about much more than flag-waving jingoism. At night, when I looked out of my hotel window, I could see endless strings of bright lights out at sea. They were the lures used by hundreds of Japanese trawlers to attract the shoals of squid (Falkland Sound is one of the world's richest breeding grounds for squid) into their nets. The right to fish for squid in these waters is governed by the Falkland Islands Company, and anyone wanting to harvest this bounty has to pay them a hefty fee for the licence. So far, so profitable, but the key reason the British government decided the islands were worth fighting over was because of their mineral exploration rights. Under international agreements, the sector allocated to the Falklands extends all the way down to the South Pole, and although at present there are comprehensive treaties protecting the Antarctic from commercial exploitation, can you guess how effective they'll be when our present sources of oil start to run out?

When all the location scenes were completed, we once again boarded a big grey 737 back to Brize Norton. After our experience of in-flight hospitality RAF-style, we were a little more prepared this time, and despite knowing that anyone found in possession of alcohol would not be allowed to board the plane (court-martialled, if you were a serving officer), most of us carried a bottle of Coke or Pepsi laced with vodka in our cabin baggage. Ian Richardson, who played the islands' governor Sir Rex Hunt, had formed a mutual aid society with his on-screen wife Rosemary Leach, and arm in arm they swept past the scowling stewardess, toting a couple of 1.5 litre bottles labelled lemonade, but whose actual contents were gin with a soupçon of tonic water. Thanks to our ingenuity, the return journey was a lot more pleasant than the outward leg – apart from when we stopped over at the RAF airbase on Ascension Island. When the stewardess ordered us to exit the plane and wait in the compound until refuelling was completed, it was clear that Ian was having more than a little difficulty walking down the aisle in a straight line. Sensing disaster, my fellow actors and I quickly formed a tight phalanx around Ian to prevent him from keeling over. With a slightly baffled look on his face, he was hustled down the steps and over to the farthest corner of the compound. Glancing back, I caught sight of our stewardess talking to a couple of burly security officers and jabbing her finger animatedly in Ian's direction. Oh God – we were due to start filming the interiors at Ealing Studios the following day, and the next flight to London wasn't for another week. If they refused to let him back on the plane, we were in serious trouble.

The two officers marched over to Ian. 'Excuse me, sir,' said one of them. 'Have you been drinking?'

Drawing himself erect – well, as erect as he could manage given the fact he was totally pissed – Ian's patrician nostrils flared, and he fixed the MPs with a look of utter disdain, saying in his finest Francis Urquhart manner, 'Drinking? How dare you insinuate I have done anything of the sort!' At least, I *think* that's what he was saying. What actually came out was, 'Dirrkngg? Hauw drryo issuniate avedonn anthnng uffasord!' The redcaps looked at each other and nodded. Despite Ian's assurance to the contrary, they seemed to be in no doubt as to the state he was in. I could see the look of blind panic in Stuart, our director's eyes as he pictured himself having to explain to the Governor General of the British

Broadcasting Corporation why *An Ungentlemanly Act* would have to be rescheduled at great expense.

'If I might have a word,' he said to the redcaps while steering them as far away from Ian as possible. As he tried to reason with them, I heard the words 'Famous actor – National Treasure – mystery virus – heavily medicated – BBC – production delays – huge cost.' The 'heard it all before' look on the officers' faces indicated they were not of a mind to reconsider.

'Royal Air Force regulations clearly state that no one considered to be in a state of intoxication is permitted aboard a military aircraft under any circumstances,' growled the senior of the two.

'He's not intoxicated,' said Stuart in desperation, 'I'm telling you the honest truth, he's caught a terrible flu, and has been taking heavy duty medi—' His explanation was interrupted by a loud braying sound from the corner of the compound where Ian, his legs buckled and his fingers clinging to the wire for stability, was giving an award-winning display of projectile vomiting through the mesh of security fence.

What phone calls were made to the top brass at the BBC, what strings were pulled or what favours were called in, I have no idea. All I know is that Ian, minus his two bottles of 'lemonade', was reluctantly allowed back on to the plane for the final leg of the journey, and to Stuart's great relief *An Ungentlemanly Act* was completed at Ealing Studios on schedule and on budget.

43

Top of the Cops

1995 was a noteworthy year for me in many ways – some memorable, others eminently forgettable. After much heel-dragging on my part, Sally and I had made a huge leap of faith and upsized to a five-bedroom period house near the park in London's trendy Stoke Newington. Although we made a small profit from selling our wee three bedroom house in Dalston (if we bought it now, we'd have to shell out around half a million quid!), I was having panic attacks wondering how the hell I was ever going to make enough money to meet the huge increase in our mortgage repayments. Temporary salvation arrived in the form of *Backup* – a justly forgotten cop-opera for BBC Birmingham. Even before filming started I felt deeply uncomfortable as I was fitted for my blue serge uniform at Berman and Nathan's, the long-established theatrical costumiers in Camden Town. When I saw myself in their full-length mirror, I thought I looked like one of those out-of-work actors who turn up at parties pretending to be a bobby before surprising everyone by singing Happy Birthday and stripping down to their Union Jack boxer shorts. Still, it was work, and at that point in my life a decently paid series was exactly what I – and my mortgage company – needed. Sadly, it didn't prove to be the salvation I thought it would be: after its initial six episodes, I found myself unceremoniously dumped from the series (the show only lasted for one more season before it too got the chop). Despite the friendliness and camaraderie of its cast, *Backup* has to be one of my least loved and least lamented jobs.

Our first episode was set in a shopping mall, where a crazed gunman had opened fire from an overhead walkway, killing a security guard and wounding a few unlucky passers-by. Our director was fond of shooting scenes in one long, continuous take with a Steadicam (a device which, as its name implies, allows the camera operator to walk or run without jiggling the camera) and decided to lump the three opening scenes together and shoot them in a single sequence. Rehearsing and choreographing the five-minute shot took up most of the night, with the cameraman following the fast-paced action up and down moving escalators, along gangways, in and out of shop doorways and through groups of extras pretending to be panic-stricken shoppers. The scene concluded with our commanding officer running into the mall and getting a swift summing-up of the situation from our sergeant, played by Martin Troakes. Martin had the scene's final lines, which were: 'Some nutter shot the security guard, then he headed off before anyone could stop him.' Just as we were about to go for the take, Martin called the director over. 'That line of mine, "then he headed off" – I think we should change it.'

'Why?' asked the director. 'What's wrong with it?'

'I think it might sound a bit, well, er – sexual.'

The director seemed puzzled. 'Sexual?' he said. 'How do you mean?'

'Well,' said Martin, 'I think it might sound like I'm saying, "Then he had it off" – you know, like "had it away".'

The director seemed dubious, but decided to give Martin the benefit of the doubt. 'What would you rather say then?' he asked.

Martin thought for a moment and said, 'How about, "Then he legged it"?'

As time was of the essence, the harried director agreed to Martin's rewrite before addressing everyone through his loudhailer. 'OK, listen up,' he called. 'The mall opens for business in about ten minutes, so we've only got one chance to shoot this scene – so, everyone set and ready? Right, good luck, and – ACTION!'

Huddled by the entrance, the rest of the squad and I began psyching ourselves up for our dramatic entrance as the camera performed its intricate manoeuvres through the labyrinth of corridors and stairways before swooping down to capture our section of the scene. When our cue came, we charged at full tilt through the precinct. As per rehearsals, our commanding officer sprinted up and asked Martin to brief him on the situation. 'Well, Sir,' Martin replied breathlessly. 'Seems some nutter shot the security guard and then, er, then he er . . .' His eyes widened as he struggled to recall the line that he had so rashly altered at the last minute. Oh Jesus, it was every actor's worst nightmare to screw up the final line of a one-time-only, five-minute-long take. We all said a silent prayer as Martin's mouth opened and closed soundlessly. I can only guess that some neural wiring short-circuited in his memory, and 'headed off' got mixed up with 'headed away' and 'legged it', because the line he finally blurted out was, 'And then he – had it away on his leg!'

'CUT!' yelled the director through his megaphone. 'CUT, CUT, CUT!' At least I think that's what he yelled . . .

The other event that year worthy of a mention was working with Mel Gibson on *Braveheart*. I'm always a little reluctant to talk about my part in the film for two reasons: one, I only had what we actors call 'a cough and a spit' in it, and two, small as my part was, it was entirely due to another actor's misfortune that I got the job in the first place.

Fiona, my latest agent,[1] had sent me the script of *Braveheart* to see if I wanted to go up for a part in it. I have to be honest and say that when I read it, I thought as a period action movie it was pretty good, but as a telling of the William Wallace story, I thought it was complete baloney. However, I wasn't about to let a little thing like personal taste get in the way of a possible part in a big Hollywood movie,

---

[1] Michael Foster had left Duncan's agency to become a highly successful producer by this point.

which explains why I found myself waiting in the foyer of London's famous Claridge's Hotel where, under a pseudonym, the equally famous Mel Gibson was staying. So many of the Scottish acting fraternity had been up to see him about *Braveheart* that the hotel's management really should have equipped his suite with a revolving door. When the receptionist called me over and gave me instructions how to get to 'Mr Williams" suite, I took the lift to the top floor, where Mel's assistant ushered me in to meet the great man. I must say, I took to him right away. Despite the dozens of hopefuls he was seeing every fifteen minutes or so, he had a real down-to-earth quality and friendly manner that immediately put me at my ease. He explained that at this point he just wanted to meet as many Scottish actors as he could before starting to cast the main characters, which was fine by me. After reading Randall Wallace's screenplay, I hadn't singled out a part that I thought I would be absolutely right for anyway. As we chatted, I told him I had been in possibly the worst version of the Wallace story ever (while thinking to myself that if Randall Wallace's script wasn't seriously rewritten, John Prebble's version might turn out to be the second worst). He asked me about the Borderline production and guffawed when I told him the story about vainly trying to conceal my nuts behind my lute while singing a medieval ballad. When I learned that filming for *Braveheart* was underway near Inverness, I figured I wasn't what he was looking for, gave a shrug and forgot all about it.

'Hello, darling,' said Fiona when I answered the phone a few weeks later. 'Mel Gibson's just been on the line, asking if you would fly up to Inverness to meet him.' I told her I was a bit perplexed – since the movie had started shooting, what could he possibly want to see me about? 'You can ask him yourself when you see him,' she said. 'There's a flight tomorrow morning. Shall I tell him you'll meet him for lunch?'

'I thought you were great when we met,' said Mel over a healthy vegetarian lunch in his trailer. 'The thing was, I really needed big, hairy-assed Highlanders for the movie – you know, the wilder-looking the better.'

I thought it was a category that Mel fitted rather well, having transformed himself from the well-groomed, smartly dressed figure I had met at Claridge's into a long-haired, kilted warrior chief who could have been a blood relative of Dougal McAngus, my character from *Blackadder*.

'The thing is,' he went on to explain, 'Alan Tall, the actor I cast as the bride's father, had an accident with his horse and is in hospital. I need someone to take his place for the wedding scene next weekend and wondered if you would be interested.'

I said I would, and we shook hands, with Mel dashing back to the set and me heading back to the airport.

The following Friday, after a frantic rush of make-up tests and costume fittings in London, I was once again on a flight up to Inverness. As I sipped at my complimentary G&T, I looked through the script that had arrived in the post that morning. That's when it dawned on me that I had agreed to play a character who only had one line – and not even a long one at that! Basically what happens in the scene is that the English lord comes to claim *primae noctis* on the young bride to be. Her father (me) steps forward and says, 'No, by God, sir, you will not!' before being clubbed senseless by an English man-at-arms. That was it – that was the sum and substance of my part in *Braveheart*. On the one hand, I was happy to add a major credit to my CV, while on the other, I knew the gossip would be, 'Oh aye – I see Norton's reduced to doing one-line parts these days . . .'

Well, what the hell, I had accepted the part, and when it came down to it, I figured it was better to be in the movie that not to be – besides, if I had turned it down my uncle Willie, who is honorary guardian of the Wallace Society, would never have forgiven me.

An authentic and highly detailed thirteenth-century Scottish village had been constructed on the banks of a river, and as I looked up towards the trailers and dining marquees that stood on a nearby hill, out of sight of the cameras, I saw Mel sprinting past all the actors and extras who were warily picking their way down the muddy hillside. As soon as he arrived, and without pausing for a second to catch his breath, he immediately launched into directing the scene. I was awestruck by the amount of energy he seemed to generate without any apparent effort – you could almost see the sparks flying off the man. After setting up the scene and discussing the shots with the cameraman, he switched roles and became Mel Gibson, actor and movie star, as the first assistant called action for the first take of the day.

At the end of the following day, when my scene was complete, Mel asked me into his trailer. I assumed it was to say thanks and goodbye, but to my surprise, he asked me if I wanted to stay on for the rest of the film. 'I want to have a core team around me,' he said. 'There's no specific parts, but we'll be doing a lot of improvising and if you come up with some good lines, they'll be in the movie.' I thanked him and said I would talk it over with my agent as soon as I got back to London. I think he was a little surprised that I hadn't jumped at the chance, but the truth was that although I was genuinely flattered by his offer, I felt like I had been there twenty-seven years before when I was just one more member of the squad on *The Virgin Soldiers*. I remembered being told then that we would all be given featured cameos throughout the film, but the bottom line was we were really just glorified extras.

On the plane home, I pictured myself standing in the middle of nowhere day after day, screaming Celtic curses at proud Edward's army, while clouds of ravenous midges swarmed up my kilt in search of a tasty snack. By the time my plane landed at Heathrow, I had already made my mind up and the following day, despite my agent's astonishment and Sally waving the latest batch of household bills before my eyes, I said no to Mel's proposition. And that, ladies and gentlemen of the jury, explains why I have such a tiny wee part in such a great big movie . . .

44

Ah, Tissue . . .

Bill Paterson and I were reminiscing about our careers over a pint one evening. 'What was your finest hour?' he asked. 'The part you would most want to be remembered for?' To his surprise, the answer that sprang to my mind was Malky 'Tissue'[1] Mulherron in *Bad Boys*. Although it may not have been one of the highest-profile jobs I've ever done, *Bad Boys* stands out in my mind as an example of how ill-served the public are when it comes to making TV programmes they actually want to watch.

For those of you who have never seen *Bad Boys*, the premise for Ian Pattison's darkly comic take on Glasgow gangsters grew out of a series of adverts for Tennent's Lager, featuring Karl Howman and my old pal Freddie Boardley. The ads began with Howman being released from a grim-looking English prison. As he stands in the rain, clutching a brown-paper parcel containing all his worldly goods, Boardley pulls up in a flash Mercedes convertible and whisks him away to Glasgow. Pattison's series began where the ads left off. Who are these two guys? What's their back story, and how does Howman's cockney chancer cope when he finds himself in Glasgow?

In *Bad Boys*, it's revealed that Karl and Freddie were once cellmates, and although he now considers himself reformed and

---

[1] He was nicknamed Tissue because he had performed a skin graft on himself in order to cover up an old tattoo – using his cellmate's skin.

'posh', Freddie's character retains a tenuous connection to a Glasgow criminal underworld, ruled by the iron fist of the 'Gaffer di Tutti Gaffers' – the fearsome Malky Mulherron. I had never felt so absolutely at home in a role as I felt playing Mulherron – one minute a vain, pompous figure of ridicule, the next a seriously scary psychopath. On paper *Bad Boys* had everything going for it. It was innovative, it was unique and Ian Pattison's scripts were some of his finest work – so why, despite the great reviews and the wonderful public response, did the BBC pull the plug on it after only one series? I've never found out the real reason, but I suspect the Politically Correct brigade, who seemed to have had a stranglehold on the Corporation back in the eighties and nineties, had a strong say in its demise.

Fortunately, I managed to clamber relatively unscathed from the wreckage, but Freddie wasn't so fortunate – Fraser Hood, the character that Pattison had tailored for him like a bespoke suit, was the part he had been waiting all his life to play. When *Bad Boys* went down the pan, it took my old pal's self-confidence with it, dealing his once busy career a blow from which it never really recovered.

So yes, even with my eight years as Matt Burke in *Taggart*, it's Malky Mulherron I would most want to be remembered for. He was the best-written character I ever played, and in my opinion *Bad Boys* was one of the funniest, most original television programmes ever made in Scotland. Yet despite the glowing reviews and the fact that the public loved it, my suspicion is that The High Heid Yins at the BBC scuppered its chances by deliberately shifting its transmission dates around without any prior warning. Since nobody knew when it was on, the viewing figures were so low that it justified their decision not to let the Scottish public (whose licence fees paid their wages) see *Bad Boys* again. Ever. So there!

45

Losing the Plot

It was Mark Twain who said, 'Never let the facts get in the way of a great story' – a phrase I wish I had taken to heart before I tried to turn the tale of Johnny Ramensky into a TV drama. I imagine it was the success of the three plays[1] I'd written for STV that prompted Robert Love, their Head of Drama, to ask if I would be interested in writing the script for a documentary that Alan MacMillan, one of his staff directors, had been researching.

When I met with Alan in Robert's office he handed me a thick folder filled with his research material, asking if I had ever heard of a chap called Johnny Ramensky. Like most Glaswegians of my generation, I had a distant memory of 'Gentle' Johnny Ramensky and his daring exploits, as his life story had been serialised in one of the Glasgow evening papers when I was a boy. My recollection was that he was a top safecracker who, during the Second World War, had been sprung from jail and parachuted into Germany on a top-secret mission that involved blowing a safe at some top Nazi's headquarters and stealing valuable secret papers. Other than the fact that he was regarded as a bit of a folk hero and had made some spectacular escapes from prison, I knew very little about him – but as soon as Alan mentioned his name, I knew his story would make a great screenplay.

---

[1] The third play I wrote for STV, *Stan's First Night*, was about my comedy hero Stan Laurel's first appearance on stage at the Panopticon Theatre in Glasgow's Trongate. Once, when I was out in Hollywood, I went to lay down some flowers at his burial place in Forest Lawn cemetery. The guide who directed me to the grave told me that Buster Keaton had delivered Stan's eulogy, saying, 'Chaplin wasn't the greatest, I wasn't the greatest. This guy was the greatest.' I couldn't agree more.

Although Robert and Alan envisaged the project as a one-off documentary, I suggested to them that we should go for broke and turn the project into a movie-length drama. Won over by my genuine enthusiasm for the subject, Robert allocated a budget for our research, and Alan and I set out on a voyage of discovery that ranged from talking to Ramensky's widow in her Gorbals high rise, through interviewing old (some of them *very* old) Glasgow villains, to taking afternoon tea with an elderly marquesa at her family estate in Italy.

One of the first things we discovered was that his name wasn't Johnny Ramensky. His police file (which a senior figure in the Scottish Security Services allowed us access to on an 'eyes only' basis) stated that his real name was Jonas Ramanauskas and he was born in Scotland, the son of Lithuanian immigrant parents.

While serving a lengthy sentence in Peterhead prison for a robbery at an Aberdeen laundry, the Second World War broke out, and after a lot of persuasion, Ramensky agreed to use his unique skills in the service of his country. According to the legend, he was sprung from Peterhead prison by the British Secret Service, and parachuted into Germany on a top-secret mission that involved breaking into Reichsmarschall Göring's castle in the Bavarian Alps. As the Nazi elite wined and dined in the next room, Ramensky blew Göring's safe and slipped silently away with a haul of vital military secrets. In reality, as a classified Home Office file revealed, he was required to serve out the remainder of his prison sentence before being allowed to join the army. Once free, he was given a new identity – John Ramsey – and trained as a commando at Achnacarrie. When his training was completed, he was assigned to a commando unit in Italy, where he lived in the mountains and worked with the partisans (who, according to his memoirs, he had little time for), harassing the Germans and blowing up the odd bridge. Interesting enough, but not really the kind of story on which to base an exciting war drama – in fact, according to a classified document I was granted access to, Major Strachan, the leader of Ramensky's unit, officially requested that his squad be sent elsewhere, as he felt they were pitifully under used. Nevertheless, given the nature of the project I knew I had to write the kind of scenes that would keep the viewers on the edge of their seats. I'll give you a typical example of the difficulties I faced. Looking through his unit's records, I discovered that Ramensky had blown a record number of safes in one day at the German embassy in Rome – now that was more like it! I wrote a key scene with Ramensky working against the clock to silently crack open the massive steel vaults, as with every second that passes he risks discovery by the SS guards who patrol the underground corridors with snarling Alsatians at their jackbooted heels. However, after reading my first draft, Alan insisted that I write the truth – which was that he blew all the Embassy safes after the Germans had pulled out. Without the threat of imminent discovery, the scene had no dramatic tension to keep an audience on the edge of their seats.

And so it went on. Every new piece of research we uncovered seemed to pull the rug from under the feet of the tale that had first fired my imagination. The more facts I uncovered about Ramensky, the less I liked him. He was anything but the dashing Raffles-type character who robbed only the rich and gave to the poor as the folk myths portrayed him. To feed his gambling addiction Ramensky would have lifted your granny's purse from her message bag without a second thought. And although it was true that he made some dramatic and exciting escapes from Peterhead prison, it was his own pig-headed stubbornness and stupidity that put him there in the first place. For a writer to fall out of love with the hero of his screenplay doesn't usually bode too well for the project, and as I struggled on, desperately trying to turn the material Alan and I had gathered into a gripping drama (in the end, there was so much material that my one-off screenplay had become a four-part series), I wished with all my heart I had kept my bloody mouth shut and gone with the original idea of a sixty-minute documentary. I had plenty of colourful background material, but I desperately needed to employ a fair bit of dramatic licence in order to write a screenplay that would entertain and enthral an audience. We had collected plenty of anecdotal tales about Ramensky's exploits – like the time in the Libyan desert when he blew the safe at Rommel's HQ and stole a book listing the names of all the British pro-Nazi aristocrats, like the Duke of Hamilton and the Duke of Windsor, who would govern the country after a successful German invasion. The Swedish ex-army officer who told the story also added that he had disobeyed an order to execute Ramensky after he had looked at the contents of the file before handing it over. Now that's powerful stuff, but without any source to corroborate it, Alan wouldn't agree to its inclusion in the script, and the artistic licence I so desperately needed was never granted.[2]

Robert Love had negotiated the major part of his production budget with the ITV network, but the offer came with a time clause, and as the final deadline grew ever closer I ploughed on, trying not to give in to despair as I struggled to transform the facts of Ramensky's life into what Alan kept insisting was 'a cracking good yarn'. By the time I had written around two-thirds of the script, the final deadline had passed and the window of opportunity slammed firmly shut. I carried on regardless, hoping that by the time I reached the final page, a miracle would have occurred and the production would still go ahead. Like so much about the Ramensky project, I was wrong about that too: the series never did get made, and despite the awards and acclaim my previous work had garnered for STV, Robert never again asked me to write another screenplay for his drama department. I try not to look back on my failures with too much regret, but opportunities to write something as potentially fantastic as *Ramensky* don't land in your lap every day. Robert had commissioned me because he had faith in my ability to bring the story of Johnny Ramensky to life, and, with

---

[2] At a point when things had started to go very wrong, I came across a *Garfield* cartoon strip that said it all. In the first panel, Garfield is watching TV as a voice from the set says, 'The following is a Made for TV Drama.' In the second panel, the voice continues, 'The story you are about to see is true.' In the last panel, the voice says, 'Apart from the stuff we made up to make it more interesting.' It's a principle I dearly wish Alan had embraced.

hindsight, if I had only argued more forcefully for the necessity of a little dramatic licence, I just might have.

Every now and again I look through the four thick scripts that have been sitting on my office shelf since the day I got the phone call telling me the plug had been pulled on the project, and painful as it is to flick through the pages and think of the blood, sweat and tears that went into their writing, I still find myself captivated by the story of this extraordinary individual, and I fantasise that someone, some day, will commission me to blow the dust off my overlong and overwritten scripts and condense them into an exciting three-part drama that would sweep the board at the television Baftas. But to get any producer interested, I'd need a name attached to the project – some young Scottish star who resembles Johnny Ramensky at the mid-point of his life. So, James McAvoy, I'm sorry I turned you down for a part in the King's panto all those years ago, but if by chance you happen to be reading this, and you've found it in your heart to forgive me – boy, have I got a part for you!

46

Things to Come

With Rachel Weisz's luminous beauty and Simon Donald's brilliant and original screenplay, *Beautiful Creatures* had a lot going for it. Like most of Simon's inspired writing, the film mixed together elements of comedy and tragedy in equal measure. I was cast as Detective Inspector Hepburn, a thoroughly nasty piece of work whose investigation into the mysterious disappearance of Rachel Weisz's husband leads to the sort of gory climax so beloved of Tarantino fans.

Graeme Gordon, the film's first assistant director, had spent most of his life in the film business, working his way up the greasy pole from runner to first AD. I liked his unpretentious attitude and admired his down-to-earth sense of values – something of a rarity in the film world. It was Graeme who was given the unenviable job of trying to persuade Rachel to do the revealing shower scene called for by the script. Despite the fact she had agreed to it when she signed her contract, as zero hour approached she stayed put in her trailer, making excuse after excuse as to why she was unable to set foot outside the door. After about a dozen attempts to persuade her to change her mind, the director finally realised he was fighting a losing battle and, to the dismay of every straight male in the crew, surrendered to the inevitable and abandoned the scene. I did, however, get to have a bit of a memorable encounter with Ms Weisz in a scene where DI Hepburn creeps into her darkened bedroom and terrifies her by slipping a shotgun under her sheets and slowly sliding it up her bare leg. The atmosphere on the set was so heavy with sexual tension that when the scene was complete and I handed the heavy weapon back to the prop man, his hands were so sweaty it slipped through his fingers and almost broke one of his toes.

Maurice Roëves, who played Rachel's suspicious brother-in-law, had given me a huge bear hug when we met at the read-through, although if he had foreseen how, thanks to our first AD Graeme Gordon, our lives would come together again in such a dramatic way a few years later, I doubt my welcome would have been quite so warm . . .

47

Soap Opera

Tony Roper and I had been good friends since the early seventies, and in the late eighties I spent a pleasant weekend with him and his partner Isobel at the cosy wee cottage they shared in Lanarkshire. After lunch Tony took me fishing, and as we dangled a couple of rods in a nearby pond, he mentioned that he was thinking of writing a play. 'What's it about?' I asked.

'It's about a bunch of women in a Glasgow wash house in the fifties,' he said. 'No big dramatic thing – just a wee gentle piece about their lives.'

I wished him well with it, thinking that just about every actor I'd ever known had said they were going to write a play, although few of them ever did. As it turned out, Tony was the exception. He called me up a few years later to ask if I remembered him mentioning the play he was planning to write about the wash house in Glasgow. I told him I did. 'Well,' he said, 'I've finished it, and I wondered if you'd be interested in taking a wee look at the script – see if you might fancy having a go at directing it.' The play was, of course, *The Steamie*, a phenomenal piece of work that rightly deserves its special place in the annals of Scottish theatre.

When I agreed to direct it, I thought *The Steamie* would be a really good piece of community theatre – a delightful piece of nostalgia that would attract a largely female audience who remembered going to the Corporation wash houses with their mothers. I imagine Tony must have thought along similar lines, as he had given the production rights to 7:84's offshoot company, Wildcat, to let them tour the show in community halls around the Greater Glasgow area. Dave Anderson, by this time Wildcat's joint artistic director, had agreed to write a number of songs that could be slotted in at various points in the dialogue. Although I can't honestly say I was a big fan of Wildcat, I had the utmost respect for Dave's musical talent, and knew I could rely on him to come up with songs that would enhance Tony's script.

As director, the first two things I had to focus on were the set design and the casting. Knowing that the set would have to be capable of fitting into an assortment of differently sized locations, I decided I needed something that wasn't a bad attempt at realism. The Citz production of *Can't Pay? Won't Pay!* when faced with a similar challenge had gone with a simple, graphic-style set that could be easily adapted to fit in all sorts of community venues, and since *The Steamie* was set in the mid fifties, I thought of the great Glasgow cartoonist and illustrator of that period, Bud Neill. To me, Neill's cartoons, with their deceptively simple style and dry wit, somehow captured the very essence of post-war Glasgow. With that in mind, I called up the inheritor of Bud Neill's mantle – the Glasgow cartoonist *du jour*, Malky McCormick. I had known Malky since he designed the poster for Billy Connolly's play *An' Me wi' a Bad Leg Tae*. He had since been asked to design posters for quite a few shows over the years, but had never been asked to design anything as complex as a stage set. However, as we talked over the practicalities and potential problems involved, I could tell the notion really appealed to him. I left him a copy of Tony's script, and the following day he called to accept the commission.

Because Tony's dialogue was so authentic, I knew that casting would be key to the production's success or failure. Elaine C. Smith, my dear friend and fellow member of the Smith/Norton mutual admiration society, was already on board. Elaine had elected to play Dolly, a wee force of nature who's always on the go and likes nothing more than a good blether (although whatever made Smithy think she might be right for a character like that I can't begin to imagine . . .).

Wildcat provided me with a shortlist of actresses who had worked for them in previous productions, and among them was Katy Murphy. I had seen Katy as Miss Toner in John Byrne's *Tutti Frutti* and thought she was a wow – but could she sing? After listening to her stunning rendition of 'Cry Me a River' at Wildcat's HQ in Jordanhill College, I knew there was no point in seeing anyone else for the part of Doreen.

Magrit was a gift of a part for the right actress. Despite a life blighted by poverty and despair, beneath Magrit's 'hard ticket' exterior beat a wounded heart of pure gold. My own heart skipped a beat when Dave MacLennan, Wildcat's co-founder, told me that Dorothy Paul was coming in to audition for the part. Dorothy Paul! My mind flashed back to a dreich autumn morning in 1961 when my pal Billy McDermott and I dogged school to queue up outside the Theatre Royal to be among the audience for a live transmission of STV's popular lunchtime show *The One O'Clock Gang*. As we stood chittering in the chill morning air, a taxi pulled up to the kerb, and the most impossibly glamorous female I had ever seen smiled and waved to the crowd as she wafted through the stage door in a confection of carefully coiffured blonde hair and a mink coat. I was captivated. Now I was about to meet the Golden Goddess in person. Over twenty-five years had passed since the day Dorothy made my knees tremble below the frayed edges of my short trousers – surely she couldn't possibly live up to the image I had of her in my head. How wrong I was. When she walked into the rehearsal room, the aura of glamour she still carried with her instantly turned me back into the shy eleven-year-old who had lost his heart to her one long-ago morning in Hope Street. Concealing my nervousness as best I could, I asked if she would mind reading a couple of scenes for me. She made a great show of faffing around with her reading glasses and let me know in no uncertain terms that cold readings weren't really her forte.[1] However, she gave Magrit's dialogue a quick once-over before making a decent job of playing the scene. Never having seen Dorothy play a dramatic role, I wanted to know how she took to direction. I shared a few of my thoughts about the character and asked her to have another go – to my joy, her second reading was superb, and when she sang, with Dave Anderson accompanying her on the piano, I knew I had found my Magrit.

I only ever had one actress in mind for the part of the frail and elderly Mrs Culfeathers – Ida Schuster, whose long and distinguished career began when she was a young girl in the Avron Greenbaum Players, Glasgow's Jewish amateur theatre group. I knew Ida had a bit of a reputation for being, as she said herself, 'a director's nightmare', but I had seen her work over the years and knew she had exactly the qualities I wanted for old Mrs Culfeathers. Thankfully (although there were times during rehearsals I might not have felt *too* thankful) she consented to accept the role.

The final character I had to cast was Andy – the only man in the entire cast. Freddie Boardley had dropped a very large hint that he wanted to do it, but Freddie was a seriously good-looking stud who had the ladies running after him in droves, and much as I appreciated his talent, I knew Andy needed to be played as someone who *thought* he was Freddie Boardley. I had known Ray Jeffries since I worked with him in my very first panto at Motherwell Civic Centre. Ray was primarily a club entertainer who specialised in small character parts (he was the drunk guy in the phone box in *Local Hero*). Andy wasn't a big part, but as soon as Ray agreed to play him, I knew I had a first-class cast that would bring Tony's exceptional writing to life.

It was clear from the start that my maiden voyage as a director was not going to be plain sailing. Apart from Ida letting me know in no uncertain terms that she considered herself far too good to work with 'all these variety people', Dorothy seemed to be having

---

[1] Much later, she confessed to me how nervous *she* had been that day.

serious problems remembering her dialogue: any time she had a longish speech, she would say the first few words followed by 'scamson scamson scamson' before jumping to her final line.[2] Although funny at first, by week two it was beginning to drive me nuts, and I began to think I might have let my admiration for her cloud my judgement.

As anyone who's known me over the years will tell you, I'm not awfy good at hiding my disappointment, and when I went back to see the cast after the show's first public preview, I must have had a face like thunder. Something had happened in the brief interval between the dress run and the performance. Every moment we'd painstakingly polished till it sparkled and every nuance of Tony's meticulously crafted dialogue seemed to have flown out the window. At the heart of it was Dorothy. Despite the times in rehearsal when her performance made my heart soar with joy, when it came to delivering the goods in front of an audience, it seemed to me that her nerve had gone. Despite my frustration, I knew it would probably destroy what little spark of confidence she still had if I gave her a rocket in front of the company, so when I walked into the communal dressing room after the curtain had come down and Elaine C. asked me how I thought it had gone, I said tersely, 'Complete run-through. Ten o'clock tomorrow morning,' before walking out.

I was discussing the fiasco with a grim-faced Tony Roper in the now empty auditorium, when I suddenly found myself pinned against the wall. 'You *bastard*!' roared Dave MacLennan. 'I've just been to the dressing room – those women are in floods of tears. Who the *fuck* do you think you are?'

'I'm the director,' I answered as calmly as I could. 'So please take your hands off me right fucking now.' Since my arms were

---

[2] I later learned that this was an old variety thing – on tour, whenever a performer did a run-through for the benefit of the technical crew, to save time, they would 'top and tail' their act, so things would go along the lines of: 'Right – ah come on fae this side – patter patter patter – she comes on fae that side – scamson scamson scamson, then business business business, song and off. OK?'

pinioned, I could only see two possible outcomes from this ugly confrontation – one involving a broken nose. Thankfully the situation ended without blood and snotters, and I shook with emotion as I walked back to my digs through the dark and empty streets. It had all gone wrong, and the simple truth was I had no idea how to make it right again.

The following morning I sat down with the company and gave them my thoughts on the previous night's performance, finishing up by telling them that the play was solid gold and from the performances I had seen at rehearsals, every one of them (by which I really meant Dorothy) was more than capable of stepping up to the plate. 'The show is great,' I told them. 'And if you want to get off the bus at great I'll get off your back right now – but if you want to stay on board till you get to terrific, then let's roll up our sleeves and get tore in.' Although they were tired and resentful from being called so early after the first performance, the company ran through the play once again with very few interruptions from me. It was all there – everything we had worked so hard on in rehearsal; all the beats, the moments, the reactions and, most importantly, the laughs. As long as Dorothy's nerve held, I knew we had a fighting chance.

That night, as the curtain fell at the end of our second preview, I was the first on my feet. Whether or not my 'pep talk' and extra run-through had done the trick I can't say. All I knew was that we had cracked it – every single one of them had given their absolute best, and Dorothy soared on eagle's wings. It was one of the greatest nights of my life, and when the curtain finally fell after a ten-minute standing ovation, the cast knew from the size of the grin on my face when I rushed into the dressing room, showering them with hugs and kisses, that for all the panic and despair, it had been worthwhile – we had a big fat hit on our hands.

And so *The Steamie* toured to rapturous reviews and packed theatres, Dorothy was deservedly elevated to the rank of Scottish National Treasure and everyone lived happily ever after . . . Well, no, that's not *quite* the happy note I'd like to leave this chapter on. A few months after the first tour ended I got a call from Wildcat, saying they planned an autumn tour of the show, culminating in a two-week run at the Pavilion Theatre. I had accepted a low fee for directing a wee show that would tour round community halls, but now that *The Steamie* was a commercial success, I expected a reasonable slice of the profits for the part I played in giving Wildcat their biggest hit ever. Instead I was offered a handful of small change to come up for a week and get the show in shape for the new tour. When I said their offer was unacceptable, I was told that all the profits from the two-week run at the Pavilion would just about cover the company's losses on the community tour. I saw the logic in this and settled for a sum that, although not much higher than the initial offer, seemed a bit more reasonable. Shortly afterwards, I learned at second hand that after its run at the Pavilion, *The Steamie* had been booked for an extended run at the 1,785-seat King's Theatre, netting Wildcat a small fortune. For a company that traded on its socialist principles, it seemed like a confirmation of the old truism, 'When the money comes through the door, the principles fly out the window.'

I suggested to Tony that we set up our own production company and record the show at the Pavilion, selling the DVD through video stores and leasing the broadcasting rights to the highest bidder. When he turned me down, saying he had agreed to let STV make their own version of the show, I remember seeing in my mind's eye an image of myself trying to hold on to a handful of beautiful golden sand as it poured rapidly through my fingers.

A year or so later Tony asked me to direct a London production of *The Steamie* in hopes of a successful West End run. I had my doubts about the show's ability to fill one of the big London theatres, but after losing out to Wildcat and STV, I was damned if I was going to let this opportunity pass me by. When the producers told me they didn't want any of the original cast, and insisted that I recast with Big Names and tone down the Glasgow accents (dear God, if anything the play was a *celebration* of the Glasgow accent), I knew in my heart it was doomed. To my eternal regret, I took the king's shilling, gave in to the producer's demands and set about trying to engage a cast that would put well-upholstered bums on plush West End seats. Sadly, all the proposed Big Names (like Lulu and Gudrun 'Supergran' Ure) turned me down, and instead of the dream cast I once had, I found myself trying to play in the premier league with a team of last-minute substitutes. Despite everyone's best efforts, after an initial three-week run at the Greenwich Theatre, *The Talk of the Steamie*[3] went down with all hands. It was years before Tony and I spoke to each other again.

When I started rehearsals for Wildcat's 'wee community show' I hadn't the slightest notion of just how big a hit *The Steamie* would turn out to be, and despite yet again being on the receiving end of the Big Bucket of Shite, I'll always be beholden to Tony for the opportunity he gave me to cut my teeth as a director. It led to me directing the wonderful Elaine C. Smith in her finest hour as the Glasgow incarnation of Willy Russell's Shirley Valentine, followed by four unforgettable years directing the grand family pantomimes at the King's Theatre. Thankfully, Dave Maclennan and I patched up our differences over a glass or two at the Oran Mor, the venue for the phenomenally successful A Play, A Pie and A Pint, which he founded and ran until his tragically early death while I was writing this book.

---

[3] As it was now titled, to avoid confusion with Nell Dunne's recent West End hit, *Steaming*.

48

One Door Closes

The first inkling that my life was about to undergo a radical transformation was when my brother Dougie phoned me to say he'd read in the papers that I was among a list of actors being considered for the role of the new Chief Inspector in a forthcoming revamp of STV's long-running detective series *Taggart*. It was certainly a surprise to me, and I told Dougie there was nothing in it and not to believe everything he read in the papers. Nevertheless, the following morning I called my agent to ask if she had heard anything about me being considered for the part. She seemed as baffled as I was and agreed that the story was probably just a piece of journalistic fluff, cobbled together to fill an empty space on a slow news day. The thing was, even though I dismissed Dougie's story as a daft fantasy, a wee voice would whisper in my ear every now and again, 'What if . . . ?'

A month or so later, I flew up to Scotland to start work on *Rose's Patch* – a pilot for a prospective BBC series about a Jewish Glasgow detective. Denis Lawson was playing DI Morris Rose, and the producer Lesley Hills, an old friend from my Edinburgh days, had offered me the part of Lawrence, Morris's loyal and long-suffering brother who runs a kosher deli and helps Morris solve the case. I loved the script and the characters – at last, here was something new and fresh, a pair of Jewish Glaswegians solving crimes together – so what's not to like already? On the first morning of filming, as I was being driven to the location by my old friend from *Bad Boys* days, Jas 'Chauffeur to the Stars' Brown,[1] he looked over to me and shook his head sadly. 'Bloody shame aboot *Taggart*, son,' he said. 'Bloody shame.' I asked him what he was talking about. 'Ach, ah don't know a' the ins an' oots o' it,' he said, 'but Eric Coulter's the new gaffer at STV, an' he's brought in Graeme Gordon tae take ower as *Taggart*'s producer. James MacPherson's leavin' the series an' they need a new boss. Apparently it wiz between you and Maurice Roëves fur the part, but in the end they went wi' Maurice. Ah think you'd huv been awfy good, son, but there ye are. Bloody shame, though.' I tried my best to appear nonplussed, but it felt like an ice-cold hand had just gripped my heart.

'Ach well,' I said, with feigned nonchalance. 'What's for ye'll no' go by ye, eh? And I'm sure Maurice'll be terrific in it.'

Although I tried not to think about it, I was distracted for the rest of the *Rose's Patch* shoot, and couldn't get over the gut-churning knowledge that I had come within spitting distance of being the new boss in *Taggart*. I wished that Jas hadn't given me the bloody news in the first place! Still, the word was that *Taggart*'s viewing figures had been on the slide for a while, and the series would be lucky if it managed to stagger on for another couple of years. Given its clever and quirky originality, I thought *Rose's Patch* stood a real chance of blossoming into a long-running series that would up my status from jobbing actor to high-profile telly star and give STV's tired old cop show a run for its money. *Taggart* – who needs it?

The morning after *Rose's Patch* (now retitled *The Fabulous Bagel Boys* – a name I had jokingly come up with on the set one day and which, to my surprise, had been gleefully adopted by the producers) went out, Lesley Hills called me up to read me the reviews. Every

---

[1] There's a best-selling book waiting to be written about Jas. Whenever there's a big movie shooting in Scotland, you can guarantee the leading actors will have been driven around by living legend Mr Jas Brown esquire. Jas is such a one-off that on umpteen occasions he's been begged by big-name movie stars to travel back to LA with them and be their personal chauffeur. So far he has refused to trade the glitz and glamour of Hollywood for his beloved Denistoun. As he said to me once, 'If they ever open a Greggs the bakers in Malibu, Ah might think aboot it . . .'

one of them praised the show to the skies. Apparently the overnight viewing figures were terrific and Lesley said she was positive that the series would be commissioned. After I put the phone down I jumped for joy – I had three kids (our third son, Jamie, was born in '97) to feed and clothe, the mortgage was overdue, my bank account was in the red and at that point in my life a good role in a long-running TV series was *exactly* what I wanted. Hugging each other with relief, Sally and I splashed out on a bottle of bubbly and toasted our financial salvation. A few weeks later, and sounding as if she was on the verge of tears, Lesley called back to tell me that despite the glowing notices and the high viewing figures, the BBC had, in its wisdom, decided not to commission *Bagel Boys* after all.

49

If the Hat Fits

One of the most interesting aspects of an actor's life is getting the opportunity to portray real-life characters. Over the years I've played Robert Owen, the eighteenth-century philanthropist and manager of the New Lanark mills; Keir Hardie, one of the founders of the modern Labour Party; Max Beerbohm, Victorian author, wit and contemporary of Beardsley and Wilde; 'Jamie the Sax', better known as King James the first of Scotland and England; Robert Burns, our national bard and one of my personal heroes; and Joseph Stalin, leader of the Soviet Union, despot and psychopathic mass murderer – or, if you're still a member of the Communist Party, Uncle Joe, the People's Champion.

The most challenging and exciting historic character I've ever played, though, has to be Napoleon Bonaparte. I've played the great man three times so far – once in Murray Grigor's wild and wacky film *Scotch Myths*, once with Leslie Nielsen in a crazy TV commercial for a Dutch telephone company, and finally – and for real – in director Kevin Reynolds' 2002 Hollywood blockbuster *The Count of Monte Cristo*. For that, I really did my homework, learning to my surprise that at five foot six and a half inches, Napoleon and I were the exactly the same height. I discovered his eyes were grey, and had a pair of coloured contact lenses made to disguise my own greeny-brown irises. Next, the nose – from all the various portraits and caricatures I found, I decided to have a prosthetic aquiline hooter made by a specialist. Finally, the voice. Discovering that, as a boy, Napoleon Bonaparte was frequently made fun of for his Corsican accent and knowing that I would be speaking English, I worked on giving him a slight Italian inflection that would set him apart from the French characters in the story. When I turned up on set, all costumed and ready to go, Kevin Reynolds whooped with delight. 'Good God!' he yelled. 'You're Napoleon to the life. After this movie comes out, you're gonna have a whole new career, playin' this guy for the rest of your days.' Fantastic – all my research and attention to detail seemed to have paid off – until he added, 'Oh, and by the way, the French characters will all be speaking in mid-American accents, so I guess Napoleon should too.' That was it – I was in at the deep end. No time to rethink my performance or practise my new accent – just get on there and do it. After a minute or two of heart-pumping panic, I quietly repeated the mantra that Roy Hanlon, an old actor buddy from my Edinburgh days, used to say before making his entrance on a first night – 'Right! Niminy fuckin' piminy – here we go!'[1]

Fast forward five years and I'm on location for *Taggart* in Ardgowan House, a stately home near Inverkip. The housekeeper who was showing me round told me the family had a connection with Napoleon, in that their great-great-grandfather had known Napoleon's mother, and after his exile to Elba had assisted her in arranging to have some of his most cherished possessions shipped out to him. As a reward, she had given the family a huge portrait of her son, along with one of his iconic hats. Napoleon's portrait was hanging on the wall of the main entrance hall, while his hat sat inside a large glass case on top of a regency table. I couldn't let an opportunity like this pass – I told the housekeeper

---

[1] I should explain that 'niminy piminy' is one of a series of diction exercises taught at drama schools. Classically trained actors often repeat it quietly to themselves in the wings to loosen up their lips and tongues before making an entrance.

I had played Napoleon in a movie and asked if there was the remotest chance that I might try it on. After a moment's consideration, he carefully lifted off the case and I gingerly placed the great man's hat on my head.

It fitted like a glove.

50

My Life in (Tagg)art

One day, early in 2001, I was in the middle of leading a raid on an underground Masonic temple when my mobile phone, which I had forgotten to switch off, rang loudly, bringing the raid to an embarrassing halt. On the screen was a text message from my agent. It read: 'Please call when you have a free minute. Fiona xx'. Six months had passed since *Bagel Boys* had gone down the pan, and I was charging in to a Masonic Temple as part of the plot of *Murphy's Law*, a TV drama starring James Nesbitt as a brilliant but unstable detective plagued by his inner demons. Like *Bagel Boys*, its producers were hoping that it would be the first episode of a long-running series. I have to confess that I had accepted the part of DCI Murdoch, Nesbitt's short-tempered Scottish boss, with some reservations. Never having been a big fan of detective fiction in general and TV cop shows in particular, I was scunnered with playing polismen and certainly didn't want to find myself with a dead-end career as yet another telly 'tec. However, with my debts piling up and the wolf at my door so often the kids had started calling it Rover, I knew I had little option but to set my personal feelings aside and be thankful that *Murphy's Law* was buying me a little breathing space before the bailiffs came a-calling.

'Hello, my darling,' said Fiona when I rang her back during a tea break. 'I've just had a call from Graeme Gordon and Eric Coulter at STV, asking if you would be interested in meeting them with a view to going into *Taggart*.' To say I was surprised would be an understatement – I knew Maurice Roëves was playing the new DCI, so what could they possibly want me for? Then it clicked – Robert Robertson, the elderly actor who had played *Taggart*'s forensic pathologist for the past eight years, had recently passed away, so obviously they were looking for someone to step into his shoes. I groaned inwardly at the thought of playing a pathologist – the annoyingly eccentric boffin who spouts reams of medical jargon while nonchalantly poking at the stab wounds on a partially dismembered corpse with his biro. Thanks but no thanks. And besides, given James Nesbitt's rising popularity, I thought that *Murphy's Law* stood a better than average chance of going to series.

'Please give Graeme and Eric my best wishes,' I said to Fiona. 'And tell them I'm grateful for their interest in me, but I really, *really* don't want to play a boring bloody pathologist!'

'Pathologist?' said Fiona, sounding slightly puzzled. 'Oh no, it's not for the pathologist. They want to talk to you about playing the lead . . .'

Over lunch in a Soho restaurant, Graeme and Eric put me in the picture. Maurice had accepted a verbal offer from *Taggart*'s previous producers to take over as the new boss. While negotiations with his agent were still ongoing, there was a regime change at STV, with Eric replacing Robert Love as Head of Drama, and Graeme taking over as *Taggart*'s new producer. Although they both wanted me for the role, they felt obliged to honour the pre-existing agreement with Maurice – but when the original deal was rejected, Graeme and Eric felt the verbal agreement was no longer binding, and they were free to make their own decision about who should play the show's new DCI. However, before they became involved in what might prove to be a costly and acrimonious legal wrangle, they wanted to know that if they *were* to offer me the part, would I be prepared to walk away from *Murphy's Law*? I didn't keep them waiting too long for my answer.

A few weeks later, as I signed my name on the dotted line of the *Taggart* contract, the disagreeable sensation that I had stabbed an old friend and colleague in the back was tempered by the thought that if our situations were reversed, Maurice, being the professional he is, would probably have signed the contract without a second thought. For any readers contemplating a life in the business, a word of caution – it's a tough game, this acting lark, and if Dame Fortune should pay you an unexpected call, be aware, before you start dancing round the kitchen (as Sally and I did, much to the embarrassment of our kids), that her beneficence might involve a swift reassessment of your moral and ethical standards.

As the day of the first read-through approached, I began to feel a twinge of anxiety about how I would be received by the regulars. Since I hadn't watched the series for years or met any of the cast socially, I wondered if there might be some strong feelings of resentment towards me. For all I knew, they might have been rooting for Maurice and were far from happy when the role went to me instead. However, from the moment I walked through the door of STV's main conference room on a chilly Glasgow morning, John Michie, Colin McCredie, Blythe Duff and James MacPherson gave me a welcome that gladdened my heart and immediately dispelled my doubts.

After the read through I was led off to the first of my appointments. I had an important meeting with Brucie, and didn't want to keep him waiting. Brucie was the name that Fiona, the head of the make-up department, had given the expensive and beautifully made little toupee I had requested.[1] I had decided to wear a hairpiece not out of vanity, but because I was losing my hair at an accelerating rate and I didn't want anyone watching the repeats in years to come and being able to tell how old the episode was by the size of the baldy bit on my napper. With the exception of period dramas where they're an essential part of the look, I hate wearing syrups (rhyming

---

[1] As the amount of grey in my hair increased over the eight years I spent in the series, a new rug was produced at the start of each new season. Every one of them was named in honour of some TV or movie star who deluded themselves that the public couldn't tell they had a teenager's hair on a pensioner's face. My two favourites were Bill (Shatner) and Chuck (Heston). I won't shatter any of your cherished illusions by revealing who the rest of them were named after . . .

slang: syrup of figs – wigs), but my decision to sport one on *Taggart* resulted in years of annoyance and irritation as the make-up assistants faffed, fiddled, footered and fannied about with the bloody thing before and after every take.

From the scene where DCI Burke makes his first entrance to the dramatic climax where DCI Jardine's killer is captured, I knew, if I wanted to make a real impact, I had to charge in with all guns blazing. I had thought long and hard about the character. Who was this man? What was his background? Where had he grown up and why did he join the force in the first place? True, there were a few pointers in the script, such as when DI Ross asks Burke, in an effort to get to know him, if he has a wife and kids. 'Used to be married,' Burke answers tersely. 'Used to have a family – that's all you need to know.' Likewise, DS Reid's friendly overtures are similarly rebuffed. DI Fraser, after a spot of discreet snooping, reveals that as part of the London Met's elite special branch, Burke has spent most of his career in the shady and secretive world of anti-terrorism. As always, when trying to find the heart of a character, I first look for the key within myself. What kind of person would I have become if I had followed the path Burke had taken? How would a career as a cop have shaped my impression of my fellow man? How cynical and hard-bitten would I be if I dealt with the basest aspects of the human behaviour on a daily basis, like Burke did? I concluded that it was of no importance to Burke whether he was liked or disliked by his colleagues, and that beneath his tough exterior there beat a heart of solid stone.

Besides casting me as the new DCI, Eric and Graeme had decided to kick *Taggart* into the twenty-first century by hiring top directors and crews from the Scottish film business in an effort to add a level of finesse they felt had been lacking in the show over the past few years. Ian Madden, a film buff with an encyclopaedic knowledge of forties Hollywood film noir[2] (and who, twenty years previously,

---

[2] Along with our enthusiasm for old movies, the fact that we both played acoustic finger-style guitar made us blood brothers for the rest of the series.

had been first assistant director on *Gregory's Girl*), was brought on board to direct the first episode and set the style for the new series. From my first entrance – when an angry and frustrated Mike Jardine yells, 'Matt Burke? Who the hell's Matt Burke?' and from the doorway of the incident room comes the answer, 'I'm Matt Burke; who the hell are you?' – I sensed that my debut as the new boss of *Taggart* couldn't be in a safer pair of hands.

Blythe and James had formed a close friendship over their years in the show, and when it came time to film James' final scene, Blythe had arranged a very special surprise for him, having primed the rest of the cast and crew to act out a little scenario for his benefit. After making sure the scene was safely in the can, the assistant cameraman checked the camera as usual before announcing there was a 'hair in the gate' and we would have to shoot the scene again. With much grumbling and groaning everyone went back to their first positions, but this time when Ian called 'action', instead of the extra who was meant to come in with an urgent message, James' musical idol, John Martyn, walked on instead. I'll never forget the look on his face as John walked over to him and launched into James' favourite song, one of his finest compositions, 'Solid Air'. As leaving presents go, they don't get much better than that. As I got to know Blythe over the eight years I spent on the series, I found that it was very much part of her thoughtfulness and generosity of spirit to organise unique and memorable gifts like that for people she cared about.

We were still hard at work filming the series when the first episode was scheduled for transmission. I had been given an advance copy on DVD, but I didn't relish the idea of viewing it on my own, so I was grateful when John Michie invited me over to his flat to watch the broadcast and share a glass or two of fizz to help calm the butterflies. As the clock ticked towards the fateful hour, I guessed from John's tuneless humming and rapid foot tapping that I wasn't the only one with the jitters. My heart skipped a beat as the new title sequence blasted on to the screen, backed by an edgy arrangement of *Taggart*'s familiar *No Mean City* theme, and I felt everything I'd ever done in my career had led to this moment: the difficult and often painful decisions I had taken; the solitary paths I had followed; the dead ends I had cursed myself for getting into and struggled to find my way back out of; the friends and loved ones I had left behind in my self-centred quest to become a bit rich and a bit famous. There was no going back now – this was it. Like a kid watching *Doctor Who* for the first time, I wanted to hide behind the settee and peek out between my fingers, ready to duck down if it all got too scary.

As the final credits began to roll, John and I exploded with joy and relief and cracked open another bottle of champagne. Graeme and Eric had done us proud. Thanks to Ian Madden's deft touch as a director and Ali Walker's remarkable skill as a lighting cameraman, the episode had the production values of a big-budget movie. Every beat and every nuance of the gripping storyline had been translated into a skilfully edited whole. In particular, the shots of Glasgow were visually stunning: the producers had shrewdly chosen to bring Glasgow, the uncredited star of *Taggart*, back to centre stage. If you were watching that first episode in a foreign country and knew nothing of Glasgow, you would wonder where in all of Europe there existed such a unique and hauntingly beautiful city.

The following morning, as we gathered to start the day's shooting, Graeme and Eric came out to the location to tell us that our first episode had been watched by over six and a half million viewers – the show's highest ratings in years. The reviews in the major newspapers couldn't have been better, praising the show to the skies and singling me out as a worthy successor to Mark McManus. I floated through the rest of that day. After so many years of 'and might I have seen you in something?', I had achieved the recognition I first sought as a thirteen-year-old would-be actor in my stage debut at the Eastwood Parish Church Hall. My only sorrow was that my mother wasn't there to have her changeling child, the cause of so much anguish in her short life, hug her and thank her for the faith she'd had in him all those years ago.

I wasn't used to the demands of working on a long-running drama series, and as we neared the end of the tightly packed schedule I found my stamina starting to flag. I might have felt like I'd won the first battle, but there was still a war to be fought. Working on the series was a bit like being served a delicious three-course meal, only to be told when you'd finished it that another three-course meal was on its way to your table. After a third or fourth serving, even Heston Blumenthal would have a hard time trying to stimulate your appetite. However, following my dad's attitude to life, I squared my shoulders and got on with it, spending six months of the year living on my own and trying to avoid the temptations of spending my evenings in the convivial atmosphere of the local pub. (Like Banquo's ghost, the image of Mark McManus often appeared before me, as a reminder of the consequences of going down that particular road.) Usually my evenings were spent dining alone in a café or restaurant with a paperback for company, or sitting in front of the telly with a takeaway, and on Friday evenings (assuming I had finished in time to catch the last plane to Heathrow) I would head back home to spend the weekend with Sally and the boys, even though most of the time would be taken up with learning lines for the following week's schedule. Since becoming a dad, I cherished every minute I spent with my three wonderful wee pals, and when I went back to a rented flat in a city that hadn't been my home for the past thirty years or so, I missed my family terribly and felt that, big career break or not, I couldn't carry on living this way – I found the enforced separations were beginning to put a serious strain on my relationship with Sally, and some weekends I would come home so stressed and short-tempered that she must have felt the boundaries between my on-screen character and my real self were starting to become more than a little blurred. I knew that if I were fortunate enough to be asked back for a second series, there would have to be some serious and life-changing decisions to be made.

There was a distinct end-of-term atmosphere as we were about to shoot the last scene of the series. The scene was set in the incident room, with John Michie sitting at his desk, speaking on the phone to an informer, while Blythe and Colin listen attentively. Halfway through, I march in to tell John about an unexpected breakthrough in the investigation. During the break, as the crew were tweaking the lights and setting up the camera, I nipped off to the wardrobe department. As the camera turned over and I stood in the shadows waiting to make my entrance, no one seemed to have clocked the fact that I was wearing a dressing gown over my costume. When I heard my cue, I quickly slipped off the robe and strode on to deliver my lines. It was only when he noticed Blythe and Colin struggling to keep their faces straight that John became aware something was amiss. Seasoned pro that he is, he carried on with the scene until it finally dawned on him that although Detective Chief Inspector Burke was dressed in his usual jacket, shirt and tie, below the waist he was wearing stiletto heels, a sequinned thong and a pair of black fishnet stockings held in place by a lacy suspender belt. Since the camera kept running, I can only pray the footage never finds its way on to YouTube . . .

A few weeks after the series ended, I took my family on an all-out, to-hell-with-the-expense holiday to Mexico's beautiful Yucatan peninsula where, on the cool, coral sand of a sun-dappled beach, Sally and I finally legitimised our union and tied the knot. It was the most memorable holiday we'd ever had, and after six months of putting up with a greetin'-faced partner and absentee father, I felt that my newly wedded wife and our three newly legitimate sons bloody well deserved it.

When the call came that the series had been recommissioned, Sally and I discussed the possibility of selling up in London and moving back to Glasgow. I was all for it, but Sally felt it would be a wrench for the boys to be uprooted from the lovely wee local primary school where they were happy and settled, and start their lives over again. Although I argued that they would be completely at home within a few months, I saw her point of view and with some reluctance agreed to carry on as before.

I couldn't face another six months in a rented flat, so Sally reckoned the smart thing to do would be to buy a two-bedroom flat somewhere off Byres Road that would give me a wee home from home – and if, for whatever reason, the wheels should suddenly fall off the cart,[3] we could always rent it out. I saw the sense in her proposal and began to search through the *Glasgow Herald*'s property pages. To cut a long story short, I put in what I considered to be pretty generous offers on three different flats, but thanks to Scotland's 'offers over' system, I lost them all. I can well understand the advantage of Scots property law in that you can't be gazumped, but who, apart from solicitors and surveyors, benefit from Scotland's archaic property laws? Why should buying a second-hand house be any different from buying a second-hand car? You want a thousand quid for your Vauxhall Astra and, after driving it round the block and kicking the tyres, I offer you £850. After a bit of horse-trading, we shake hands on £920. I hand you the money, you hand me the logbook and the car is now mine. Where's the flaw in that system? But when it comes to buying a house in Scotland, once the envelopes with the bids inside are opened and you've lost by a couple of quid (or a couple of thousand – you'll never find out), you're not given the opportunity to revise your original offer. Now, I'm sure there are plenty of Scottish solicitors who would be happy to explain to me why the Scottish system of house-buying is the best in the world – well, save your breath, folks. After losing a sizeable amount of cash on three expensive but futile surveys, Sally suggested that instead of doing the smart thing and buying a place in Glasgow, we should do a daft thing and buy a place in France. I was so hacked off by then that I agreed. So, after a couple of months' searching, we found a location we both loved, and for less than the price of a room and kitchen in Dowanhill, we ended up buying a medieval house in one of the most beautiful areas in the south of

---

[3] Having spent over fifty years in the business and known once-busy actors who found themselves back in rented bedsits, I've learned to live in daily anticipation of just such an event.

France. And – Scottish property lawyers please note – the transaction was as simple and straightforward as buying a used Vauxhall Astra.

The thought of our unique house, with its ancient stone walls, huge marble fireplace like something from the giant's castle in a panto, and its medieval *pigeonnier* (doocot), gave me a warm and fuzzy feeling that kept me buoyed up during many a long night shoot. I'd be standing in a sleety drizzle, poking at yet another mutilated corpse in a bin bag up a back lane in Maryhill, when suddenly a vision of Sally and I sitting on our top terrace, sharing a chilled bottle of white wine with a few friends while watching the sun set over the hills beyond the valley, would fill me with joy and make the endless takes and retakes a lot more bearable.

However, having a house in France hadn't in any way changed the fact that I still had to go back to a cheerless flat in Glasgow each evening. Everything took an unexpected turn for the better when, on one of my weekend flights back to London, I found myself sitting next to an old friend. I had known Rhoda MacDonald since the mid seventies, before she became head of Gaelic output at STV, producing and presenting her own highly popular series, *Speaking Our Language*. I hadn't seen her for ages, and as we talked, I happened to mention my futile search for cosy digs in Glasgow. 'I don't know if you'd be interested,' she said, 'but I've got a lovely flat in the west end that I hardly ever use since I moved to London. Would you like to have a look at it?' The following week, as I opened the door with the set of keys she had given me, I couldn't believe my eyes – the place could have featured on the cover of *Homes and Gardens*. A passionate admirer of contemporary art, Rhoda had hung the walls with a collection of paintings that wouldn't have looked out of place in the window of a Bond Street gallery. At last I had a place that would be a pleasure to come back to each night.

I would still be on my own, though – not something I particularly relished. This problem was solved at a stroke when Bill Paterson mentioned that he was looking for somewhere to stay in Glasgow during the filming of his supernatural drama series *Sea of Souls*. As soon as I showed him around Rhoda's flat, he called her to ask if she fancied having another lodger. And so, after a gap of thirty-odd years, and in a scenario that, if you were pitching it as a series, would be best described as *The Odd Couple* meets *The Sunshine Boys* meets *Still Game*, Bill and I became flatmates once again – although our tenure almost came to an abrupt end when, a few days after we'd moved in, the phone rang. I was busy making our tea, so Bill took the call – it was Rhoda.

'Hi Bill,' she began breezily, 'just ringing to see if everything's OK for you two.'

'Oh, everything's just great, thanks,' said Bill.

'And isn't my flat simply beautiful?' she purred.

'Oh yes,' said Bill, with a slightly camp inflection. 'And I just *know* you're going to love what we've done with it . . .'

I could hear Rhoda's horrified shriek from the far side of the kitchen.

Shortly before each new series of *Taggart* was due to be broadcast, STV's publicity department would set us all up with a series of interviews with the local and national press. One of the questions we were asked on a regular basis was 'Has anything funny ever happened to you while you were filming?' My standard answer was that the amount of sheer hard graft involved in trying to complete each episode on schedule didn't leave much time for fun and games. In truth, though, we did have some wonderfully funny moments – like the time we were on location and an elderly lady came over to Blythe during one of the breaks. 'Excuse me, dear,' she said, 'but do you know what they're filming here?'

'It's an episode of *Taggart*,' Blythe replied.

'Oh, *Taggart*,' she said, looking round at the camera and the lights. 'And tell me – is it a repeat?'

One incident that had us all in stitches was when an extra who had been hired to play a murder victim fell asleep in the make-up chair while the realistic-looking slashes and stab wounds were applied to his neck and face. When he woke up and saw himself in the mirror, he promptly passed out with shock and had to be sent home in a taxi while a replacement was found at short notice. Despite my stock answer to the press, in truth we always tried to find an opportunity for a bit of a laugh. During rehearsals, John and I would occasionally play our scenes as Arthur Lowe and John Le Mesurier in *Dad's Army* – two actors we admired tremendously in a show we were both big fans of.

JOHN

You wanted to see me about something, Sir?

ME

Yes, Wilson, I did. It seems there's been a murder.

JOHN

A murder? Oh I say, Sir, how frightfully unfortunate . . .

A memory that still makes me smile was the time when the family came up for the weekend and I took my two older boys to the Barras. Wandering around the busy market, they couldn't help but notice the number of heads that swivelled in my direction as we passed by. Finally, Jock tugged at my arm and whispered, 'Everybody's looking at you, Dad – are you really famous now?' Before I could answer, a wee guy selling dodgy packets of fags called over to me. 'Heh – you're the new Taggart, urnt ye?' I nodded and smiled, with a wink to Jock as if to say, 'Well, does that answer your question?' As I walked on, feeling quite pleased with myself, the tobacco baron called after me: 'Aye, ye're no' bad, but McManus wiz the best.' Ah yes – there's no' much chance of gettin' above yersel' in Glesca.

Most of our fun and games usually came in the form of a good wind-up. Colin McCredie was usually the biggest culprit when it came to winding up an innocent victim (nine times out of ten,

314

said victim being yours truly), but I still don't think he's forgiven me for the pain and humiliation he suffered when I found the perfect opportunity to even the score. Lorraine McIntosh had made her name as the singer in the hugely successful Scottish band Deacon Blue, before reinventing herself as an exceptionally talented actress. When we learned she had been cast in the next episode, Colin could barely contain his excitement. 'Oh my God!' he yelped. 'Lorraine McIntosh! I've been in love with her since I was a teenager.' He told me about the first time he saw her perform at the Caird Hall in Dundee and how, as she sang one of his favourite numbers, he felt sure that she had been aware of him, sitting in the middle of the third row. 'I mean, I'm sure she didn't really,' he said wistfully, 'but at that moment, I really believed she was singing just for me.' As he finished his poignant little tale and begged me not to mention it to anyone, a wicked little voice began to whisper in my ear . . .

As we all trooped off to lunch one day after shooting one of Lorraine's scenes, she sidled over to Colin. 'I feel a bit stupid asking you this,' she said. 'But were you ever at a Deacon Blue concert in Dundee, back in the late eighties?' Colin's eyes became perfect circles and he started to turn a funny colour.

'Er, um, yes – yes I was actually,' he stammered. 'It was at the Caird Hall in 1987.'

'I knew I recognised you!' said Lorraine triumphantly. 'You were sitting in the middle of the third row, weren't you?'

By now, Colin had lost the power of speech and was reduced to jerking his head backwards and forwards in agreement.

'And,' she continued, 'I don't suppose you would have been aware of it, but I remember I sang a song just for you.' Colin's legs had given up trying to support him at this point and he was leaning against the make-up truck, struggling to breathe. It was only when he glanced up and saw me doubled over with laughter that the penny finally dropped. 'You rotten shit!' he croaked. 'You evil spawn of Satan – I'll get even with you for this, you horrible, horrible bastard!'

315

Despite Colin's many, many attempts to even the score, the dear little ginger rascal never did manage to top that cleverly devised and perfectly executed little scenario.

51

All at Sea

It was 2005 and we were approaching the final episode of my fifth year with *Taggart* when I got a call from Fiona, my agent. 'Hi,' she began. 'Priscilla John sends you her love and asks if you'd like to meet her for the new *Pirates of the Caribbean* film they're about to start shooting.'

I first met Priscilla back in the seventies, through my old flatmate Stephanie Davies, who had worked alongside her when she was an assistant in Granada TV's casting department. Since leaving Granada and striking out on her own, Priscilla had become one of the biggest and most influential casting directors in the film business and could take credit for kick-starting a lot of highly successful movie careers. 'I've still got another month to go on *Taggart*,' I said to Fiona. 'Even if I did get offered the part, there's no way I'd be able to do it.'

'I've looked at all the dates,' she answered, 'and they wouldn't need you until after you'd finished your final episode, so it should all fit in quite nicely before you start back on the next series of *Taggart*.'

When I was a wee boy and dreamed about being a movie actor, it was really Disney ones I had in mind. Without exception, it was their summer blockbusters my pals and I would run to see at the Pollok Picture House: *The Swiss Family Robinson*, *20,000 Leagues Under the Sea*, *Darby O' Gill and the Little People*, not to mention *Rob*

Roy, *Davy Crockett*, *Greyfriars Bobby* and one of my all-time favourites – *Treasure Island*. I had taken my kids to see the first Pirates of the Caribbean film, *The Curse of the Black Pearl*, and sat there watching it with all the excitement and enthusiasm of my ten-year-old self. I thought it was a masterpiece, easily matching up to, if not outdoing, the best of the classic Disney canon – and now I was being offered the opportunity to audition for a part in the sort of Disney movie I loved when I was a kid. If, by some miracle, I actually landed it, how fantastic would *that* be?

I was up for Bellamy, the captain of a merchant ship named the *Edinburgh Trader*. At the casting meeting, Priscilla outlined the story, telling me how Elizabeth Swann sets out to search for her lover, Will Turner, by disguising herself as a cabin boy and stowing away aboard my ship. My heart missed a beat when she added that the writers still hadn't decided whether or not Captain Bellamy would carry on into the third film of the series. This was news to me: I was under the impression (assuming I landed the part) that I would be in just the one film – *Dead Man's Chest*. If Bellamy was going to be in two movies, I realised I was going to have to make a very difficult decision regarding my future with *Taggart*.

Priscilla recorded me playing a couple of Bellamy's key scenes[1] and sent them off to the film's director, Gore Verbinski. A couple of days after I returned to Glasgow to start work on the final episode of the current series, the call came through that Gore had loved my audition and had told Priscilla not to bother seeing anyone else for the part, and that due to script rewrites, Captain Bellamy would appear in only one film after all. This was the best news I could have wished for – it meant I would be free to accept Disney's offer without having to resign from *Taggart*. My boyhood dream of being in a big Disney blockbuster was about to come true. When I told the team, Blythe squealed with delight and gave me a huge hug. John slapped me on the back and gave me a congratulatory handshake,

---

[1] Including one where he lies mortally wounded on the deck and offers his soul to Davy Jones – which meant he would appear as one of the living dead in the third film.

while Colin simply sighed and told me it was all a terrible mis-understanding – what I had actually been offered was a small part in a low-budget workout video called *Pilates of the Caribbean*.[2]

At one point, during the final episode of the series, I had to go to the wardrobe truck to change costume for one of my scenes. As I walked back on to the set, I was stopped in my tracks by a sea of cardboard pirate hats, black eye patches and Jolly Roger flags as the entire *Taggart* cast and crew launched into a rousing chorus of 'yo-ho-ho and a bottle of rum' and, with a crate of bubbly generously provided by Eric and Graeme, raised their glasses and wished me all the luck in the world. As I was soon to discover, I would need it . . .

The fact that my starting date had been delayed by a few weeks didn't overly concern me when my driver dropped me off at the entrance to the Walt Disney Studio complex in North Hollywood. 'You head straight along Goofy, hang a right at Donald, and turn left on Dopey,' said the friendly security guard at the gate. As I headed to my trailer, along streets named after their founder's favourite creations, it occurred to me that the Disney Studio complex gave a whole new meaning to the phrase 'Taking the Mickey'.

My first scenes were set in the interior of my ship, the *Edinburgh Trader*, and in one of the studio's biggest sound stages, teams of skilled craftsmen had painstakingly constructed a replica of an eighteenth-century captain's cabin that was authentic in every detail, even down to the irregular surface of the glass in the big transom windows. I had hardly slept a wink the previous night, fighting a rising tide of panic as I tried desperately to learn my new lines, and now, as I sat in the semi-darkness of the massive sound stage with a full-sized replica of Captain Jack's ship the *Black Pearl* at one end and Davy Jones' ghost ship the *Flying Dutchman* at the

---

[2] As a close friend once remarked to him, 'Colin, it's a good job you're adorable, otherwise you'd be a really annoying wee bastard.'

other, I felt like my forty-odd years in the business counted for nothing. I was a bag of nerves.

For most actors, the first day on any new movie is a fairly nerve-wracking business. Unlike a play, where you have a rehearsal period to explore and develop a character, on a movie set, once the director calls action, whatever choices you've made, whatever decisions you've come to about your performance, are about to be set in stone. Unlike theatre, you don't get the opportunity to polish your performance during the run of the play. From personal experience, I've found the best way to prevent the heebie-jeebies from getting the better of you is to learn the lines until you're sick of them – and then learn them again. Believe me, when the camera starts rolling you'll have enough to worry about without wondering what the hell you're supposed to say next. So, having spent the best part of the previous week alarming total strangers by wandering round my local park mumbling to myself as I memorised Bellamy's dialogue, picture my delight when the evening before my first shooting day an envelope containing what amounted to a complete rewrite of my dialogue was delivered to my hotel room. I'd love to have you believe that actors live in a kind of never-never land where it's always playtime and you don't ever have to grow up and become a boring adult. The stark truth is that an actor's life is a lot like being a soldier on active service: ninety-eight per cent boredom and two per cent terror.

When everything was finally ready to go, I took a big, deep breath, walked on the set and in the few remaining minutes before the first take, while the lights were given a final tweak and the lenses on four huge Panavision cameras were minutely adjusted, I ran silently through my lines for the final time. The first assistant yelled for quiet, the warning bell rang, the cameras began turning and in the moment before the director called 'action' I softly whispered the actor's prayer: 'Oh God, don't let me fuck up.'

Somebody upstairs must have put in a good word for me that day, as once the opening scene was in the can and the flop sweat had dried a little, I was able to take over the controls again and the rest of the day's shoot went just fine.

A fortnight later, having completed the first part of my schedule, I was flown back home again. Despite feeling disappointed with myself for being such a Nervous Nellie on the first day of the shoot, I mentally gave myself a wee pat on the back for having faced my fears and overcome them.

I gained a valuable insight about fear at a life-changing seminar I had attended some years before. When I signed up for it, I had no idea that the event would culminate in a fire walk. I knew there was absolutely no way I was going to be talked into risking serious injury by doing something as terrifying and potentially dangerous as a fire walk, but later that evening, as I stepped barefoot from the end of a thirty-foot bed of burning coals, unharmed and whooping with triumph, the speaker, Anthony Robbins, said the point of the exercise was not about the fact that I actually did the fire walk; the point was that I had conquered my fear of doing it. How much more, he continued, could we achieve in our lives if we refused to allow ourselves to be governed by fear? Fear of failure, fear of how others might judge us and even – odd as it might seem – fear of success.

Things began to take on a slightly worrying aspect when I learned that, due to unseasonal weather conditions in the West Indies, my next section of filming had been delayed yet again. Added to the initial delay in starting, it meant that my revised schedule was drawing uncomfortably close to the start date for the next series of *Taggart*.

I think it's fair to say that Kingstown, the capital of St Vincent, the largest of the Windward Islands, is not one of the Caribbean's top tourist destinations. The beaches that fringe the island are mainly composed of black volcanic sand, most of which, until legislation was drawn up to retain what little was left, had been removed for use in the building industry. Nevertheless, St Vincent was the base for much of the filming of *Dead Man's Chest*, and it was where I would be quartered for the next two weeks while filming my exterior scenes aboard the *Edinburgh Trader*.

As a lover of all things historical, my heart soared when I boarded my ship for the first time. From the moment I saw her sitting at anchor in the bay, I thought her graceful lines seemed familiar. I realised why when her captain told me she had been built for the Marlon Brando version of *Mutiny on the Bounty* – a film that completely enthralled me when I first saw it as a twelve-year-old at the Waverley Cinema in Shawlands. Then he told me that the beautifully made teak and brass ship's wheel was from the 1935 film starring Clark Gable and Charles Laughton. As I stood at the ship's wheel first used by Clark Gable, then Marlon Brando and now me, I felt connected to a historical chain that stretched back to Hollywood's golden era.

I had become less panicky about the last-minute scene changes and the fact that there was no point in learning the lines as they appeared in my original script – in fact, I was even bold enough at one point to offer Gore Verbinski a rewrite of my own. After being handed a rewrite that looked to me like it had been hurriedly stitched together from several previous drafts, Stevie Spiers, the brilliant Welsh character actor who played my first mate, and I spent the rest of the evening having a go at rewriting the scene ourselves. I think we made an excellent job of it – far better (at least in our view) than the version that was slipped under our doors – but I suspect the writers' noses were put slightly out of joint since our submission was politely rejected and our budding career as top Hollywood script doctors ended as swiftly as it had begun.

To my regret, the scene where Keira Knightley, disguised as a crew member, tries to persuade me to alter course for Tortuga had been ditched. I never found out why, although I suspect it's possible the studio bosses found it hard to believe that a hard-bitten old sea dog like Bellamy would be duped for a moment by the exquisitely beautiful Ms Knightley's attempt to pass herself off as a lad. It was a pity, as I could have played a whole subtext, with Bellamy puzzled by the unexpected stirrings he feels every time his young doe-eyed cabin boy brings him another tot of grog . . .

Still, I did have a scene with Orlando Bloom. In the story, we come across his character, Will Turner, drifting in a lifeboat in the middle of the ocean, half dead and babbling something about being pursued by a ghost ship. We blocked the scene through without Orlando, who was off doing a pick-up shot with the second unit. Once the scene had been set to Gore's satisfaction, an exhausted-looking Orlando joined us for a final run-through.

'So,' Orlando asked Gore, 'what's this scene about?'

'It's the scene where you're being questioned by Captain Bellamy aboard his ship,' said Gore.

'Oh yes – yes, of course,' said Orlando. Then after a brief pause, 'And why am I on Bellamy's ship?'

'You've just been rescued from a lifeboat . . .'

Orlando seemed slightly perplexed. 'A lifeboat?'

'Yes, they come across you in the lifeboat after you managed to escape.'

'Escape – yes, that's right, I've escaped.'

There was another, slightly longer pause during which Orlando seemed to be doing mental arithmetic. Finally, he looked up at Gore. 'And who have I escaped from again?'

Now, I've worked with actors who don't like to be too familiar with their lines, using the feeling of not quite knowing what comes next to keep their performance fresh and vital – but I have to say, not being too sure what movie you're in, never mind what scene, was a new one on me.

After my exterior scenes aboard the *Edinburgh Trader* were finished I had a longish break at home before I was due to complete the final part of my schedule. This was to be the special-effects sequence where the legendary sea monster, the kraken, attacks my ship, dispatching me and dragging the *Edinburgh Trader* to Davy Jones' locker. Disney's special-effects team had been busy designing and building a full-sized replica of the *Edinburgh Trader*, mounted on hydraulic ramps that would snap the ship in two and drag it to the bottom of the huge tank that was under construction in the

Bahamas. As a result of previous delays, my filming schedule had edged dangerously close to *Taggart*'s start date, and if there were any more delays, being swallowed up by the kraken would be the least of my problems. As I sat at home, chewing my fingernails, I got the news I had been dreading – the special-effects tank wasn't going to be ready on time, and as a consequence my schedule had been put back for at least a month.

If you were a regular *Taggart* viewer, you might recall an episode called, ironically enough, 'Running Out of Time' where, in the very first scene, DCI Burke gets shot and wounded, spending the rest of the episode in a coma while the team set about tracking down his would-be assassin. Can you guess why I spent most of that episode off screen? That's right – so I could complete my last section on *Pirates of the Caribbean*.

The delay with the tank meant that Disney now wanted me to work for them during the period I was supposed to start work on the first episode of the new *Taggart* series. My agent, God bless her, had been doing her level best to sort things out and try to keep everybody happy, but the way things were going it was obvious that somebody – me, most likely – was going to end up with skint knees and a sore face. Graeme and Eric had made it clear to Disney that my contractual obligations meant they had first call on me, so Disney would just have to work around the *Taggart* schedule and lump it. The next salvo in what seemed to be a rapidly escalating battle was when Disney came back with the ultimatum that they were not prepared to alter the schedule of their multi-million-dollar Hollywood blockbuster in order to accommodate a regional television company, and unless STV agreed to release me, they would have no option but to reshoot all of my scenes with someone else. At a tense meeting with Graeme and Eric, I practically went down on my hands and knees, telling them how much being in the movie meant to me and begging them to write me out of *Taggart*'s first episode – adding that if the storyline required me for the odd day or so, I would be happy to work for nothing. After negotiating a financial deal with Disney, to cover the cost of commissioning a new script with a plausible storyline that would cover my absence, Graeme and Eric agreed to release me from the first episode.

As it turned out, my grateful thanks were a little premature. A few weeks before the newly written episode was about to start shooting, I got news that the tank in the Bahamas had been destroyed by a hurricane and the final part of my schedule had been put back yet again. All the Machiavellian manoeuvring and deal making that had gone on to ensure I would be free to complete my work for Disney had been for nothing. The nightmare had returned with a vengeance and I was right back at square one.

After another flurry of transatlantic phone calls between Graeme and the Disney executives, a compromise was reached – instead of the fortnight Disney had requested, Graeme had somehow persuaded them to complete my final scenes in a single weekend. Because of the pressure I was under, the joy I felt at being in one of Disney's all-time greatest movies had long gone and, knowing how much had to be shot in such an impossibly short space of time, my mind was in panic mode as I boarded a flight to Miami on a Friday morning – and flew straight into the tail end of Hurricane Katrina.

I was supposed to disembark at Miami airport and board a small local plane bound for Nassau, but as the jumbo jet approached Florida and battered through the raging storm clouds like a bucking bronco on crack, the part of my brain that was still rational figured that even if I survived the white-knuckle ride from Hell, I wouldn't be flying out of Miami that afternoon.

I was right. When we finally touched down with a bang that must have necessitated a total refurbishment of the plane's undercarriage, I made my way to the transfer desk only to be told that all flights to the Bahamas had been cancelled until further notice. I sat morosely in an airport hotel room that night, emptying the minibar, watching the TV weather reports and wondering how much higher the interest rates were going to get on the cosmic debt I was being asked to repay.

The following afternoon, thank God, the storm had abated just enough for the Bahamian flights to resume, and after another trip through the kind of lightning storm usually reserved for seventies disaster movies, I landed safely at Nassau, where a waiting limo whisked me straight to the now completed tank to start rehearsals aboard the replica of the *Edinburgh Trader*.

I was still feeling a bit woozy from jet lag when Gore called action for the first take of what proved to be a long and arduous night shoot. However, thanks to the skill and professionalism of the technical crew, we ploughed through my scenes at a rate of knots. When it came time to shoot my final appearance (or rather disappearance), they could only film me from one side, or else the camera would have caught dawn's rosy glow peeping over the horizon.

While every other actor had signed a Run of Film contract – meaning that no matter how many weeks (or even months) their schedules overran, they were contractually obliged to be available until their scenes were completed – I was the only actor who, because of my *Taggart* commitments, had to have a definite finishing date. My scenes absolutely had to be completed over that final weekend. So I guess the words in bold capital letters at the top of the shooting schedule that read 'THE ALEX NORTON WEEKEND!' must have been added with some irony.

My scenes were shot in record time, and less than twenty-four hours after I was grabbed, hurled skyward and devoured by a giant squid while my ship was snapped in half and dragged under the sea, I was back in the *Taggart* interview room, grilling a suspect over a grisly murder about which – thanks to a rich brew of jet lag, fatigue and disorientation – I had only the vaguest notion.

Later that year, as the publicity machine began to gear up for the film's eagerly awaited opening, I spent a lot of time giving interviews to showbiz journalists who would inevitably say to me at some point in the proceedings, 'It must have been great fun, working on a Disney movie.' My standard reply was that it was a sheer joy from start to finish, although what I really wanted to say was, 'Let me tell you something – being in a Disney movie isny like watching one!' The other thing I was constantly being asked was what Johnny Depp was like. Sadly, we had no scenes together, and I met Captain Jack Sparrow for the first and only time the night of the film's London premiere. Despite being pressed for time (the PR people were steering him from one photo opportunity to another) he was very pleasant, and after introducing himself to Sally, he asked me where I'd got my sporran with the skull and crossbones on the front (it had been specially sourced for me by the *Scottish Sun*'s showbiz writer, Georgina Reid), and at the risk of sounding a bit light on my loafers, may I add that I thought he was the handsomest man I had ever seen in my life. After he'd moved off, I turned to ask Sally if she thought so too, but annoyingly she had fainted.

Despite being stressed to the max for most of the time I worked on *Pirates of the Caribbean: Dead Man's Chest*, it was, without question, one of the absolute highlights of my career. When I sat in the dark, watching the film for the first time at its glitzy premiere in Leicester Square, I thought back to when I used to sit in the Pollok Picture House with a bag of Butterkist and a Kia-Ora, dreaming about being an actor in a Disney film, and I wondered if maybe one day, some wee lad with a head full of dreams might be sitting in his local cinema, thinking to himself, 'That guy playin' Captain Bellamy's from Glasgow – if he can get tae act in a big Disney picture, maybe I can as well.' And who knows, maybe one day he might look back and write a book about the weird and wonderful journey *his* dream took him on . . .

52

The End?

Giving an after-dinner speech one evening to an audience that included several of STV's top board members, Tam Cowan, the well-known writer, broadcaster and wit, drily remarked, '*Taggart* – a show that managed to carry on for fifteen years without Mark McManus, but only six months without Colin McCredie – d'ye think somebody might have made a wee mistake there?'

Rewind to a year before, when I got a call from *Taggart*'s new producer, saying there was good news and bad news – the good news was that the network had commissioned another series. The bad news was that we would be going ahead without Colin. I was stunned by this unexpected bombshell. Colin and I had become close friends over the years, and I had never heard him say he wanted out of the show. I asked why Colin had decided to leave. 'I'm afraid it wasn't his choice,' I was told. 'A decision was taken to make a few important changes in the show's format that we hope will revitalise it and keep it running for another twenty-five years, so for Colin's sake we think it would be best if you don't call him right away, as we want to give him time to decide what story he'd like to tell the press.'

I remembered how devastated I had felt years before on discovering I had been dropped from the BBC cop series *Backup*, and I had only been in half a dozen episodes, while Colin had been a regular in *Taggart* since 1995. When I rang him to commiserate, he told me that ten minutes after being told he was out of the series, a journalist had called him, asking how he felt about being sacked. When the story hit the headlines, he said his life became unbearable. He couldn't get into a taxi, have a quiet drink in a pub or even take his children to school without somebody making a comment along the lines of, 'Ah heard ye got the elbow fae *Taggart*, wee man – that's a bloody shame,' before adding with a certain amount of relish, 'Ye must be gutted, eh?'

You might ask, since John, Blythe and I were really all such friends with Colin, why didn't we call a meeting with the producers and demand his reinstatement? Well, as Ralph Richardson once said about actors, 'We're all just taxis, driving round Sloane Square with our "for hire" signs on.' Not a very romantic view of the profession, but spot on nonetheless. Although the three of us were deeply upset about the offhand way we felt Colin had been treated, we had all been in the business long enough to know we had no power to influence the producers' decision. The only real power an actor has is the power to turn down an offer – other than that, their status can be summed up by the fact that some cynical directors have been known to refer to them as 'walking props'.[1]

On the morning of the read-through for the first episode of the new series, Blythe, John and I gathered in STV's conference room, meeting and greeting the new cast, chatting with the production team and catching up with each other's lives as we normally did before sitting round the big conference table and starting the read – all of us acutely aware of Colin's absence and knowing it could have been any one of us sitting at home that morning, looking out the window and wondering why we had lost not only our livelihood, but our dignity too.

For the first time in *Taggart*'s history, a show runner had been brought in to oversee the storylines and weave some plot strands

---

[1] Or, as a friend of mine once overheard a director say to the first AD, 'Right, bring on the meat puppets.'

that would come together to provide a dramatic climax to the final episode. Instead of a single camera, two cameras now covered each scene, which meant we could overlap the dialogue, giving our performances a more naturalistic feel. When the series was broadcast in October 2010, I watched it with a more critical eye than usual, and it did seem to me to have a sharper edge to it – the pace was brisk, the hand-held camera shots gave it a feeling of immediacy and the scenes were tightly focussed and dynamic. Controversial as some of our new producers' decisions may have seemed, it looked like they had achieved the results they were after. Maybe the show would carry on for another twenty-five years after all.

The critical response to the new series was enthusiastic and the viewing figures excellent, so why, apart from repeats on the digital channels, did *Taggart* disappear from the nation's screens in 2010? I can honestly say that unlike my on-screen counterpart, DCI Matt Burke, I haven't a clue – all I can say is that the answer to the question I get asked every time I get into a Glasgow taxi – 'So when's *Taggart* comin' back then?' – lies in the complex funding agreements between the ITV network and the few remaining regional companies like STV. Basically, the ITV network, who provided the lion's share of the show's production costs, decided, for reasons best known to themselves, to discontinue their funding – so, no more network money; no more *Taggart*. Despite rumours that Channel 5 were going to part-fund a new series, or that the show was going to relocate, lock stock and barrel to Australia, where it's still hugely popular (when I heard that one, I pictured myself wearing a hat with corks hanging off it and saying, 'What's that, Skippy? There's been a murder?'), nothing came of it, and the longest-running detective series on British TV seems to have ended without a whimper, never mind a bang.

To this day, no one has ever called Blythe, John or me to say the show has definitely been cancelled. *Taggart* may have vanished forever, or it may return with or without any of its recent cast. Who knows? But if there *is* a chance it might make a reappearance, here's a wee notion that came into my head – why not kick off the new series by having the team, whoever they might be by then, investigate the sudden and mysterious disappearance of the *old* series? I can see it now:

AN ABANDONED BUILDING ON THE CLYDESIDE. NIGHT.

In a dark and derelict office, the team pull on latex gloves before examining the old and dusty folder marked: THE TAGGART FILES. HIGHLY SECRET. MUST NOT BE OPENED WITHOUT WRITTEN AUTHORISATION. Glancing nervously at each other, the team cautiously prise off the crumbling seal and withdraw the yellowing contents. The DCI scrutinises them closely, his brow furrowing as he reads the dusty pages.

DC
Well, Sir? Any clues as to what became of the old series?

DCI
Aye. It's just as I suspected.

FEMALE DI
Oh no – you don't mean—

YOUNG DS
Sir, please don't say it . . .

DC
Somebody has to—

The DCI looks straight into the camera lens.

DCI

There's been a murder!

**CUE THEME MUSIC. ROLL CREDITS
AND FADE TO BLACK . . .**

Postscript

At the time of writing, it's been five years since we finished the last series of *Taggart*. Thanks to Graeme Gordon and Eric Coulter's decision to cast me as the show's new boss, my life changed immeasurably. Not only did it raise my profile as an actor, but more importantly it meant that I was able to provide a comfortable and stable family home for my wife and our three wonderful boys – something I so desperately longed for when I was a youngster.

The thing I always loved most about being an actor was the variety it brought to my life. I never knew from one month, one week, or sometimes even one day to another what I'd be working on next, and while I'm grateful for the eight wonderful years I spent as a member of the *Taggart* team, my career path seems to have come full circle, and I can honestly say I'm more than happy to be back once again as a taxi with my 'for hire' sign lit up.

Oh, and by the way, if you were the irate, red-faced chap who came up to me in the Trongate branch of Marks & Spencer a few years ago, and snarled, 'Aye, it's a' right for you, in't it? Talk aboot an easy life! Well ye can jist take yer money and fuck off back tae London as soon as ye like.' I'd just like to say thank you and I'm glad I resisted the temptation to plant my boot up your backside as you walked away – if I hadn't mulled over the fact that you passed judgement, knowing nothing about me or my life, I might never have got round to writing this autobiography.

As film director Hugh Hudson once said, 'My life might have been a roller coaster, but at least I got a ride,' which is an observation I can entirely relate to. Although some of the dips have been unimaginably terrifying, the view from the peaks has been more thrilling than I could ever have imagined. So, dear reader, thank you for spending time with me on the roller coaster that's been my life so far. This is where I let you off, but if you'll excuse me, I think I might just take another couple of turns around the track before the fairground closes for the evening.

Acknowledgements

My profound apologies if you were part of my life and searched the book in vain for your name. There's a limit to how long an autobiography can be before the reader takes a scunner to you, so I had to be ruthless in terms of what to include and what to omit. Among those without whom my life would have been much the poorer for not knowing them are, in no particular order:

My primary school pals, John Wylie and Jim Clarke. My tormentors at Shawlands Academy, John Mackintosh and Tommy Nelson (if you only knew how often I channelled you when playing nasty pieces of work). My fellow rogues and vagabonds, who either inspired me, showed me a little kindness along the way, or both – Paul Humpoletz, Phillip Davies, Lizzy McInnerny, Melanie Parr, Tessa Hatts, Ronnie Letham, Charlie Kearney, Stanley Baxter, Phyllis Logan, Sue Wilson, Nancy Meckler, Maureen Lefevre, Danny Webb, Michael Maloney, Elspet Gray, Tim McInnerny, Jimmy Chisholm, Jimmy Yuill, Ken Drury, Peter Kelly, Paul Young, David Robb, Richard Wilson, Kevin McNally, Ron and Jenny Bain, Julie Graham. Stuart Mungall, Michael Gambon, Susan Hare, Brian Linnie, Aly Bain, Anne Louise Ross, Forbes Masson, John Sampson, David Hayman, Andy Gray, Mandy Patinkin, Mel Gibson, Liam Neeson, Teddy Kempener and Jimmie McGregor – even though I've already mentioned him in the book, our friendship

335

goes a long way back, and his is invariably the first name that springs to mind when I think on P.D. Ouspensky's book *Meetings with Remarkable Men*.

Old friends who will always have a place in my heart: Martin and Rutie Burstyn, Mel McLean, Pip Hills, Archie Forrest, Bill Copeland, Anne and Charlie Collinson, Jackie Ambrosini, Simon and Rachel Cosyns, Kathy Arthur, Richard Vaughan Davies.

A special mention for Kerry Gardener, who told my future agent, Duncan Heath, to go and see me in *Writer's Cramp* at the Bush Theatre.

My Scottish relatives: my wonderful Auntie Betty, my cousin Maureen and Willie Hanlon and their beautiful and talented daughter Lindsey, my Uncle Hughie, my cousin Margaret and last but far from least, my uncle Willie, without whose influence, inspiration and sense of the absurd my autobiography would probably have been called *Round the Bend: the Rib-Tickling Memoirs of a Glasgow Plumber*.

'The Rellies' down under: my uncle Alec (after whom I'm named), my auntie Yvonne, my cousin Bill and his wife Rosie, my other cousin Penny, her son Lee, his wife Sarah and their son, wee Angus – a real chip off the old block.

My love and thanks to everyone from the Granada casting department who showed such kindness to me when I lived in Belsize Park – Anna Callaghan, Suzie Bruffin, Lin Cordoray, Doreen Jones and Malcolm Drury.

All my friends and acquaintances in our wee village in France: Steve and Jane Young, Bill and Pam Foster, Christopher and Josephine Campbell-Howes, Mark and Sophie Cornelius and finally, the couple who made it all possible, our fairy godmother Pauline and her inspirational husband, Didier Ponsard.

Finally, for all the wonderful lassies who flitted in and out of my life over the years, I dedicate these lines from Robert Burns' 'The Parting Glass' to you:

ACKNOWLEDGEMENTS

Oh, all the comrades that e'er I had
They're sorry for my going away
And all the sweethearts that e'er I had
They'd wish me one more day to stay
But since it falls unto my lot
That I should rise and you should not
I'll gently rise and softly call
Good night and joy be with you all.

337